g No!

"Beverly provides much-needed strategies, information, and support for every woman who has or is still being traumatized by any kind of sexual misconduct, whether it is in the workplace or elsewhere. I strongly recommend it for all women no matter their age or circumstances."

—**Gretchen Carlson**, television journalist, best-selling author of *Be Fierce* and empowerment advocate

"This book is an excellent resource that helps women who have experienced sexual assault, sexual harassment, and sexual pressure to use their voice to speak truth and take a stand. An empowering book that I highly recommend."

—**Raychelle Cassada Lohmann**, author of *The Sexual Trauma Workbook for Teen Girls*

"In her latest book, Engel provides readers with useful guidance for saying no to would-be sexual abusers and encourages readers to practice what it feels like to use those two simple but imperfect letters—N-O!—a skill that benefits people of all ages."

—**Holly Kearl**, founder of Stop Street Harassment

"It's easy enough to tell women to 'say no' but, in reality, there is nothing easy about saying no if you are a woman. Engel's book doesn't only shed light on why this remains true, even in the age of MeToo and TimesUp, but it provides readers with critical, pragmatic tools and strategies designed to confront and report gender harassment, sexual assault and childhood abuse effectively."

—**Soraya Chemaly**, author of *Rage Becomes Her: The Power of Women's Anger* and Director of the Women's Media Center Speech Project

I'm Saying No!

I'm Saying No!

Standing Up Against Sexual Assault, Sexual Harassment, and Sexual Pressure

Beverly Engel

SHE WRITES PRESS

Published 2019
Printed in the United States of America
ISBN: 978-1-63152-525-4 pbk
ISBN: 978-1-63152-526-1 ebk
Library of Congress Control Number: 2018964766

For information, address:
She Writes Press
1569 Solano Ave #546
Berkeley, CA 94707

She Writes Press is a division of SparkPoint Studio, LLC.

Dedicated to all the brave women who have taken up the challenge of changing the way women are seen and the way women are treated in the world.

Contents

Preface

When I was four years old, my little friend Joey and I were taken under a large bush by a teenage boy. Once there, he proceeded to get us to take off our clothes and to show us "what grown-ups do when they get married."

When I was nine years old, I was sexually molested by the new husband of my mother's best friend, Ruby. He was babysitting me while my mother and Ruby were at work. The abuse continued over the span of several months.

When I was ten years old, a Peeping Tom was caught lurking outside our windows, watching me as I took a bath. I had felt someone watching me for months, but when I told my mother she'd just laughed at me and said I was being silly.

When I was eleven years old and on my way home from school a man exposed himself to me.

When I was twelve years old, I was brutally raped while on a "date." The man who raped me was twenty-four years old.

The fact that I was sexually violated so many times before I even reached adolescence may seem unusual to some of you, but unfortunately, it really isn't that uncommon. Many of my clients have had similar experiences, starting when they were young girls. And unfortunately, throughout the world, the question doesn't seem *whether* a girl will be sexually violated but *when* she will be.

You may be one of those women. You too may have been violated in large and small ways, from being sexually harassed by men on the street to being molested or raped.

Just because sexual violations occur so often doesn't mean they should be normalized. No young girl should have to suffer from any of these intrusions. One by one, these events traumatize a girl, making her feel more and more helpless, more and more objectified and used. Each sexual assault is also an assault on her self-esteem, her self-confidence, her self-concept. With each violation, she becomes more convinced that she has no power.

If you identify with me or with the situation of being violated, this book will be especially beneficial for you. It will encourage you to realize just how damaging sexual violations are to girls and women and teach you to have compassion for your suffering instead of minimizing the damage or blaming yourself for what is clearly only one person's fault—the perpetrator's. It will hopefully help you to connect with your righteous anger and empower you to begin to stand up and say "NO!" to sexual assault, sexual harassment, and sexual pressure.

Hopefully, this book will also help you to feel less alone. Many of us who have suffered these types of violations feel isolated. I hope that reading the chapters to come will make you feel more connected to other women and girls who have gone through similar traumas. I hope you will learn from their experiences and become empowered by their experiences.

Introduction

For everything that gets taken from you,
Don't let your voice be one of them.

—Anonymous

The #MeToo movement has provided a safe avenue for more women to tell their stories of sexual abuse, sexual assault, and sexual harassment anonymously. It is empowering women because it's making them feel less alone, and because they're finally getting the opportunity to tell their story and feel heard. Now, more than ever before, we are having important conversations about the rampant abuse of power in nearly every industry, including: the entertainment industry, the music industry, the political world, the sports world, and academic and military communities. It has become abundantly clear that the climate of secrecy we've all lived within for years has continued to exist due to the fact that women have been afraid that should they tell their stories, they wouldn't be believed.

In many cases, it has become clear that their fear was warranted.

Now we have the Time's Up movement—another sign that things are changing. With the money and attention the celebrity founders of this new movement have access to, it is likely that real change will come regarding sexual harassment in the workplace.

While it is possible that the tide may be turning and we may actually be looking at a major cultural shift when it comes to the way men treat women, it is also possible that this, too, will pass. We are already experiencing signs of a major backlash as men begin to push back and the focus has changed to worrying about men being falsely accused.

There certainly is a risk that people will tire of hearing about sexual harassment and assault and will focus on something else to distract themselves from the problem. After all, the rampant sexual violation of women is a very uncomfortable subject, especially for men. And any real change can only come from exposing the roots of the pervasive problem of powerful men systematically taking advantage of less powerful, and therefore vulnerable, women.

Another roadblock to effecting enduring change is the fact that women can't do it alone. Men have to take part in the discussion and the change. And while some men are stepping forward to support the women making allegations against their abusers, it will take more than this kind of support to actually change the culture. It will take men actively listening and learning while women explain to them what boundaries they should never cross and how it makes women feel when they do. It will take good men taking offenders aside and explaining to them what they are doing wrong. It will take men setting time aside for some real soul-searching and asking themselves, "Have I ever been guilty of sexually pressuring women?" and even more important, "Have I ever sexually assaulted a woman?" If the honest answer is "yes," it will take these men stepping forward and sincerely apologizing in public, in posts, and most important, if possible in person. It will take companies making it crystal clear what the rules of appropriate behavior in the workplace are, and that anyone breaking these rules will be terminated. It will take criminal offenders, such as Harvey Weinstein and Bill Cosby, being convicted of their crimes. And finally, it will take fathers acting as positive role models for how to treat women and girls, and it will take mothers and fathers teaching their sons how to grow up to be good men who respect and value women and girls.

The #MeToo Movement has clearly advanced from a moment to a full-fledged movement, galvanized by Trump's election and now by the nomination of Judge Brett Kavanaugh and the events surrounding his confirmation hearings. It is clear that we are now experiencing a cultural shift, but at the same time we are embroiled in a divisive cultural issue that threatens to stall the movement. In order to prevent this more women need to become involved in creating the change. We need more people to join the political and social fight to help victims, change laws, and garner support for the changes to our political system we so desperately need.

In addition to all the roadblocks named above, there is still another obstacle in the way of creating enduring change for women. There is a missing piece when it comes to creating the changes that will make women safe. That missing piece is what *"I'm Saying No!" Standing Up Against Sexual Assault, Sexual Harassment, and Sexual Pressure* is all about. My focus here is on helping women make the kinds of changes within themselves and in their personal lives that will really make the difference.

News commentators are saying that "women have finally found their voices." But is this really true? Yes, there is safety in numbers, and as more and more women come forward to report sexual harassment or assault by powerful men, more women are feeling empowered to speak up about the sexual misconduct they have experienced in their own lives. And because many women are now being believed (unlike when the Bill Cosby accusers first came forward), more women are feeling emboldened to speak out. But this isn't really the same as "women finding their voices." Although their bravery should not be minimized, these victims of powerful men are experiencing an unprecedented amount of support. The average woman is not likely to receive the same support when she speaks out—at least, not yet.

Take, for example, the young single mother working as a waitress who gets harassed every day by her male coworkers in the kitchen. Can she speak up and tell the men to stop? Can she tell her boss about how she's being treated? Can she risk being labeled a "troublemaker" and possibly lose her job?

What about the women who are trying to break into industries like construction—women who have to work around men who are threatened by their very presence? Can they speak up about the way their coworkers tell sexual jokes around them or "accidentally" brush up against them?

What about women in law enforcement or the military, who need the support of their male colleagues in order to function in their job?

What about young college women, who are still being sexually assaulted in record numbers? Can they get past their fear of not being believed and not being supported by their college administration, even though they continually hear about other young women who are treated badly when they report the crimes perpetrated against them, and who consistently see the perpetrators walk free?

Is this "moment of change" going to help these women? Hopefully. But I don't think women can depend on that. I believe women still need to work on truly finding their voices, once and for all. That's where *"I'm Saying No!"* comes in. In the upcoming chapters you'll learn about the work that still needs to be done to empower women to speak up when they are being sexually pressured, harassed, or assaulted, the work that needs to be done to empower women to report sexual harassment, sexual assault and childhood sexual abuse.

Women in general, even those who don't work for powerful men, are still afraid to say no to men—period. Many were raised to be "nice girls" and to not "rock the boat;" many were raised to never challenge authority; many were sexually abused in childhood and don't have the tools or the emotional strength to stand up for themselves.

Although some women are feeling empowered by the #MeToo and Time's Up movements, many are still feeling *afraid, hopeless, and helpless.* And for good reason. Women are feeling afraid because:

- 321,500 Americans twelve and older are sexually assaulted or raped each year.

- 1 in 3 women have been sexually assaulted in their lifetime.

- As many as 70 percent of women are sexually harassed at work or at school.

Street harassment is at a record high, with 65 percent of all women experiencing it, starting when they are children. Women of color and women outside the US tend to experience this harassment—and more aggressive forms of it—at an even higher rate.

These statistics reveal a very ugly truth. Despite today's more "progressive" climate, it is not safer for women to freely walk the streets, attend social gatherings, and generally go about their lives today; women are not being respected and protected more than ever before. In fact, the reverse is actually true: women today are more in danger than ever before and have less protection than ever before. Rape culture, the war on women, women being blamed for their own dilemmas, and internalized shame have ensured that this will be the case.

Almost every woman knows at least one other woman who has been sexually assaulted. This is especially true of young women, since the majority of sexual assault victims are under thirty. Young women are more at risk because they tend to go out to bars, night clubs, and parties—places where they are exposed to men who are actively looking for their next conquest.

Female college students are particularly afraid because they are among those who are at highest risk for sexual assault. As one client who recently started college told me, "I notice that my friends are buying pepper spray and rape whistles, while the guys are buying condoms."

Most college-bound young women have heard horror stories of girls being drugged and raped at fraternity parties, often by a number of men. In some cases, not only do other males at these parties not attempt to rescue a girl who is in trouble, they actually stand idly by and watch. There have even been cases where young male bystanders have recorded incidents and shared the videos with their friends.

Women who have already been sexually assaulted or sexually abused in childhood are especially fearful, and they have reason to be. We know that survivors of previous abuse and assault are at a higher risk for being sexually assaulted again. For example, research shows that 38 percent of college-age women who have been sexually violated were first victimized prior to college.

Women are not only in danger of being sexually assaulted by strangers and acquaintances; they're also at risk within their ongoing intimate relationships. The rate of partner rape is up, as is the rate of sexual assault as an aspect of domestic violence. Statistics reveal that one in ten women has been raped by an intimate partner in her lifetime. And when domestic violence is a part of a relationship, the chances of spousal rape occurring rises by 70 percent.

Sexual assault isn't the only type of violation women experience. Women are also sexually harassed and touched in public, on public transportation, and on the way to work or to class. Even confident women can feel afraid and uncomfortable in their own bodies after being harassed. Street harassment—defined as unwanted comments, gestures, or actions, usually of a sexual nature, that one stranger forces upon another stranger in a public place without the other's consent, is rampant today.

According to the National Street Harassment Report, a survey conducted in 2014 involving 2,000 women in the US, street harassment is a significant and prevalent problem.

Most women surveyed said they were afraid, when the street harassment occurred, that it would escalate. Two-thirds (68 percent) said they were very or somewhat concerned that the incident would escalate into something worse. And street harassment is not only frightening, it can be life-changing. A solid 4 percent of the respondents of the survey reported having quit a job or moved due to being harassed.

Many women take various means to alleviate their fears of being sexually assaulted, from avoiding walking alone at night to avoiding eye contact to carrying pepper spray in their handbags. Measures such as these can help them to feel more prepared for an attack, but it does not take away the over-arching fear that witnessing and experiencing the consistent objectification of women, as well as the rape culture that currently permeates our country, has taught them to feel.

In a recent study, researchers found that the treatment of women as sex objects contributes to their fears of sexual assault. According to Dr. Laurel Watson, a psychology professor specializing in traumatology at the University of Missouri-Kansas City, "Our research supports previous findings that the rampant sexual objectification of women, what some consider an act of sexual terrorism, can heighten women's fear of incurring physical and sexual harm."

Women feel helpless. In spite of the #MeToo and Time's Up movements, many women still feel that they are on their own when it comes to protecting themselves from men's sexual misconduct. While they may feel somewhat empowered by the number of women who have stepped forward to tell their stories and by the fact that more women are now being believed when they do so, overall, they still feel helpless about changing the overall situation. They feel helpless about protecting themselves against street harassment, sexual assault, and date rape drugs. They feel helpless when it comes to saying no to unwanted sexual advances from men, including strangers, their dates, or even their boyfriends.

Some women don't have the emotional strength to stand up to intense manipulation, sexual pressure, or threats of rejection. Others feel helpless when it comes to stopping their spouses or boyfriends from raping them or forcing them to engage in sexual activities they find abhorrent. Women who have already been sexually assaulted or harassed feel especially helpless since the chances are extremely high that they did not receive the justice they so desperately needed.

The term "rape culture" doesn't just refer to the act of rape itself; it also refers to society's trivialization of sexual assault and normalization of male dominance over women. This rape culture is glaringly evident on college campuses in the US. For example, in 2016, the Kappa Alpha fraternity at the University of Richmond made headlines for an email that urged members to prepare for the "type of night that makes fathers afraid to send their daughters away to school. Let's get it." The Delta Kappa Epsilon fraternity at Yale University was suspended in 2011 after a video of pledges chanting, "No means yes! Yes means anal!" went viral.

Women feel helpless because they feel that they have nowhere to turn for help. More and more, young girls and women who are being harassed or assaulted can't depend on men to step in to help them. In spite of programs like Bystander (an intervention program promoted under the Obama administration), men still tend to stand by while a woman is being sexually harassed or even assaulted, especially in college environments like fraternity parties.

Women feel hopeless. Many women feel hopeless when it comes to teaching men to treat them with more respect. They feel hopeless when it comes to changing the sexist, misogynistic attitudes of so many men, especially young men. They feel hopeless about men coming to view them as more than just bodies, sexual partners, or receptacles for their shame and anger. Some women report feeling hopeless because a man who openly admitted to grabbing women's "pussies" was elected President of the United States. Others feel hopeless because an accused child molester was able to run for the Senate in Alabama. They feel hopeless about changing a society that still gives men permission to oppress women, disrespect them, use them, and discard them. A culture in which so many men still don't recognize that every woman they disrespect, sexually harass, or sexually assault is someone's mother, sister, or daughter.

Women have reason to feel hopeless. In the current administration, they have less protection under the law than they've had in the past. The former White

House stance, with its "It's on Us" organization (launched by President Obama and Vice President Biden) was the first major indication that there might be hope and help for sexual assault victims, especially young women in college. But the current administration is not inclined to support such programs, and many existing programs have gone by the wayside since Obama left office.

Women are *afraid*. They feel *helpless*. They feel *hopeless*. They need help, but they don't know where to turn to get it. I've written *"I'm Saying No!"* to provide women with what they are so desperately looking for: support and validation that their feelings of fear, helplessness, and hopelessness are understandable, and *powerful strategies for prevention and empowerment.*

I'm Saying No! will encourage women to turn their fear and helplessness and hopelessness into action in the form of standing up and saying "No!"—*no* to unwanted sexual pressure, *no* to street harassment, *no* to sexual assault. Women need to be given permission to turn their fear and anxiety into righteous anger—anger that will motivate them to refuse to be mistreated any further.

We women have within us the power to speak up against sexual violence in all its forms. We have the ability to find our voices, no matter how silenced we have been in the past. We have the strength to let our voices be heard to say "No!" to sexual assault, sexual harassment, and sexual pressure. And we have within us the power to access our righteous anger and insist that we be treated with respect and consideration.

Chapter 1:
Empowerment from the Inside Out

Words are singularly the most powerful force available to humanity. We can choose to use this force constructively with words of encouragement, or destructively using words of despair. Words have energy and power of the ability to help, to heal, to hinder, to hurt, to harm, to humiliate and to humble.

—*Yehuda Berg*

No. It's such a simple word, and yet such a powerful one. It's a word that many people say easily, without much effort: "No, thank you"; "No, I don't want to do that"; "No, I don't like that." But for many women, "no" is a very difficult word. A word they seldom speak. A word some don't even know how to say. A word they are afraid to say.

"No" is perhaps the most important word in our language—especially for women. "No," after all, is the word we most often use to protect ourselves—to stand up for ourselves. In order for women to be able to stand up for what is important—their safety and their integrity, for example—they have to be able to say "no": "no," to a sexual request or demand that is unwelcome; "no" to a behavior that is inappropriate or abusive; "no" to a situation or system that is not working or is not fair. Yet for many women, this is hugely challenging.

Many women have a hard time saying no because they fear they will be rejected, abandoned, or punished if they do so:

"I have such a difficult time saying no to a guy I really like if he wants sex right away. I'm afraid that if I say no he won't think I like him and he won't ask me out again."

—Jessica, age 18

"My boyfriend is always pushing to get me to try new things sexually. I've gone along with some things, but I don't like most of them. He even wants me to do some things that actually repulse me, but I try them anyway. I want him to be happy and he tells me that if I don't do these things, he'll find someone else who will."

—Selena, age 23

"My manager always finds a way to touch me whenever we're alone. He sits next to me and puts his hand on my knee or leans in too close. When he walks past me his hand will 'accidentally' brush by my butt. And he always looks at me like he's undressing me. I hate what he does but I'm too afraid to say anything. I need my job and I'm afraid he'll fire me if I don't just keep my mouth shut and go along with him."

—Melanie, age 32

Other women are unable to say no because they have already been traumatized by sexual abuse as a child or sexual assault in adulthood:

"I was sexually abused as a kid and it affected me in many negative ways. One of those ways is that I sometimes freeze when a guy approaches me or when a guy makes a move on me. I just stand there like my feet are in cement. If he starts touching me, instead of telling him to lay off, I end up just letting him. I want to learn how to stop reacting this way, because every time I let a guy touch me when I really don't want him to, I feel re-traumatized."

—Mandy, age 24

And still others can't say no because they were raised to be "nice girls"—i.e., to go along with whatever men tell them to do:

"My parents were very religious. They raised me to view the man as the head of the household and to do whatever he says. I don't like some of the things my husband does to me sexually but I just can't bring myself to tell him to stop. I no longer believe he has the right to use my body any way he chooses, but the old thinking just stops me in my tracks from ever resisting him."

—Marlena, age 36

"I'm ashamed to say that I can't leave my husband even though he physically abuses me when he gets drunk. He comes home from the bar and either starts a fight or immediately starts manhandling me. Either way he ends up raping me and doing things to me that I detest. I don't know why I stay except that when he isn't drinking, he's a really good man and I love him."

—Elizabeth, age 45

As different as these women are in terms of their ages and circumstances, they all have something in common: They all lack the ability to stand up for themselves, to say "No!" to unwanted sexual advances, or to report sexual harassment or assault. Even confident women often find that when it comes to knowing how to say no in the sexual arena, they feel inadequate. And those women who have already been sexually assaulted as adults or experienced sexual abuse as children or adolescents find that when it comes to sexual assertiveness, they simply can't find their voice.

You may be one of these women. It may be that with all the talk about sexual harassment these days—with all the talk about the #MeToo and Time's Up movements in the news—you have realized that you are not comfortable saying no to men who approach you sexually. You may sit quietly while other women talk about how they have been sexually harassed or sexually assaulted, all the while feeling bad about yourself because you can't speak up about what happened to you—or, even worse, what is still happening. Or perhaps all the talk about men's sexual misconduct is triggering for you because you were sexually abused as a child and you have never told anyone about it. It may be terribly upsetting to you to hear about former victims who were harassed or abused for years because it reminds you of how long you have been keeping your silence.

If you find that saying no to sexual pressure is difficult for you; if you are assertive in other areas of your life but find that you lose your voice when you are around men; if you find that you continue to put the desires and needs of men ahead of your own, this book will help you. It will help you become more comfortable saying "No!" to unwanted sexual advances from strangers, dates, and even partners, and it will help you to say it loud and clear—to say it proudly, without hesitation or embarrassment—so there is never any confusion about your message.

Every woman has a "No!" buried inside of her, no matter how deep. By the time you finish this book, you will have found that "No!" buried under your fear and shame, you will understand that you have an absolute right to say it at any time, without apologizing for it. You will also learn how to say "No!" metaphorically; no to women being treated like objects, no to: young girls being taken advantage of and used by selfish men who put their own desires first, no to men viewing their female partners as their property and feeling they have the right to treat them any way they wish, and no to men sticking up for each other and not standing behind women who report abusive men.

"I'm Saying No!" is a declaration. It is about gaining the courage to speak out, to get angry, to say no more! It is about joining with other courageous women to put a stop to women and girls being mistreated, abused, and assaulted by men. And it is about saying "No!" to remaining quiet, to not speaking out against the mistreatment of women, to remaining silent and letting the sexual misconduct of men go unreported.

"I feel like such a coward. Ever since the #MeToo movement began all these women are coming forward to tell their stories, but I still can't tell mine. I'm still afraid of my abuser. He doesn't even know where I am but he told me he would kill me if I ever told and I believed him. Somehow I still believe him. I wish I had the kind of courage that these other women have."

—Amelia, age 35

"I was raped in my dorm room at college. When he started coming on to me I resisted him, but he just kept holding me down so I couldn't get up. I was too ashamed to call out to someone for help. I thought if I kept resisting he'd stop,

but he didn't. When it was all over I was just happy to be alive. I didn't tell anyone because I was too ashamed. I did text him to tell him he raped me but he texted me back and told me it was consensual, that he would never rape a girl because he didn't have to. I knew no one would believe me so I just kept quiet and didn't report it. Now I feel really guilty because I'm sure he's raping other girls and getting away with it."

—Lila, age 19

"I'm afraid to get angry about the things that have happened to me. I've even gone to a therapist, but I could never express my anger. I'm afraid to. I'm afraid that if I start to get angry I will go insane or I'll become like all the monsters who have hurt me."

—Angela, age 30

Sadly, at a time when women are finally being heard and believed; when women are standing together and making their voices known; when women are feeling a collective empowerment as one victim after another comes forward to report the sexual violations she has been subjected to; there are still women who are currently being sexually abused in their intimate relationships and yet are unable to say "No!"—unable to report the abuse or even to walk away. There are still college students who are being raped and are afraid to report it. There are still women who are being subjected to sexual harassment, sexual bullying, and sexual pressure every day but are unable to speak truth to power.

There are also women who are so triggered by all the talk about sexual assault and harassment that they have retreated inside themselves, not wanting to be seen or heard. Women whose personal histories of child sexual abuse or sexual assault as an adult have wounded them so much that they have lost their voice. If you're one of the many women who have been silenced by past trauma, were raised to believe they didn't have a right to say no, or have spoken out in the past and not been heard—I wrote this book for you.

Questionnaire: Do You Need This Book?

If you still aren't certain whether this book is for you, the following question-naire will help you decide:

1. Are you afraid to go to parties or to go out with your friends to clubs or bars because you are afraid someone might slip you a date rape drug or that you might end up drinking too much and having some guy (or guys) take advantage of you?

2. Have you heard horror stories of girls getting gang raped at parties and are afraid it might happen to you?

3. Are you petrified every time you have to walk from your car to your apartment or house at night?

4. Are you frequently harassed as you walk down the street by men making lewd comments, "assessing your body," or trying to pick you up?

5. Have you ever been sexually harassed in a job or at school?

6. Do you think the only way to keep a man is to go along with whatever he wants?

7. Are you unable to say no to a guy when he comes on to you because you don't want to be seen as a bitch or accused of being cold?

8. Do you tend to freeze whenever a guy makes a move on you, even when you don't like the guy or he is being inappropriate?

9. Do you let guys fondle you or have sex with you so you can be popular or fit in with the group?

10. Have you ever "gone along" with whatever a guy wanted you to do sexu-ally, even if it repulsed you, because you were afraid he would stop seeing you if you didn't?

11. Have you been sexually assaulted as an adult?

12. Were you sexually abused as a child?

13. Do you blame yourself for having been sexually assaulted as an adult or sexually abused as a child?

14. Were you triggered by the way Trump talked about women or by his behavior toward them as shown on the *Access Hollywood* tapes?

15. Have you been triggered by all the talk about sexual harassment and assault surrounding the #MeToo and Time's Up movements?

16. Do you put yourself in dangerous situations by drinking too much in public places or allowing yourself to be taken advantage of by men?

17. Does your partner frequently put pressure on you for sex or for sexual activities that you don't want to engage in, and do you have a difficult time saying no to him?

18. Has a partner ever forced himself on you sexually but you continued seeing him anyway?

If you answered "yes" to even one of these questions, this book is definitely for you. *I'm Saying No!* will help you in the following ways:

- If you are afraid of being sexually assaulted to the point where it has hindered your social life, this book will help you develop a mindset that will embolden you while still keeping you safe.

- If you are frequently intimidated by street harassment, this book will teach you how to respond in ways that will discourage this kind of treatment.

- If you are currently being sexually harassed at work or at school, this book will teach you how to respond in assertive ways and help you decide whether to report these incidents and how to report them.

- If you tend to allow men to touch you or to go further than you are comfortable with, this book will help embolden you to stand up against unwanted taunts, approaches, and advances.

- If you have been reckless with yourself, this book will help you to recognize dangerous situations and avoid them. More important, it will help you to understand why you have tended to be reckless and help you develop the willingness to take care of and protect yourself.

- If you blame yourself for previous experiences with sexual abuse or sexual assault, this book will help you understand that these violations are never the victim's fault and help you heal your shame surrounding the trauma.

- If you believe you deserve to be mistreated by men, this book will help you get to the roots of this belief and instead begin believing that you deserve to be treated with respect and consideration.

- If you allow men to do whatever they want to you sexually, this book will help you begin to honor your feelings and your body.

Empowerment as the Key to Prevention

A major thesis of this book is that *empowerment is the key to prevention*. But empowering women to stand up, find their voices, and fight back against sexual assault and harassment is easier said than done. Before that can happen, women need to do the following:

Women need to learn that we have the right to say "No!"

Women need to remember, and in some cases discover, that we have the right to stand up, speak out, and fight back against inappropriate comments, touches, and sexual approaches. We need to come to believe that our words can be powerful and that saying no can be an effective way of deterring men from speaking to and treating us in offensive, aggressive, and harmful ways.

Every girl and every woman has the right to stand up against sexual assault and sexual harassment. Unfortunately, many women don't know they have this right. Some need to be told that they can say "No!" when they don't want to go any further, when they don't want to engage in a particular sexual activity, or when they aren't in the mood for sex, even if they've engaged in sex with that man in the past. Some women also need to be told, or reminded, that they have the right to say "No!" when a man is trying to talk them into engaging in a sexual activity that feels demeaning (including anal sex, sex without a condom, and sex that involves bondage and discipline) or that turns them off sexually, (including being talked to by their partner in degrading ways or other ways that feel unacceptable to them).

Women need to be taught how to say "No!"

Some women know it is their right to say "No!" but find they are unable to do so even when they try. This is especially true for women who have already been traumatized by child sexual abuse or by sexual assault as an adult. As one client shared with me, "Time after time I just freeze when a guy makes a sexual advance, hoping it will stop him or he will walk away." This "freezing reaction" is a common reaction of those who were sexually abused in childhood.

Women need to be educated about the price they pay when they don't say "No!"

Some women know they have the right to say "No!" but are reluctant to do so—often because they are afraid they won't be able to keep a man unless they do what he wants. Too many young women today have such low self-esteem that they believe a young man will only want to be with them if they go along with whatever he wants sexually. Competition among young women for men is so intense that it is common for young women to agree to or even instigate sexual acts that are repugnant to them, not realizing the damage this does to their self-esteem. And peer pressure can even play a part in a young girl's response to unwanted sexual advances, as evidenced by one young client I worked with, who told me, "What do you do when a guy starts touching you and you don't like it? I get paranoid about saying no because I don't want to come off as 'bitchy.' And besides, if I don't go along with what he wants, some other girl will."

Women need to recognize that speaking up and standing up is not only their right but their obligation—to themselves and to other women. When girls and women allow men to treat them with disrespect and even disdain, it becomes a major wound to their self-esteem and self-concept. The more a girl or woman puts up with, the more distorted her image of herself becomes. Little by little, acts of disrespect, objectification, and shaming whittle away at her self-esteem until she has little regard for herself and her feelings. There is a huge price to pay for "going along" with sexual exploitation. When a woman gives away her body, she also gives away her integrity.

Learning to say no can empower you and help prevent sexual victimization.

Research shows that being able to say no in a way that communicates to the other person that you mean it can be a powerful weapon against sexual assault and misconduct of all kinds. A study called, "Reducing Sexual Victimization among Adolescent Girls" found, for example, that women who firmly resist unwanted sexual advances stand a greater chance of escaping a sexually coercive situation. Saying no in a strong, assertive way can also provide you with the needed strength and motivation to continue resisting. (There are some situations where a woman needs to not resist in order to save her life; I will address this later).

Knowing how to say no not only eliminates so-called "misunderstandings" and empowers women to push away those intruders who just won't go away, it also helps women with their shame. If a woman is clear that she said a firm "No!" she isn't as likely to blame herself if a man continues to push her for sex to the point where he sexually assaults her, after all, she told him "No!" and there was no confusion about that. While she will still have to deal with the shame of being sexually violated, of feeling defiled and made to feel powerless, she won't have the added burden of wondering whether she "led him on" in any way. And it's this type of self-blame that is one of the most damaging aspects of having been sexually violated.

Every Woman Needs This Book

Whether you are young or old, highly successful or just getting started, married or single, assertive or passive, sexually experienced or new to the dating scene, you need this book. No matter what your ethnicity, you need this book (although some ethnic groups need it more than others). For example:

While 80 percent of rapes are reported by white women, women of color are more likely to be assaulted than white women. (www.endrapeoncampus. org)

- Native American women are 2.5 to 3.5 times more likely to experience sexual assault compared to all other races. (Women of Color Network)

- The National Violence against Women Survey found that 34.1% of Native American women report rape in their lifetime.

- And according to a 2014 study, about 22% of black women reported being raped and 41% experienced other forms of sexual violence. (www. endrapeoncampus.org)

While white women find it difficult to report rape, women of color find it even more difficult. For example, for every one black woman that reports her rape, at least fifteen others do not. Asian/Pacific Islander women tend to report lower rates of rape and other forms of sexual violence than do people of color from other racial backgrounds.

Women of color also have a higher rate of marital rape and are less likely to report it. For example:

- Married Latinas are less likely than other women to immediately define their experience of forced sex as rape and terminate their relationships; some view sex as a marital obligation.

- An estimated 29.1 percent of African American females are victimized by intimate partner violence in their lifetime (rape, physical assault or stalking). (Women of Color Network)

Women need to feel empowered to stand up for themselves and to strengthen their resolve to keep themselves safe from sexual assault. They need to learn effective strategies for handling sexual harassment at work, school, and on the street. They need to learn better ways of handling sexual pressure and coercion. In essence, they need to take the next step in their evolution of becoming the most powerful woman possible—a woman who can and will protect her body and her integrity against sexual attacks of any form.

While this book is written for every woman, it specifically applies to the following groups:

1. **Young women ages 16-30.** High school girls, young career women, and girls going off to college are the women who are most vulnerable to being sexually assaulted and harassed and the ones who are most often in search of help. "I'm Saying No" is designed to prepare these women for the hazards they will likely face especially when it comes to protecting themselves at parties, on dates, on the streets, and in the workplace.

2. **College students.** This population of women is particularly at risk for

being sexually assaulted. According to RAINN, women aged 18-24 who are college students are three times more likely than women in general to experience sexual violence. It's estimated that in the fall of 2016, a total of 20.5 million students attended American colleges and universities, females making up the majority of students—about 11.7 million students. Most parents don't sit their teenage or twenty-something daughters down and explain the possible risks they'll face at college or the best ways to protect themselves from sexual assault or sexual harassment. Most don't explain their rights, how and whom to report an incident to, and how and whom to seek counseling from if they are sexually assaulted or harassed. This book is the primer every young women needs but is not likely to get anywhere else. Every young woman should have a copy of this book before entering college or starting a job. In particular, every student going away to college needs this book. So much can happen that first year, when young adults are first introduced to a world away from the (hopefully) watchful eyes of their parents; in fact, studies show that college freshman and sophomore women are at greater risk for becoming victims of sexual assault than are upperclassman, and 84 percent of women who have reported sexually coercive experiences have said that it occurred during their first four semesters on campus.

3. **All the girls and women who are having difficulty managing the sexual pressure they continually experience.** Young women today are constantly pressured and coerced at school, at parties, and whenever friends gather. This category also includes women who are continually pressured by their intimate partners for sex or to engage in sexual activities they find repugnant.

4. **Those women who have already been sexually assaulted or sexually abused in childhood (one in three women).** The information and advice contained in this book will help victims heal their shame, become clear that it was not their fault, and arm themselves with knowledge that will empower them and help prevent them from being abused again (the average woman who was sexually abused as a child is more vulnerable to being sexually assaulted later on in life, as are women who are sexually assaulted in adulthood).

5. **Those women who are upset about sexual harassment, on the job and in school settings.** Shockingly, research reveals that *70 percent of women experience sexual harassment on the job.* Those women who are currently being sexually harassed at work will be especially interested in this book, as will women who are just entering the job market. Women have reported being shocked at hearing the complaints against the powerful men like Roger Ailes, Harvey Weinstein, and Charlie Rose and said that hearing about them was a wakeup call. One client shared with me, "I was feeling really confident that I would be able to know how to deal with unwanted advances from a man, even someone in power, but now I'm not so sure. These women aren't passive little wallflowers. They are assertive, successful women. And yet they didn't know how to say no to a powerful man. The truth is, I really don't know how I'd handle myself in the same situation, and I don't like that."

6. **Women who are plagued by street harassment.** Street harassment is of great concern to many women, so much so that organizations such as Stop Street Harassment, Hollaback, and The Street Harassment Project are very popular. According to a 2014 Stop Sexual Harassment national survey, 65 percent of women experience street harassment.

7. **Victims of intimate partner sexual assault.** This is a problem that occurs more than most people are aware of. Statistics reveal that:

- 38,028,000 women have experienced physical intimate partner violence in their lifetime (huffingtonpost.com)

- 4,774,000 women in the US are victims of physical violence perpetuated by an intimate partner every year. (huffingtonpost.com)

- 45.9 percent of the battered women who report abuse each year also report being forced into sex by their intimate partner.

Even though the majority of sexual assault victims are under thirty, make no mistake about it, it is not only young women who are at risk. According to RAINN statistics:

- 15 percent of victimized women are 12–17 years old

- 54 percent are 18-34

- 28 percent are 35-64

- 3 percent are 65 and over

Mature women in their thirties and forties are being given rape drugs when they go to bars with their friends or when they go to parties; women in their forties are being sexually assaulted when they are on date; and women in their fifties are being raped on the streets. Women of all ages need help when it comes to the issue of sexual harassment in the workplace. And in the current culture, women of all ages need to know how to handle themselves in a variety of situations that women didn't have to deal with in the past.

Becoming Empowered from the Inside Out

Learning to say "No!" is not just about learning to say no verbally; it's also about saying no with your mind, body and spirit. And this is not just a "prevention" book; it is a true empowerment tool. It is meant to empower women to stand up to all forms of sexual violation, whatever their age, race, or situation.

The chapters to come will offer you information and strategies that will help you make important internal changes—changes that will help you become empowered from the inside out in the following ways:

- Come out of denial and recognize the dangers all around you.

- Stop blaming yourself for past experiences of sexual violation and put the blame and shame where it belongs—on the perpetrators.

- Gain self-compassion for all the suffering you've already experienced due to the sexual misconduct of men, starting when you were a little girl.

- Become more comfortable with anger and more empowered to express your righteous anger.

- Find a way to express your anger and rage about having been sexually abused in childhood or sexually assaulted as an adult, and to let this anger empower you.

- Realize that you have a right to put your own needs ahead of the needs of men.

- Learn to appreciate, value, and respect your body more—and therefore feel more inclined to protect it.

- Come to know, on a deep emotional level, that you have a right to say no to unwanted sexual advances and defend yourself.

- Become clearer about what it is you do and do not like to do sexually, and begin to believe that you have a right to say no to sexual partners and sexual acts that are not comfortable for you.

- Rid yourself of beliefs and behaviors that make you more vulnerable to sexual attacks.

Becoming empowered from the inside out means that you are willing to look deeper inside yourself to discover why you prefer to ignore the dangers around you; why you have been careless with your body, putting it and yourself in risky situations; why you may even hate your body and think it is ugly, and therefore think that any attention is better than none. Becoming empowered from the inside out means that you are open to learning the reasons why so many women behave in these less-than-life-affirming ways, and that you are willing to do the work required to change these behaviors. It means you are willing to be transformed into a warrior and to join the army of powerful, assertive, brave women who have taken up the challenge of changing the way women are seen and the way women are treated in the world today. And it means that by the time you reach the end of this book, you will insist upon being treated with respect by the men around you.

Moving From a Moment to a Movement

Even though we now have the #MeToo and Time's Up movements and things are changing somewhat when it comes to recognizing the problems women suffer in the workplace and beyond, there is still a lot to do when it comes to changing the minds and hearts of women and men alike. In order to turn this moment into an actual movement, men need to get involved and become better educated about how women feel when they cross boundaries. Many men need to learn just what those boundaries are. Good men need to begin to back women up and to speak up for them when they witness inappropriate behavior and hear inappropriate words coming out of the mouths of other men. More laws need to be passed to protect women, and we need to make certain that the laws that are already on the books are upheld.

But as a group, we women also need to do our part in creating change, both in the world and within ourselves. We need to begin to believe, on a deep level, that we have a right both to *be* protected and to protect *ourselves*. And each individual woman's task is to find her voice—to speak up when someone crosses her boundaries, whether this means asking her to do something she doesn't want to do or trying to manipulate or force her to have sex when she doesn't want to.

If you don't feel like you can do all these things at this point, you are not alone. Many women have not found their voice. Many are still afraid to speak up to defend themselves. Many haven't set their boundaries around sexuality and don't even know what healthy boundaries look like. In fact, there are more women like you than there are women who feel strong enough and confident enough to speak up for themselves in the sexual arena.

There is no shame in not knowing how to say "No!" No shame in being afraid to speak up. No shame in not being able to report abuse. There are good reasons for your reluctance and fear, and we will discuss these reasons throughout the book. No woman or girl should feel ashamed about not being able to assert herself. It takes an enormous amount of self-respect, determination, courage, and strength to do so—and unfortunately, many girls and women have already had their store-house of these important qualities depleted by the constant verbal, emotional, and physical attacks they have endured in their lifetime.

In general, women have more power than they know. We can protect ourselves, make our wishes known, and say "No!" to unwanted sexual advances. We just have to learn how. And that is the focus of this book: helping you recognize the power you already have.

In the chapters to come I'll walk alongside you as you go through all the steps you need to take in order to gain the self-confidence, self-respect, will, and courage to start saying "No!" with conviction. My hope is that as you read this book, you will become stronger and stronger, and your resolve to take your life—and your sexuality in particular—into your own hands will increase to the point where you will become confident in your ability to stand up and protect yourself in any situation. You will recognize that doing so is your job and yours alone, and you will feel proud to take on the task.

That being said, I want to make it very clear that the problems of sexual assault, sexual harassment, and sexual pressure are not the creations of women. They are the creations of men. Women should be able to walk freely on the streets with no fear of being harassed or assaulted. Women should be able to go to parties or bars and not have to watch their drinks. Women should be able to get drunk and not fear that a man—or several men—will take advantage of them. It should be up to men to make the world safer for women, not the other way around.

Nevertheless, there is tremendous value in loving yourself and respecting yourself enough to make yourself safer. There is value in taking responsibility for your own actions. And there is value in doing *everything in your power* to prevent being sexually traumatized or retraumatized.

A Note about Terms Used in This Book

Victim versus Survivor. As you will notice, I use the term "former victim" as opposed to the term "survivor" throughout this book. I do this even though it has become politically correct to use the word "survivor" when describing someone who has been abused or assaulted and who survived the experience. The argument is that this term is more empowering than the word "victim," which has the connotation of someone who is weak or damaged.

I completely agree that the word "survivor" is far superior. But over the years, I have received feedback from many clients who have said they are actually offended when someone calls them a survivor, especially when their victimization happened very recently or when they are just beginning to heal from the violation they experienced. They've shared with me that they want to be the ones to decide what they call themselves and that the word survivor doesn't fit for them until they have experienced some substantial recovery. Still others object to being called a survivor by others because they feel like their victimization is being glossed over and that the word survivor makes other people more comfortable than acknowledging they have been victimized.

I use the phrase "former victim" not because I don't want you to feel empowered, or because I don't want to give you credit for surviving horrific abuse or assault. I use the phrase "former victim" because I don't want to minimize the abuse or assault that you experienced by avoiding the term "victim." You have, in fact, been a victim, with all that implies.

That said, if you consider yourself a survivor, please substitute that word in your mind whenever I use the phrase "former victim." Please know that I respect whatever your choice is. But if you have a strong reaction to the word victim, I also ask you to question why that is. Is it possible that you are still struggling with the fact that you were, in fact, victimized? Is it because deep down inside, you are still blaming yourself? Is it that you hate the idea that someone could overpower you and make you feel so weak? If so, you may have some work to do.

Audience

For the most part, I am addressing women and older girls in this book. I realize that there are many male victims of sexual violations and they have much in common with female victims. But I purposely chose to write this book for the female sex because there are so many issues at play that are specific to women and girls and need to be addressed.

I'm also primarily addressing women who have been sexually victimized by men in this book, though I understand that there are some of you who may have been sexually violated by female abusers. This is especially true when it comes to childhood sexual abuse, as well as adult relationships between two women where one abuses or puts sexual pressure on the other. In some sections, therefore, I will sometimes use the phrase "he or she" to include those of you to whom this applies—but overall, I address the reader as "she" and the abuser as "he,' since that most accurately describes the reality of the majority of the situations I describe. There certainly are female abusers in the world, but their numbers don't compare to the number of male abusers in the world.

Trigger Warning

I will be naming the various forms of sexual violations and giving real-life examples of how women have been sexually abused and assaulted in this book. This may trigger memories of past trauma for you. If this is the case, I recommend that you practice the grounding technique below. For those of you who were severely abused in the past, focusing on your trauma can be especially triggering. It can bring up feelings of fear and shame that at times may feel overwhelming, causing suicidal thoughts and behavior such as: recklessness and self-mutilation. It is very important that you seek professional help if you experience any of these symptoms while you are working your way through the book.

A trigger is any sensory information you take in that causes an overwhelming emotional and/or physical response that you associate with a trauma. A trigger is not merely anything that reminds you of the trauma. Some of the symptoms of rape triggers can include anxiety, panic attacks, rage, intense sadness, the urge to drink or drug, the urge to self-harm, dissociation, and even a strong sexual urge.

How to Cope with Being Triggered or Having a Flashback

1. Tell yourself that you are having a flashback. Remind yourself that the actual event is over and that you survived.

2. Breathe. Take slow, deep breaths by placing your hand on your stomach and inhaling long breaths. You should see your hand move out with the inhalations, and watch it fall in with the exhalations. When we panic, our body begins to take short, shallow breaths, and the decrease in oxygen can make you feel more panicked. Deep breathing is important because it increases the oxygen

in your system and helps you move out of an anxious state more quickly.

3. Return to the present by using your five senses (sight, smell, sound, taste, touch).

   Look around you.

   - What do you see? Count the items in the room; count the colors or pieces of furniture around you.

   - What do you smell? Breathe in the smells around you. Light an aromatic candle or light incense.

   - What do you hear? Listen to the noises around you, or turn on music.

   - What do you taste? Eat or drink something you enjoy. Focus on the flavor.

   - What does it feel like? Hold something cold, like a piece of ice, or hot, like a mug of tea.

4. Think about what would make you feel safer. Wrap yourself in a blanket, or go into a room by yourself and close the door. Do whatever it takes to make you feel secure.

How to Get the Most Out of This Book

This book is based on a program designed specifically to help you move from one mindset to another. I recommend that you practice each step and complete the exercises in each chapter before moving on to the next. Readers of my previous books have reported that they got much more out of my books when they took the time to complete the exercises. Some read the book in its entirety and then went back to complete the exercises, while others said it worked best for them to complete the exercises as they read each chapter.

Navigating the Structure of the Book

As you will notice, there isn't one specific chapter devoted to learning to say "No!" in this book. Instead, I offer information and strategies in each chapter that, collectively, will move you toward being able to say "No!" both literally and symbolically. I specifically focus on sexual assault, street harassment, and sexual pressure here, but the advice I offer applies to all forms of sexual violation.

At the end of each chapter I offer two ways to focus your attention concerning what you have just read:

- I summarize the goal of the chapter.

- I provide you with an exercise or way to practice saying "No!"

Part I

Making Changes from the Inside Out

Chapter 2
Why It Is So Difficult For Women to Say No

Each person holds so much power within themselves that needs to be let out. Sometimes they just need a little nudge, a little direction, a little support, a little coaching, and the greatest things can happen.

—Pete Carroll

There are many reasons why women have so much difficulty saying no, and we will discuss these reasons throughout this chapter. But the most important message I want to communicate in this chapter is that it is not a woman's fault if she has difficulty standing up for herself and saying "No!" to sexual misconduct. Girls are essentially raised and conditioned not just by their parents but by society in general—to always say "yes." As I wrote in my book *The Nice Girl Syndrome*, girls are raised to be passive, compliant, and agreeable, to put their own needs aside, and to worry more about other people's feelings than about their own.

There are four major reasons why many women behave in Nice Girl ways. These include:

- *Biological predisposition*, i.e., women are hardwired to be patient and compassionate and to value connection over confrontation.

- *Societal beliefs* passed on to a child by the culture or society in which she is raised.

- *Familial beliefs* passed on to a child by her family, either directly or by witnessing parental and other family members' behavior.

- *Experiential beliefs* a child forms as a result of her personal experiences, including childhood trauma.

Let's focus on these one at a time.

Biological Predisposition

Some scientists argue that women are hardwired to be patient and compassionate, and to value connection over confrontation. In her landmark studies, Harvard University professor Carol Gilligan came to the conclusion that what has previously been considered "female passivity" is often the woman's need to seek a solution that is most inclusive of everyone's needs—"as an act of care rather than the restraint of aggression."

Another important UCLA study suggests that women actually have a larger behavioral repertoire than the fight-or-flight response men are limited to. When the hormone oxytocin is released as part of the stress response in a woman, it buffers the fight-or-flight response and encourages her to tend to children and gather with other women. This same stress response can overshadow a woman's need to protect herself.

Societal Beliefs

Even today, girls are typically socialized to be polite, appropriate, pleasant, and agreeable—all the personality traits that characterize Nice Girls. For centuries, being nice was often synonymous with being female. Girls were supposed to be "Sugar and spice and everything nice." Unfortunately, the feminine ideal continues to be a woman who tends to please others, to be selfless, nice, and pretty, and to make herself the object of someone else's life.

In order to attain this culturally prescribed ideal, a teenage girl must put away a great many parts of herself. She stops speaking out and expressing her feelings and focuses instead on trying to please others, especially those of the opposite sex.

Familial Beliefs

Your family passed down to you certain messages and beliefs. These include everything from the way people should treat one another to the role women play in a family. These messages and beliefs have a powerful influence on your thinking and behavior and help shape who you are today.

Some women have a harder time saying no and standing up against sexual pressure and harassment because they have a more difficult time shedding this unhealthy Nice Girl behavior than others. Take Sarah, a former client of mine. She was raised in a deeply religious family where females were viewed as second-class citizens. Her father was considered to be the head of the household and he made all the decisions. Her mother never contradicted him and she had to get her husband's permission before leaving the house; he had to know where she was at all times. Sarah had to do the same, even after she became a young woman.

What did Sarah learn from her parents' messages and beliefs? She learned that as a female she needed a man to protect her from the dangerous world outside. She learned to be passive and to not trust her own judgment. She also learned that it was okay for a man to dominate her. When she grew up, her typical pattern was to date men who were controlling and who thought she should be subservient to them. This culminated in her being sexually controlled by her boyfriend of two years.

By the time she came into therapy, Sarah was in bad shape, both emotionally and physically. Her boyfriend had become increasingly sexually violent with her, even to the point of inserting foreign objects into her vagina. After one such episode Sarah went to the emergency room because of severe bleeding and was told she had a perforated uterus.

While Sarah's is an extreme case, she is not by any means alone. Many women were raised in a way that has set them up for being mistreated or abused by men.

There are several common types of family situations that can set a woman up to be a Nice Girl. These include:

- Having a passive mother

- Having an abusive or tyrannical father or older brother

- Being raised in a misogynistic family

- Having parents who place an extremely high value on being "righteous"

Experiential Beliefs

It is quite common for Nice Girls to have experienced physical, emotional, or sexual abuse in their childhood or as adults. Abuse and neglect tend to create certain unhealthy attitudes and beliefs that set women up to be Nice Girls— and often, victims. For example, those who end up becoming a Nice Girl or taking on a victim stance tend to:

- Blame themselves when something goes wrong

- Doubt themselves, including doubting their perceptions, knowledge, and beliefs

- Be overly trusting of others, even when someone has proven to be untrustworthy

- Be naïve when it comes to the motives of others

- Believe that their own needs are not as important as those of others and that they should meet the needs of others (especially those of their partner and children) no matter what the consequences or hardships to themselves

Exercise: Where Did Your Nice Girl Behavior Come From?

Look over the list of four major reasons why women are too nice and see which of these you can relate to. For example, you, like Sarah, may have been raised in a home where you were taught to be nice, compliant, or passive, or you may have grown up witnessing your mother being passive in her relationships with men. Or perhaps you were physically or emotionally abused as a child, and because of this experience you grew up being afraid to speak up for fear of being hurt.

Even if you didn't have any of these kinds of experiences growing up, think about how you may have been influenced by society to keep your mouth shut and be compliant instead of making waves by speaking up.

Making the connection between the way you were raised and the way you now behave, especially when you are around men, is very important. I suggest you write about any connections you have been able to make based on the information above.

Some of you will resonate with this information on Nice Girl behavior more than others. For those who do, I have included an entire chapter on how to overcome Nice Girl behavior later on in the book.

Another Culprit: Low Self-Esteem

In addition to girls and women being conditioned to be passive, compliant, and agreeable, another major reason why girls and women have such a difficult time saying no to unwanted sexual behavior from men is that they simply don't have the required self-esteem to do so. It takes confidence to stand up and declare that you aren't going to be bullied into sex. It takes confidence to say "No!" to getting involved with sexual activities that you are not interested in. It takes superhuman confidence to walk past a group of men on the street who are calling obscenities at you and not feel intimidated and afraid.

In the last twenty years, there has been a society-wide focus on raising the self-esteem of girls and young women. We want our young women to feel proud and strong, to walk with their heads held high. So we try to instill confidence in them. We tell them they can do whatever they set their minds to do. We send them off to college with the feeling that they are safe—that they can protect themselves, and should they find themselves in a situation where they can't, *we* will protect them. But this is a lie. They are not safe, they don't know how to protect themselves, and we don't protect them.

How ironic that we now have movements to encourage and empower girls and women all over the world and yet one in three girls are still either sexually abused or raped in their lifetime, traumas that undermine or even wipe out any gains in self-esteem they may have experienced as a result of our efforts. How can we encourage young women in the US to feel empowered enough to go to college when there is such a high risk of being raped on campus? Further, how can we expect them to "get over it" and go back to classes if they become a victim of sexual violence? The sad truth is that the average young woman who is raped at college never returns to complete her degree.

Even the most confident girl cannot sustain her sense of confidence if she is sexually violated. She feels so much shame that it is difficult to hold her head up high. She finds it difficult to find the motivation to continue on her path, whether it be college or a career.

The ugly truth is that, by far, *the single most damaging thing to young women and girls' self-esteem in the US is the way they are mistreated in our culture.* The average girl experiences unwanted sexual remarks and sexual behavior from boys and men beginning when she is just a small child. Remarks about her body and her sexuality come from boys at school and from men on the streets. Young girls today continually complain that they are bullied in school—mostly by boys who make remarks about their genitals, their behinds, and, as they get older, their breasts. In today's schools, starting in grammar school, there is a common practice of boys running by girls and grabbing their behinds or breasts and running away.

Sexual aggressors are everywhere. The men who yell out sexual comments as a girl or woman walks by them. The old man who exposes himself. The guy who sits too close to her on the bus or rubs up against her on the subway. The boys who make fun of her looks at school or who grab her breasts or butt whenever they get the chance. The men standing on the street who grab their crotches and say disgusting things to her when she walks by. You ask any woman to name the inappropriate, disrespectful, frightening, and shame-inducing things they've had to endure, starting when they were children, and you will be amazed by how much the typical woman has suffered. From the time most girls reach puberty, or even before, they have been either sexually abused, street shamed, slut shamed, or bullied sexually.

Fear

Last, but certainly not least, the reason why women have such difficulty saying no to unwanted sexual advances from men is that we are afraid –and for a multitude of reasons.

Some women are afraid to say no because of social pressure. As one teenager shared with me: "Guys are always coming on to me. Some of them are my friends or friends of friends and I don't want to make them angry and get a reputation for being a bitch. I try to push away their hands or move away from them but they just keep trying. How do I get them to stop without getting them pissed off?"

Another young client told me, "At our school, when a girl turns a guy down for sex she is running the risk of him making up lies and spreading rumors about her all over school."

And of course, we know that women are afraid to say no to sexual harassment at work because they are fearful of negative consequences, such as being demoted, passed over for a promotion, or fired. As one client shared with me,

"It got so that I hated my manager for the way he treated me. He constantly made inappropriate sexual comments and did things like lick his lips while he focused on my breasts. I never felt safe around him. It was creepy. He propositioned me more than once and was always trying to get me alone in a room. But I knew that I couldn't report him. I was just a secretary, newly on the job, and he was a very well-respected manager who made the company a lot of money. I also knew I couldn't be too forceful when I turned him down, that I always had to leave the door open so I wouldn't hurt his ego and make him angry. I felt horrible about myself for putting up with it but I needed that job."

Women who have already been sexually assaulted or sexually abused in childhood often find it especially difficult to say no to unwanted advances. Because it is likely that any attempt they made to say no to their perpetrator was ignored or even punished, they may feel it is useless to even try. And as I mentioned in Chapter 1, many women who have already been traumatized tend to freeze when a man makes a sexual pass at them, especially if he does it aggressively.

At the core of women's fear around saying no to men's sexual advances is the mere fact that as females we are the "weaker" sex—physically at least. The truth is that most men are bigger and stronger than most women and for this very reason, they intimidate us. We aren't necessarily conscious of this on a daily basis, but the fear is there nonetheless. It is similar to how a small dog feels next to a large dog. The two dogs can coexist on a day-to-day basis and even play and romp with one another, but make no mistake about it: the smaller dog knows his limitations. He knows that if the larger dog wanted to, he could overpower him.

The other factor, closely related to the size differential, is that men carry a built-in weapon they can use against women: their penis. Most men don't think of their penis as a weapon, and most women don't either. But nevertheless, an erect penis can be used to penetrate, harm, and dominate a woman. Again, it isn't that women consciously think of this on a day-to-day basis; it's simply that the inherent fear is there, just below the surface.

These two physical factors influence a woman's thinking and feeling on a subconscious basis. We know that our very safety is dependent on the good will of men. If we cross them, if we make them angry, we are risking being physically punished. While most men do not use their physical advantage against women, the possibility—and the threat—is ever-present.

Women's inherent fear of men also comes from our history of being dominated by them. Throughout human history, physical force has been used by the dominant forces in society to keep subordinate groups in their place. Men have always been physically larger and stronger than most women, and most societies have been male-dominated. Because of this, for centuries, women have been frequent victims of physical assault and intimidation by men and have learned, in response, to be afraid of men.

In ancient Roman times, a man was allowed by law to chastise, divorce, or kill his wife for adultery, or even for attending public games. During the Middle Ages, a man's right to beat his wife was beyond question—yet a woman could be burned alive for so much as threatening her husband.

It took centuries before any real efforts were made to curtail this problem, because for centuries few people viewed violence in the home as a problem. The common notion—and this is one that persists in many societies today— was that a woman was not a full human being. Instead, she was considered to be property—first of her father, then of her husband.

Girls and women continue to be so afraid today because we continue to be dominated and abused by men. Although much has been done to alleviate domestic violence and child sexual abuse, the fact is that these two crimes are still rampant in every culture in the world. Men are still physically and emotionally abusing their wives in record numbers, and the rate of childhood sexual abuse is still climbing. And once a girl or woman has been abused, whether emotionally, physically, or sexually, she becomes overwhelmed by fear and shame. In fact, many women go on to live lives characterized by the fear that they will once again be victimized.

These fears are at the core of why it is so difficult for women to stand up to men and say "No!" For this reason, I encourage you to remind yourself periodically of the origins of your fears. Don't use your difficulties with standing up to men as a reason to be critical of yourself or to shame yourself. Women who are unable to leave abusive relationships, even though they know they should, don't stay because they are weak or stupid or masochistic, they stay because they are afraid. And they are afraid for all the reasons we have discussed.

Below is a summary of the many reasons women have difficulty saying "No!" and reporting abuse and assault. These include:

1. Many women are still raised to be "Nice Girls"—to be sweet and agreeable instead of assertive.

2. Women are biologically hardwired to seek compromise over conflict.

3. Many women and girls suffer from low self-esteem, making it difficult for them to stand up for themselves. Their desire to be accepted/popular/loved overshadows their need to put themselves first or even to protect themselves.

4. Many girls and women have been sexually abused and/or sexually harassed in the past and have lost their ability to speak up as a result.

5. Many girls and women have already had the experience of speaking up and not being heard or believed.

6. Many girls and women don't believe they deserve better treatment from boys and men, either because of the way they were raised or because they are victims of previous abuse.

7. Women tend to internalize shame. When something bad happens to them, instead of getting angry they tend to blame themselves.

We will discuss all of these reasons in depth throughout the book. The important thing to understand at this point is that it is *not your fault* if you have a hard time saying "No!" or if you have difficulty standing up for yourself.

Exercise: Why Do You Have Difficulty Standing Up for Yourself and Saying No?

You may relate to one or more of the reasons listed above, or you may have another one that is not listed. Take a few minutes to consider why you have difficulty saying "No!" to men or standing up for yourself in situations where you feel uncomfortable and write about them here or in your journal.

_____

_____

_____

_____

There are effective ways to overcome your preconditioning, the damage to your self-esteem, and any other reasons you might have for being afraid. I will offer many of these in this book but the most important is to practice saying "No!" *The more you say it, the stronger you will become.*

Saying "No!" not only stops many men from continuing to touch you or pursue you, it also emboldens you to stand up and fight for yourself. Saying "No!" reminds you that you have a right to protect yourself and your body. It reminds you that you don't have to give in just because a man wants something from you sexually.

Why Don't Women Report?

Now that so many women are coming forward to report sexual assaults and sexual harassment from the past, many are being met with criticism—namely—"Why did they wait so long to report it?" and "Why didn't they speak up at the time?"

Just as women often have difficulty saying "No!" and standing up for themselves with men, they also have difficulty reporting sexual violations. Why is this? I have found that there are actually many understandable reasons why women don't report sexual assault and sexual harassment, including:

1. Victims are too ashamed to come forward. Shame is at the core of the intense emotional wounding women experience when they are sexually violated. Sexual assault is, by its very nature, humiliating and dehumanizing.

2. Victims of sexual assault blame themselves. Most victims of sexual assault blame themselves in some way and this often keeps them from reporting.

3. Victims are afraid of being blamed. This makes sense since we have a victim blaming culture in which we make the assumption that if something bad happens to you it is somehow your own fault. This is particularly true for the way we blame women. "She shouldn't have gone to that party," "What does she expect if she wears a dress that short. She's just asking for it." "It's her own fault for drinking so much."

4. Victims are afraid they will not be believed. Sexual misconduct is the most under-reported crime because victims' accounts are often scrutinized to the point of exhaustion and there is a long history of women not being believed when they attempted to report a sexual violation. Although friends and family usually believe a woman when she tells them she was sexually assaulted, when it comes to reporting the crime, it is another story. Most women have heard horror stories about how other victims have had jump through hoops in order to be believed and often the perpetrator's word is taken over hers, especially when the rape has occurred on a college campus or when the perpetrator is a popular guy on campus, such as a star football player. Young college women are afraid

to report the rape to their college administration because of a long history of cases being mishandled.

5. <u>They are afraid of retaliation by the perpetrator</u>. Eight out of ten victims know their rapist and because of this, many are afraid that if they report it to the authorities their perpetrator will retaliate in some way. In addition, rapists who are strangers often threaten to kill their victim if she reports the sexual assault. There have been only a few well-known cases of a rapist returning to harm a former victim, but enough to scare women with this possibility.

6. <u>They are afraid of having their reputation ruined.</u> Many female victims are afraid of the stigma connected to sexual assault. They are afraid of it getting out and it hurting their reputation. This is especially true of adolescents, who focus on their "reputation" obsessively. And there is good reason for them to be concerned. I've had many adolescent clients whose named were smeared after the news that they were sexually assaulted came out at school. Girls often called "whores" and "sluts" and received many rude and threatening comments and gestures from the boys at school.

7. <u>They don't believe it will do any good</u>. Most victims know that very few rapists are caught and even fewer are convicted and serve any jail time. In fact, ninety-nine percent of perpetrators walk free. With these odds, it is understandable that victims would have serious doubts about reporting and that they would question whether it is worth having their integrity and their character questioned. Those with a history of childhood sexual abuse who never received justice are particularly prone to feeling it will do no good to report a current sexual violation.

8. <u>They want to put it behind them—to forget it ever happened</u>. I often hear clients tell me that this is why they didn't report the sexual assault. "I just wanted to move on," they will say. Unfortunately, this doesn't work. Former victims can't just put it out of their minds. The pain and fear and shame surrounding sexual trauma continues to haunt them. They suffer from troubling flashbacks, nightmares and difficulty sleeping, depression, extreme anxiety, and have difficulties with issues such as trust and

low self-esteem. Their sexuality suffers, either causing them to have difficulty engaging in the sexual act or the other extreme, they become promiscuous. Many repeat the trauma by continuing to be victimized or by becoming abusive themselves.

9. <u>They don't want to go through the "hassle" of reporting it to the authorities.</u> This is an interesting excuse when you compare sexual assault to what happens when someone gets their car stolen or their house broken into. We seldom, if ever, hear people say, "I didn't want to go through the trouble of reporting the robbery to the police," in these circumstances. Most people don't get their car or other valuables back when they are stolen but this does not stop them from reporting the theft to the police. The truth is, this excuse probably reflects the victim's lack of self-esteem.

10. <u>They are too traumatized to report the assault.</u> This is more common than you would imagine and brings up some issues that not everyone is aware of. For example, most people are familiar with PTSD (Post-Traumatic Stress Disorder), a severe anxiety disorder with characteristic symptoms that develop after the experience of an extremely traumatic stressor, such as a violent assault on one self. Many understand that those who suffer from PTSD often relive the experience through nightmares and flashbacks, have difficulty sleeping, and feel detached and estranged, and these symptoms can be severe enough and last long enough to significantly impair the person's daily life. What many don't realize, however, is that PTSD is marked by clear biological changes as well as psychological symptoms and is complicated by the fact that it frequently occurs in conjunction with related disorders such as depression, substance abuse, and problems of memory and cognition.

In some cases, the symptoms of PTSD can become more debilitating than the trauma. Some characteristics of PTSD can actually run counter to a victim reporting the sexual assault. She may be so overwhelmed by avoidance symptoms such as emotional numbing, or a strong desire to stay away from anything that reminds her of the assault, that she is incapable of taking the action of reporting. Or, she may be overtaken by feelings of helplessness and passivity that can be symptomatic of PTSD.

Instead of asking why victims don't tend to report sexual assault, we need to ask, "What are we doing to make it safe for them to report?" and "What can we do to make reporting processes less threatening and more trauma-sensitive for victims?" Women have good reasons for not being able to say no to sexual advances from men. And they have good reasons for not being able to report it when they are sexually assaulted or harassed. If you have had difficulty doing either one or both of these things, please make a concerted effort to be less critical of yourself. Your behavior is entirely justified.

Goals of Chapter 2

This chapter was designed to acquaint you with the many valid reasons why women have a hard time saying "No!" and why they have a difficult time reporting sexual violations. Learning these reasons and reminding yourself of them is a first and important step toward taking away any shame you might have about your own difficulties in doing so. You are not weak; you do not lack courage. The reasons for your fear are real and universal.

No! Exercise

- Find a quiet place where you can be alone and undisturbed. Begin to say "No!" out loud several times. Pay attention to how it feels to do so. If it brings up fear, try saying it a little louder. If you feel foolish, remind yourself that this is important: you need to be able to say "No!" to unwanted sexual comments, touches, requests, and demands. Now try it again: "No! No! No!"

- Over the course of the next few days, continue saying "No!" out loud. Use different volumes and inflections, again noticing how you feel each time. For example, say "No!" while driving in your car, when you are alone at home, even when you are on a walk.

- After you have practiced saying "No!" for a few days, complete the following sentence a number of times: *When I say "No" I feel* _____.

Do not think of your answer ahead of time, just allow yourself to give spontaneous responses. Continue completing the sentence until you have no more responses (spending no more than two to three minutes in total on this).

Preliminary exercises like this one are aimed at helping you to get more comfortable with saying "No!" and to notice what happens when you do. Most of my female clients give the following types of feedback after doing this exercise:

"I didn't realize how difficult it is for me to say no. It took me days before I could say it in a strong, assertive way."

"I was very uncomfortable saying no; in fact, I felt afraid to say it."

"It felt good to say no. I don't say it enough in my life. It felt empowering."

"The more I practiced saying it, the stronger I felt."

Chapter 3
Knowledge is Power

Feminism is not about girl power. It is about equal power.
—*Whitney Wolfe*

You've no doubt heard the saying, "Knowledge is power." It couldn't be truer than when it comes to empowering women to say "No!" The more you know, the better you will become at protecting yourself. A major way of empowering yourself is by learning information that will help you to: 1) become better prepared to face the challenges you are likely to encounter, 2) stop blaming yourself for not speaking up before, and 3) understand more fully why you are reluctant to speak up and why you find it difficult to report.

The information in this chapter is intended to help you in all three ways.

Our Rape Culture

Most of us are not completely unaware that there is an alarmingly high incidence of sexual assault and harassment in our culture. But few people, most especially women, have actually taken the time to understand why this is. High on the list of things that you need to understand in order to protect yourself from sexual violations is that we are living in what is often referred to as a "rape culture"—a setting in which rape is pervasive and sexual violence is normalized due to societal attitudes about gender and sexuality.

Emilie Buchwald, author of *Transforming a Rape Culture*, defines rape culture as a complex set of beliefs that encourages male sexual aggression and supports violence against women. Rape culture creates a society where violence is seen as sexy and sexuality as violent. Kate Harding, in her excellent book *Asking For It: The Alarming Rise of Rape Culture—and What We Can Do About It* defines rape culture as:

- A culture in which most victims of sexual assault and rape never report it because they fear they will not be believed.

- A culture that condones physical and emotional terrorism against women and presents it as the norm.

- A culture in which people identify with the accused person rather than the person reporting the crime.

- A culture that encourages us to scrutinize victims' stories for any evidence that they brought violence upon themselves.

Rape culture is perpetuated through the use of misogynistic language, the objectification of women's bodies, and the glamorization of sexual violence, thereby creating a society that disregards women's rights and safety. In a rape culture, women experience a continuum of violence that ranges from sexual remarks to sexual touching to rape itself. When society *normalizes* sexualized violence, it accepts and perpetuates rape culture.

Rape culture promotes the idea of women as objects, possessions, prizes, and toys. There are many men in our culture who believe that:

- Women exist for men to pursue and use as they will

- Men are more manly when they can conquer and take

- Men are entitled to sex with any woman who happens to strike their fancy

- Men cannot help but give in to their sexual urges because, after all, they are men

- Men bear no responsibility for their sexual actions

- Submission, whether achieved through drugs, alcohol, intimidation, or physical force, is the same as consent

- Women are responsible for never being "guilty" of "provoking," "exciting," "enticing," "tempting," "seducing," or "bewitching" a male into doing what supposedly comes naturally—i.e., rape.

These beliefs are myths intended to excuse men's bad behavior and place the blame on women. You have the right to expose these myths for what they are, as well as the right to say "No!" to unwanted comments, unwanted touch, and the unreasonable expectation that you should put your needs aside in order to please men.

Symptoms of Rape Culture

- Blaming the victim ("She was asking for it")
- Trivializing sexual assault ("Boys will be boys")
- Sexually explicit jokes
- Tolerance of sexual harassment
- Inflating false rape statistics
- Publicly scrutinizing a victim's dress, mental state, motives, and history
- Gratuitous gendered violence in movies and television
- Defining "womanhood" as submissive and sexually passive
- Pressure on men to "score"
- Pressure on women to not appear "cold"
- Assuming that only promiscuous women get raped
- Assuming that men don't get raped or that only "weak" men get raped
- Refusing to take rape accusations seriously
- Making women feel preventing rape is their responsibility, not men's.

Our Dangerous World

Once you understand the damage that continues to be done to women because of our rape culture, the next step is for you to become clear about just how difficult and even dangerous this world has become for women. Women and girls face real threats every day. This country is truly out of control when it comes to the rate of sexual assault and other sexual violations women are subjected to. For example:

- One in five women will be raped at some point in their lives. If we include child sexual abuse, the figure goes to one in three.

- A rape or attempted rape occurs every five minutes in the United States (according to the US Department of Justice).

- As many as 70 percent of women are sexually harassed at work or at school, and 8 percent of rapes occur while the victim is at work.

- Street harassment is a significant and prevalent problem for women. According to the National Street Harassment Report, a survey conducted in 2014 involving 2,000 women in the US, more than half the women surveyed had experienced verbal harassment, 23 percent had been sexually touched, 20 percent had been followed, 14 percent had been "flashed," and 9 percent had been forced to do something sexual.

- Not all rape is perpetrated by strangers. In eight out of ten cases of rape, the victim knows the person who sexually assaulted them. And according to the National Institutes of Mental Health, 84 percent of victims of rape know the offender and of those, 66 percent were on a date when the rape took place. In fact, acquaintance rape accounts for the largest category of reported sexual crimes.

- Of the total sexual assaults reported in the US, 29 percent were perpetrated by a husband or lover, and 7.7 percent of American women have reported being raped by an intimate partner in their lifetime (ndvac.org). Two studies—one of married women in San Francisco and another conducted in Boston—found that 10 percent of married women had been victims of spousal rape. It has also been reported that 69 percent of women who have been raped by their spouse have suffered this violation more than once. Staff of domestic violence agencies report that sexual assault is one of the most common types of abuse in romantic relationships.

Definitions

Let's make sure we are on the same page, so to speak, about the terms I'll be using throughout this book, and go over some definitions of the different types of sexual violations young girls and women experience in their lives:

Sexual assault: This is a general term referring to any sexual contact or behavior that occurs without explicit consent of the victim. Sexual assault comes in many different forms, and is often referred to as a continuum. This is due to the fact that some incidences will overlap, and the victim will experience multiple different types of sexual assault at the same time. Others will experience sexual assault as an isolated, singular event.

Assault does not have to be penetration. It includes both fondling and molestation. Sexual assault is considered rape when it involves oral, anal, or vaginal penetration. Sexual contact is also illegal if inflicted upon a person who is incapable of giving consent because of age, physical incapacity, or mental incapacity. The terms and definitions below make up a good part of the sexual assault continuum; however, the continuum is not limited to this list. Any unwanted sexual contact, whether it is verbal, visual, or physical, is sexual assault.

Rape: The Federal Bureau of Investigation (FBI) defines rape as "penetration, no matter how slight, of the vagina or anus with any body part or object, or oral penetration by a sex organ of another person, without the consent of the victim." The age of consent differs from state-to-state and country-to-country. However, mental and legal capacity to consent is fairly easy to understand. Someone with "diminished capacity" e.g., someone with disabilities, elderly people, or individuals who have been drugged or drinking is unable to legally consent.

Acquaintance rape: This is rape committed by a person who the victim personally knows. This is also often referred to as "date rape," especially when the two parties have agreed to a romantic relationship but the victim has not consented to sexual intercourse.

Acquaintance rape is often misunderstood; people think that because the two parties know each other, it isn't a "real rape." This is incorrect, rape is a felony crime, regardless of the relationship between the people involved. A clear, consenting "yes" needs to be communicated in order for sexual contact to be legal.

Date rape: The term "date" often leads people to believe that one must be *dating* the rapist for a sexual assault to be referred to as date rape, but that is not the case. Regardless of whether two parties are in a relationship, rape is sex without consent, and it's a crime.

Marital rape: Marital rape is non-consensual sex within marriage. It is known as "partner rape" when a romantic couple is not married. Many cultures have difficulty understanding that this type of sex is sexual assault. However, even in a married relationship, any sexual act without consent is assault.

Intimate Partner Sexual Violence (IPSV): This is any form of sexual assault that takes place within an intimate relationship. This can include any unwanted sexual act, including rape, shaming a partner's sexuality or sexual preferences, threats or coercion to obtain sex, and not respecting a partner's sexual or physical privacy. Other forms of IPSV include violent sex, degrading sexual taunts, forced involvement in the making or viewing of pornography, forced prostitution, and forced participation in group sex or sex with another person.

Stranger sexual assault: This is sexual assault committed by a perpetrator that the victim does not know. This can include any unwanted visual, verbal, or physical sexual contact.

Alcohol-and drug-facilitated sexual assault: This occurs when the victim is unable to give consent because she or he is under the influence of drugs and/ or alcohol. These substances inhibit the victim's ability to resist the sexual act, and sometimes even prevent them from remembering the event.

These assaults occur in two ways: the perpetrator either takes advantage of a person's inebriation, or the perpetrator causes the victim to consume drugs or alcohol without their knowledge or consent. Again, this type of assault is not the victim's fault, regardless of how the inebriation was achieved.

Statutory rape: Statutory rape is sexual intercourse with a minor. Even if both parties are consenting, by law, an underage party is "too young" to give legal consent to have sexual intercourse; this cannot be done until someone is eighteen years of age. Consent age laws vary from state-to-state and country-to-country, but in most states, when both parties are minors, it is still considered statutory rape.

Gang rape: Also known as **a** "gang bang" or "sex train," this kind of rape is perpetrated by two or more individuals against a single person. Gang rape is sometimes used as a rite of passage or way to establish membership in a group or gang. The dynamic created by gang rape is especially traumatizing for a number of reasons—not only is the victim being assaulted, but they are being assaulted in front of an audience. The experience is horrific, humiliating, and degrading.

Oral copulation or oral rape: This occurs when a victim is forced to perform oral sex on a perpetrator, receive oral sex from a perpetrator, or both. The crime is more punishable when perpetrated against a minor. Remember that with any type of sex, including oral sex, consent is always necessary.

Same-Sex Sexual Assault: This is sexual assault where the perpetrator and the victim have the same gender identity. There is a myth that sexual assault doesn't occur in gay and lesbian relationships, but that is simply untrue. Victims of same-sex sexual assault have to deal with the same traumatic post-assault effects, with additional concerns about homophobic responses from others and/or dismissal of the seriousness of the event due to beliefs that same-sex partners cannot sexually assault each other.

Systematic Sexual Abuse: This is an organized form of sexual abuse, frequently involving numerous perpetrators and victims, that is used to control, condition, or "initiate" victims. This type of abuse is often grouped with ritualized abuse (we will discuss this further in Chapter 4, which covers child sexual abuse in greater depth). It is repeated frequently, and can be perpetuated under the disguise of initiation into a gang, a religious or spiritual expression, or membership in a secret or sexual group.

Sexual harassment: This refers to any unwanted visual, verbal, or physical sexual behavior that interferes with a victim's work, education, or life. The US Equal Employment Opportunity Commission (EEOC) defines sexual harassment as unwelcome sexual advances, requests for sexual favors, and other verbal or physical harassment of a sexual nature. In a job-related context, this type of harassment can affect an individual's employment, interfere with their work performance, or create an offensive, hostile, or intimidating work environment.

According to the EEOC, there are two different types of sexual harassment. Quid pro quo sexual harassment means "this for that." In this type of sexual harassment, the perpetrator expresses or implies demands for sexual favors in exchange for a benefit (e.g. a promotion, a pay raise, etc.) or to avoid some consequence (e.g. job termination).

Hostile environment sexual harassment arises when a person's speech or conduct is so severe and pervasive that it creates an intimidating or demeaning environment or situation that negatively affects a person's job performance. These situations are often not as easy to recognize for a victim as quid pro quo sexual harassment, because the offenses are less obvious (which also makes them more difficult to report).

Street harassment: While commonly reported in public spaces, with 67 percent of women experiencing it in places like streets and sidewalks, 26 percent also experienced street harassment in stores, restaurants, movie theaters, and malls. Most women surveyed in the National Street Harassment Report said that they were afraid the harassment would escalate. Two-thirds (68 percent) said they were very or somewhat concerned that the incident would escalate into something worse. And street harassment is not only frightening, it can be life-changing. As many as 4 percent of the survey's respondents reported quitting a job or moving due to being harassed.

In addition to the major categories of sexual assault there are dozens of other forms of sexual violations that women often don't consider harmful but simply put up with. These so-called "lesser" forms of sexual violation include:

- Catcalls

- Indecent exposure

- Peeping

- Being looked at in overtly sexual ways

- Being touched inappropriately on buses, trains, etc.

- Harassment via technology such as digital photos, videos, apps, and social media

- Unsolicited or non-consensual sexual interactions.

Catcalls: Catcalls consist of verbal advances that include whistling, shouting, and/or saying sexually explicit or implicit phrases or propositions that are unwanted by the victim. Catcalling has received a lot of media attention in the last few years; women, in particular, are fed up with being verbally harassed on the street. Many perpetrators of this types of sexual harassment believe it is a form of flattery, but victims do not perceive it this way at all. Instead, it feels to them like an objectifying, unwanted advance.

Obscene Phone Calls: Obscene phone calls consist of sexual and/or repetitive, unwanted phone calls. Law enforcement officers often consider these calls to be a trivial issue, but they are still instances of sexual harassment. The vast majority of these calls are made to anonymous recipients and only occur once, but occasionally one individual will be phone harassed by the same perpetrator over and over again. In either case, if you receive this type of call, report it as soon as possible.

Exhibitionism: Exhibitionism is a paraphilia in which a person derives sexual arousal from the act or fantasy of exposing their genitals to non-consenting strangers. In the vast majority of cases, the perpetrators of exhibitionist acts are men and the victims are women.

One common form of exhibitionism is "flashing." A typical "flasher" will set himself up in a public place where there are many people. He will conceal his genitals with a trench coat, newspaper, book, or other object. When he sees a suitable victim, he will enter the victim's line of vision and expose his genitals to her. At this point, the flasher will revel in the reaction of the victim, perhaps fantasizing about a sexual relationship with the victim or imagining that the victim is impressed with his penis. The flasher may masturbate at the scene to the point of ejaculation, or he may masturbate later to the memory of the event.

Voyeurism: Voyeurism occurs when a perpetrator, often known as a "Peeping Tom," derives sexual pleasure from looking at sexual objects or acts—specifically, from watching people who are naked. Voyeurs are usually male. Some voyeuristic activities include spying on people who are taking showers in locker rooms, looking through binoculars for people undressing by their windows, or watching people from hidden cameras.

It Isn't Normal

Being sexually assaulted or violated as an adult or adolescent in the ways listed above has become so common that most women have been victimized in at least one of these ways or know someone who has. It has almost been taken for granted among women that when they open up and share their stories, one or more women in the group will have been assaulted or violated.

The fact that these attacks are so common is absolutely horrifying. Unfortunately, because it has become so commonplace for women to be victimized in these ways, there is the risk of it becoming *normalized*.

It should never become normal for a woman to be attacked in these ways. Sexual assault and abuse are so debilitating, so life-changing, that they can rob a woman of her self-esteem, her belief in herself as worthy and loveable, and her ability to protect herself—even her belief that she deserves to protect herself.

Most women and girls have experienced some kind of sexual victimization, and yet most don't acknowledge it to themselves or others. Most have been humiliated by derogatory sexual comments or unwanted violations of their body, and yet few acknowledge the hurt they have felt because of them.

My hope is that these lists and descriptions will help you to:

1. Get past any vestiges of denial you may have about the fact that you have been sexually violated.

2. Identify the ways those around you may currently be mistreating you without identifying it as such.

3. Recognize the ways in which you have suffered because of these violations.

You may have been shocked to learn about the extent of sexual violations women endure. The truth is, it is shocking. It is shocking what the average woman has to put up with, sometimes daily. It is shocking that these types of sexual violations are as extensive and as common as they are. It is shocking that men are still allowed to perpetrate these acts. But as shocking as it is to face the truth about the extent of the attacks on women, it is important to let yourself take in this information. Ignoring, denying, and minimizing the dangers *prevents you from being able to protect yourself.*

Exercise: The Ways You Have Been Abused

Make a list of the ways in which you have been sexually violated. Take your time so that you can remember each violation. Notice any tendency to minimize a particular violation, to blame yourself for it, or to want to deny it altogether by avoiding writing your list (e.g. telling yourself you should be doing something else).

Take a close look at your list and really take in the fact that you have experienced all these sexual violations.

Write about how each and every one of these traumas affected you. Include how each one made you feel and how you were different afterwards. Keep in mind that it may take you some time to write about each trauma, and that you may need to put the project aside and come back to it if this writing brings up too many intense emotions for you. Here is what my client Lupe wrote about one of her experiences with sexual trauma:

"When I wrote about my date rape when I was eighteen [she is thirty-one now] I was shocked to discover how much it had affected me and how much pain I still feel about it. I thought I'd gotten over it years ago but I see now that I really haven't. I felt so betrayed and horrified that some guy I actually liked could do that to me. It made me distrust every guy who comes onto me after that. I assume all men care about is sex and they'll do anything to get it—lie to you, even force themselves on you. I put up a wall between me and men, a wall that, unfortunately, is still there. I don't like the way I feel, I'd like to be able to fall in love. I guess I need to do some work on this to get past it."

Once you have written about each trauma, write about your overall reaction to thinking about and writing about all the sexual violations you experienced over the years. This is what my client Angie wrote about her reactions to remembering her experiences of sexual trauma.

"I didn't realize how many times in my life I have been sexually violated. Heck, I didn't even call them 'sexual violations.' I guess I thought that every woman has had these experiences, and that this somehow made them less painful or traumatic. Each time I was violated I just tried to push it out of my mind. But the truth is, all the things men have done to me haven't gone out of my mind. I have flashes of memory every once in a while—like every time I get on a bus I remember the time a man came up behind me and stuck his hard penis up against my backside. I remember how much it scared me and how unsafe I felt on the bus

after that. And every time I have to walk past a construction site I remember men calling out obscenities at me and hope it doesn't happen again. When I go on a first date I remember the time I was date raped. I've just been fooling myself to think that all these things haven't had an effect on me. They have. I'm not as confident as I once was. And I'm not as friendly. I hold my body tight whenever I am in crowds or when I am on a first date, anticipating getting hurt again."

Angie was able to identify some of the ways she has suffered due to the sexual violations she experienced: *fear, intrusive memories, holding her body tight, being less friendly.* These are all common reactions and after-effects of sexual violence. Other, more severe aftereffects of sexual violation or violence include *suicidal thoughts or attempts, self-harm, eating disorders, substance abuse,* and *sleep disorders.*

Some additional common aftereffects of sexual violations include:

- Difficulty trusting others, especially men

- Anger and rage

- Shock

- Numbness

- Disorientation

- Helplessness

- A sense of vulnerability—feeling unsafe

- Fear

- Self-blame/guilt—blaming oneself

- Developing a negative outlook

- Feeling "damaged" or unworthy of a better life

- Drug or alcohol abuse as an attempt to cope with overwhelming feelings

- Chronic fatigue

- Involuntary shaking

- Muscle tension or pain

- Sexual dysfunction

- Feeling that these reactions are a sign of weakness

The following section describes some more serious consequences of sexual violations and violence—issues that sometimes continue to plague former victims for years.

The Damage Caused by Sexual Violations and Sexual Violence

Sexual violence can have psychological, emotional, and physical effects on a victim. It is a trauma, and as such it causes four main types of problems: 1) depression, 2) flashbacks, 3) post-traumatic stress disorder, and 4) shame.

Depression

Depression is a mood disorder that occurs when feelings associated with sadness and hopelessness continue for long periods of time and interrupt regular thought patterns. It can affect your behavior and your relationships with others.

It is normal for former victims to have feelings of sadness, unhappiness, and hopelessness. If these feelings persist for an extended period of time, it may be an indicator of depression. Depression is not a sign of weakness and it's not something you should be expected to "snap out of." It's a serious mental health condition, and former victims can often benefit from the help of a professional. (Please note: 95 percent of rape victims meet the criteria for a diagnosis of "major depressive disorder" following rape.)

Flashbacks

A flashback is when memories of a past trauma feel as if they are taking place in the current moment. Some refer to it as a sudden, intrusive "vomiting" of memory. A flashback is a sudden intrusion of *real* memories on an otherwise normal moment. You may feel as if the experience of sexual violence is happening all over again.

Flashbacks are not hallucinations, which are imagined and artificial constructs of your mind. They can, however, make it difficult to connect with reality while they are occurring. And they can make you feel like the perpetrator is physically present.

Sometimes people having a flashback may appear to be dissociated because they are sitting silently and passively and staring blankly. The difference between dissociation and flashbacks, though, is that with a flashback you feel powerful emotions. Another difference between flashbacks and dissociation is that with both you may temporarily feel "not there" because you've "faded out," but in a flashback, you're "not there" because you're mentally back in the trauma.

Flashbacks feel terrible, but they are not dangerous. They occur when the subconscious mind is trying to resolve some conflicted or painful detail about your trauma. They happen when your mind is sufficiently at ease for the subconscious to inject the troubling memory into your conscious without the defensive walls of dissociation, numbness, or intoxication holding them back. (This is why people who suffer flashbacks often abuse substances. The mind can't retrieve these memories when it is incapacitated with alcohol or drugs).

Unless conflicted memories are acknowledged, fully expressed in your mind, and resolved, they will continue to manifest as flashbacks. The good news is that having a flashback indicates that you are finally ready to resolve these traumatic memories. Although they feel frightening, they also indicate that you have the mental strength to recover from the experiences that created them.

Flashbacks may seem random at first. They can be triggered by fairly ordinary experiences connected with the senses, like the smell of someone's odor or a particular tone of voice. They are a normal response to this kind of trauma, and there are steps you can take to help manage the stress they induce. (Refer back to the exercise toward the end of Chapter 1 for one type of intervention. I will provide others as we move along.)

For now, remember this: you wouldn't be having flashbacks if you weren't emotionally ready to face your trauma. Think of a flashback as an indication that something needs your time, attention, and correction. The most potent trigger for a flashback is a self-shaming thought about your sexual violations, whether it be child sexual abuse, rape, sexual harassment, or sexual coercion. Merely thinking about your sexual violation does not trigger flashbacks; it's when self-shaming or self-blaming thoughts or beliefs rear their ugly heads that they are triggered. This is why flashbacks usually present you with the most painful, explicit, or humiliating moments of the sexual violation—the moments when you had the least power over what was happening. This is what triggers self-blaming talk like, "That's why I am responsible for what happened!" or "That's the part that makes me feel the dirtiest!"

Overcoming flashbacks requires you to do the exact opposite of what you feel like doing. Rather than avoiding these memories (by drinking, drugging, or using any other avoidance strategies you've developed in order to numb them), you need to directly examine them. In every detail. Even the most painful, yucky ones.

Journaling is a powerfully effective way of doing this.

Journaling about Flashbacks

- Write down every detail of the flashback.

- Examine it from every sense: what you felt, what you heard, what you smelled, what you tasted.

- Write down even the things that seem unrelated or bizarre ("I remember staring at some watermarks on the ceiling," or "I remember the smell of his sweat. It was rancid and sour smelling.")

Post-Traumatic Stress Disorder

It's normal for victims of sexual violence to experience feelings of anxiety, stress, or fear. If these feelings become severe, last more than a few weeks, or interrupt your day-to-day life, you may be suffering from a condition known as post-traumatic stress disorder (PTSD), which is an anxiety disorder that can result from a traumatic event. Often associated with the military, it can apply to victims of any type of trauma, including sexual violence. With PTSD, the feelings of stress, fear, anxiety, and nervousness any former victim can experience are extreme, can cause you to feel constantly in danger, and can make it difficult to function in everyday life. Research has shown that 94 percent of all rape victims meet the criteria for post-traumatic stress disorder within the first week after a rape.

PTSD is a very serious, life-altering, debilitating condition that does not tend to vanish with the passing of time. Its symptoms do diminish gradually—three months after the assault has taken place, the percentage of women with PTSD drops to about half, but this is where the improvements begin to stall. In other words, nearly all rape victims experience PTSD at some point, and about half will continue to experience it even months and years later, with no further recovery occurring without therapy.

While all victims react differently following a severe trauma, there are three main symptoms of PTSD:

1. Re-experiencing: feeling like you are reliving the event through flashbacks, dreams, or recurring or intrusive thoughts.

2. Avoidance: intentionally or subconsciously changing your behavior to avoid scenarios associated with the event, or losing interest in activities you used to enjoy.

3. Hyper-arousal: feeling "on edge" all of the time, having difficulty sleeping, being easily startled or prone to sudden outbursts.

Shame

The primary damage caused to a child or adult when they are sexually violated in any way is shame. This is true whether a woman is sexually harassed on the street or sexually assaulted in her own bed. Shame can damage a person's self-image in ways that no other emotion can, causing us to feel deeply flawed, inferior, worthless, bad, and unlovable. If someone experiences enough shame, she can become so self-loathing that she becomes self-destructive or even suicidal.

I have devoted an entire chapter of this book to how shame negatively affects victims of sexual violations, but for now, here is a summary of how the shame associated with sexual violations can affect the victim:

- Self-destructive behaviors (abusing your body with alcohol, drugs, cigarettes, or too much or too little food, self-mutilation, or being accident-prone).

- Self-sabotaging behaviors (starting fights with loves ones or sabotaging jobs)

- Perfectionism (based on the fear of being caught in a mistake and being further shamed)

- Constant self-criticism and self-blame

- Self-neglect

- Intense rage (frequent physical fights or road rage)

- Acting out against society (breaking rules or laws)

- Repeating the cycle of abuse through victim behavior and/or abusive behavior

- Repetition of the sexual violation (putting yourself in dangerous situations).

If you have been traumatized by a sexual violation, you need to seek counseling in order to heal from this trauma. There are rape crisis centers in most cities, as well as low-cost counseling centers. Please reach out to these centers if you recognize that you are suffering from any of the symptoms discussed above. Group counseling or support groups for women who have been sexually violated are especially effective and can reduce the cost of therapy.

Coming Out of Denial and Knowing the Risks

A woman's body, and especially her sexual organs, can cause her to feel extremely vulnerable, and this feeling of vulnerability is often not only uncomfortable but overwhelming. How can a woman deal with the realization that every time she walks out of her house, every time she goes out with a man or goes to a party, she is risking being raped?

The answer? She goes into denial. She tells herself that she is tough and strong and that no man will stop her from being herself, that nothing will stop her from asserting her needs and becoming everything she was meant to be—just like all the self-help books have told her.

But this denial doesn't protect women; in fact, it makes us more vulnerable to attack. Because the truth is, men have a built-in weapon—their penis. And although not all men use it in this way, the fact is, they all have it and could use it at any time (with the exception of those men who are impotent). Women, on the other hand, are an open vessel.

And so we see that it is not a coincidence that men attack women's sexuality. Our sexual organs are some of the most vulnerable parts of our body. And it is completely understandable that so many women would sink into denial about how vulnerable they really are.

Besides accepting our vulnerability, it's also important that women also need to know who among us is most at risk of being sexually assaulted or harassed. This does not imply that some women are weak or that some women "ask for it." And it doesn't mean that if you don't recognize yourself in these descriptions, you are not at risk. Essentially, every woman is at risk. But knowing that there are some situations that can increase a woman's risk can be an important prevention and empowerment strategy.

- Those women most at risk include:

- Those who have already been sexually assaulted or harassed as an adult (past sexual violence is the best predictor of future violence).

- Those who were sexually abused in childhood or as teens

- Those who were raised to be Nice Girls (including those raised in authoritarian, deeply religious households)

- Women with low self-esteem, body image issues, and those who have been fat shamed

- Women with substance abuse issues

Take note of which of the above items describe your situation—keeping in mind that the fact that you fit into one or more of these categories does not mean you are doomed to future sexual violations. Throughout this book I will offer you remedies for all these situations so that you decrease your risk of being sexually violated.

Empowerment, Compassion, and Hope

This book is not intended to be a strident, negative book full of rage against men, and it is not designed to pit one sex against the other. Although it delivers a heavy dose of reality about the dangers that surround you, it is ultimately about *empowerment, compassion,* and *hope.*

- *Empowerment* comes from knowing, deep down inside, that you have a right to protect your body and your spirit by saying "No!" to unwanted sexual remarks, sexual pressure, or sexual violations. It comes from facing the truth head-on and saying "No!" to sexual mistreatment of any kind, and from understanding once and for all that it is absolutely never the woman's fault when a man sexually violates her in any way.

- *Compassion* comes from recognizing that all women and girls live under tremendous sexual pressure and this can make it difficult, painful, and frightening to navigate through the world. It also comes from understanding the damage childhood sexual abuse, sexual assault, and sexual harassment has on a girl or women's self-esteem and self-image.

- *Hope* comes from having the courage to stand up and speak out for yourself and other women and girls. It comes from realizing that saying "No!" makes you feel more powerful and, in many situations, protects you from further harassment or unwanted sexual advances. It comes from knowing that you aren't alone—that there are many women who are feeling the same emotions you are and that there are ways to connect with other women in order to receive support from and offer support to one another.

Goals of Chapter 3

My intention in this chapter was to provide you with the information necessary to educate (or reeducate) you about rape culture in the United States and the challenges it presents to every woman, sometimes on a daily basis. I also wanted to make sure you know what the different types of sexual violations are and what to call them, as well as familiarize you with some of the damage these sexual violations can cause women. Finally, I wanted to help you come out of denial about the types of sexual violations you have suffered, as well as recognize how these violations have affected you.

No! Exercise

Think about the various ways in which you have been sexually violated as an adult. Notice what feelings come up for you when you remember each event (you may feel numb, sad, feel afraid, feel shame, feel angry, etc.).

Just note the feeling (or lack thereof), take a deep breath, and work toward accepting the fact that you have this feeling. Whatever feelings you have are okay.

Say the word "No!" silently to yourself as you continue to think about the ways in which you have been sexually violated. Say "No!" to each incident of violation. Notice how doing this makes you feel. Does it feel scary? Does it feel empowering? If you feel angry, let yourself feel your righteous anger. Let it well up inside you and help you to say "No!"

Now, if you can, say the word "No!" out loud while continuing to think about how you have been violated. Think about each individual incident, one by one—and say "No" out loud to each specific violation.

Notice any resistance on your part. Notice all the reasons you tell yourself that you can't say "No!" out loud ("Someone will hear me" or "This is silly," for instance). These are just excuses. If you are afraid of being heard, go to a place in your home where you will have privacy, or get in your car and drive to a secluded place.

If you are able to say "No!" out loud, notice how it feels. It may feel scary at first; you may say the word so quietly that you can barely hear yourself. But continue saying it until you can vocalize it loud and clear. Say "No!" to the way men have mistreated you. "No!" to the idea that they thought they had the right to mistreat you or violate you.

If you were able to say "No!" out loud, pay attention to how you feel now. Notice if you feel any stronger or more powerful—or if, on the other hand, you feel a bit shaken, like you've done something wrong. Either way it is okay. The point is that you were able to do it. You should feel proud of yourself for that.

If you weren't able to say "No!" out loud, that's okay too. Ask yourself the following questions: *Why was it so difficult for me to say "No!" What can I learn from this experience? Is there anything I can do to help myself be able to say "No!" at another time?*

Chapter 4
Facing the Truth about Child Sexual Abuse

No one wants to be inconvenienced by all the things that happen to girls.
—T.E. Carter

I n addition to the major ways in which women are sexually traumatized every day, there is another type of sexual violation we need to acknowledge: the sexual violation that so many of us suffered as children. I would venture to say that if you are reading this book, it is highly likely that you were sexually abused as a child.

The reason I've devoted an entire chapter to child sexual abuse is that we need to acknowledge just how much childhood sexual abuse influences and even forms our personalities, our ability to protect ourselves from further sexual violations, and even our motivation to do so. Former victims of childhood sexual abuse are often unable to stand up for themselves and adequately protect themselves from the dangers all around them. This is because the effects of child sexual abuse are devastating to a young girl's self-esteem, self-confidence, and self-concept. Furthermore, the trauma can make it difficult for former victims to believe they deserve to be protected and respected.

And as Judith Lewis Herman states in her classic book *Trauma and Recovery*: "Many survivors have such profound deficiencies in self-protection that they can barely imagine themselves in a position of agency or choice.

The idea of saying no to the emotional demands of a parent, spouse, lover or authority figure may be practically inconceivable."

There are still other reasons why saying "No!" can be especially difficult for women who were sexually abused as a child. When first attacked they probably didn't have an opportunity to say no—or perhaps they did, and their requests were ignored. These experiences can lead these women to believe that any future attempts to say "No!" will be similarly futile, so there is no point in trying. Other reasons include:

1. They have no basis for what a healthy relationship looks or feels like, and they believe that sex will always be forced.

2. They do not believe they have a right to say no (this is especially common for former victims who were abused at an early age).

3. They feel guilty because they don't want to be touched in certain ways or to engage in certain activities (so they go along with whatever their partner wants).

4. They fear that any attempt to say no could make a bad situation worse or more violent.

If you were sexually abused as a child, it is vitally important that you acknowledge the damage it caused you, that you have compassion for your suffering, and that you make the connection between any difficulties you have in standing up for yourself now and the trauma you experienced as a child.

Many of you already know you were sexually abused and may have already sought help for the trauma, either by seeing a counselor or therapist or by attending a support group. But some of you likely haven't faced this painful truth yet. Many people who were sexually abused as a child or adolescent go through life in denial of those experiences. There are various reasons for this:

- The trauma of child sexual abuse (CSA) is so intense and life-changing that many girls simply cannot face the pain. Instead, they "pretend" it didn't happen or they tell themselves that it wasn't a big deal.

- A trauma such as CSA can cause the victim to dissociate—to leave their body—in order to survive. Because they are not in their body while being abused, they have no memory—or at least very little memory—of the abuse. Dissociation provides an escape where no actual escape is possible. It provides a mental escape from intense experience, emotions, and memories.

- Many victims of CSA blame themselves. Children tend to blame themselves for most of what happens to them, and many perpetrators tell their victims that the abuse was their fault—that they did something to cause the perpetrator to react as he did or that they clearly wanted it. This can be especially confusing if the child experienced any kind of pleasure during the assault or if the child returned to the place or the person who molested them.

Why It's Important to Come out of Denial

In addition to helping you understand yourself better and to stop shaming and blaming yourself for not saying "No!" more often or for not protecting yourself better, the other primary reason why it is important to acknowledge if you are a former victim of child sexual abuse is that victims of CSA are particularly vulnerable to later sexual re-victimization. In fact, research over the past decade has consistently shown that *those who were sexually victimized as a child or adolescent are far more likely to be sexually assaulted as an adult than other women.* One recent study found that former victims of CSA are *thirty-five times more likely to be sexually assaulted than non-victims* (Tapia, 2014).

Why are victims of child sexual abuse more at risk of being revictimized?

- Most former victims of child sexual abuse experience a lot of shame and self-blame. These two factors are by far the most damaging effects of CSA and increase the likelihood of revictimization more than does any other effect. This is partly true because victims of sexual abuse develop certain behavioral problems, such as alcohol abuse, that make revictimization more likely. Victimized women, in particular, believe that they have brought any abuse they've experienced on themselves and that they do not deserve to be treated with respect or loved unconditionally (Filipas & Ullman, 2006). Furthermore, shame is related to an avoidant coping style, as the person who is shame-prone will be motivated to avoid thoughts and situations that elicit this painful emotional state. A victim who is experiencing avoidant symptoms may be prone to making inaccurate or uninformed decisions regarding potential danger because of the fact that the trauma has been denied, minimized, or otherwise not fully integrated (Noll et al., 2003). The reexperiencing symptoms can lead to a repetition compulsion where the failure to accommodate to a traumatic experience may lead to a subconscious drive to reenact the experience—an attempt to achieve a sense of mastery over the original trauma (Van der Kolk, 1989).

- They tend to have alcohol and drug problems. Former victims often numb their reexperiencing symptoms with alcohol and drug use, which can serve to impair judgment and defensive strategies (Noll et al, 2003). According to research, former victims of child sexual abuse are about four times more likely to develop symptoms of drug abuse, and adolescents who have been sexually abused were two to three times more likely to have alcohol use/dependence problems than non-victims (RAINN). CSA has also been identified as a significant precursor to alcohol abuse, as well as to co-occurring alcohol use (Oshri, Tubman & Burnette, 2012).

- Certain factors increase the likelihood of revictimization. Factors such as the severity of the abuse, the use of force and threats, whether there was penetration, the duration of the abuse, and closeness of the relationship between victim and offender are associated with higher risk of revictimization (Classen, 2005).

- Certain kinds of abusive men target women whom they perceive as vulnerable.

- Former victims tend to have sexual behavior problems and oversexualized behavior. Children who have been sexually abused have over three times as many sexual behavior problems as children who have not been abused (d21.org).

- They tend to have low self-esteem and poor body image. Obesity and eating disorders are more common in women who have a history of child sexual abuse. (d21.org). Girls and women who have a poor body image are more likely to feel complimented by male attention and are more vulnerable to men taking advantage of their need for attention.

- They may feel powerless because the abuser has repeatedly violated their body and acted against their will through coercion and manipulation. When someone attempts to sexually violate them as an adult, they may feel helpless and powerless to defend themselves.

- They don't tend to respect their bodies. They may feel stigmatized, suffer from a great deal of shame and feel like they are already "damaged goods," and there is no point in protecting their reputation or their body.

- They don't tend to be attuned to warning signs that a person may be a sexual perpetrator.

- They don't tend to have good boundaries.

One of the best ways to come out of denial about previous abuse is to read about the various types of child sexual abuse. ***Warning: reading this material may trigger you.*** This is one of the reasons why reading through them can be beneficial—but be aware that you may experience some of the feelings described earlier, in the section about PTSD. If this happens, practice the grounding exercise ("How to Cope with a Flashback") toward the end of Chapter 1.

Let's start with a general definition of child sexual abuse. **Child sexual abuse** includes any contact between an adult and a child or an older child and a younger child *for the purposes of sexual stimulation of either the child or the adult or older child* and that *results in sexual gratification for the older person*. At the extreme end of the continuum, child sexual abuse includes sexual intercourse. However, touching offenses, non-touching offenses, and sexual exploitation are all considered child sexual abuse. This can range from non-touching offenses, such as exhibitionism and child pornography, to fondling, penetration, incest, and child prostitution. A child does not have to be touched to be molested.

By definition, an older child is usually two years or older than the younger child, but even an age difference of one year can have tremendous power implications. For example, an older brother is almost always seen as an authority figure, especially if he is left "in charge" when parents are away. A younger sister will tend to go along with an older brother's demands, whether out of fear or a need to please. There are also cases where the older sister is the aggressor, although this does not happen as often. In cases of sibling incest, the greater the age difference, the greater the betrayal of trust, and the more violent the incest tends to be.

Child sexual abuse can include any of the following:

- *Genital exposure.* The adult or older child exposes his or her genitals to the child.

- *Kissing.* The adult or older child kisses the child in a lingering or intimate way.

- *Fondling.* The adult or older child fondles the child's breasts, abdomen, genital area, inner thighs, or buttocks. The child may also be asked to touch the older person's body in these places.

- *Masturbation.* The adult or older child masturbates while the child observes; the adult observes the child masturbating; the adult and child masturbate each other (mutual masturbation).

- *Fellatio.* The adult or older child has the child fellate him (perform oral sex on his penis or scrotum), or the adult fellates the child.

- *Cunnilingus.* This type of oral-genital contact requires either the child to place mouth and tongue on the vulva or in the vaginal area of an adult female (or older female child) or the adult to place his or her mouth on the vulva or in the vaginal area of the female child.

- *Digital (finger) penetration of the anus or rectal opening.* Perpetrators may also thrust inanimate objects, such as crayons or pencils, inside the victim.

- *Penile penetration of the anus or rectal opening.*

- *Digital (finger) penetration of the vagina.* Inanimate objects may also be inserted.

- *"Dry intercourse."* A slang term describing an interaction in which the adult rubs his penis against the child's genital-rectal area or inner thighs or buttocks.

- *Penile penetration of the vagina.*

- *Exposing a child to the act of sexual intercourse.*

- *Pornography.* Showing the child or adolescent pornography, usually for the purpose of initiating the child into sexual contact or to sexually stimulate the child, or using a child to film, photograph, or model pornography.

- *Prostitution.* Engaging or soliciting a child for prostitution.

- *Commercial sexual exploitation.* Girls, boys, and transgender youths are lured into both prostitution and other forms of sexual exploitation using psychological manipulation, drugs, and/or violence. These pimps and traffickers often forge a "loving and caring" relationship with the child or adolescent in order to gain trust, and then exploit the victim for monetary gain.

- *Ritual abuse.* This is an extreme, sadistic form of abuse of children and non-consenting adults. It is a methodical and systematic sexual, physical, emotional, and spiritual abuse that often includes mind control, torture, and highly illegal and immoral activities such as murder, child pornography, and prostitution. Not all elements of ritualized abuse are sexual, but as there is overlap, I find it fitting to include this type of abuse in this list.

Hidden or Subtle Forms of Child Abuse

Many of you already know that you were abused in childhood. But in addition to the abuse that you have already identified, I'm guessing that you may have also been abused in other, less obvious ways. Below is a description of the lesser-known, more hidden forms of abuse. These forms of abuse can be just as damaging, just as shaming, as the more obvious, overt forms of abuse. Keep in mind that it is the intention of the adult or older child while engaging in these activities that determine whether the act is sexually abusive:

- *Nudity.* The adult or older child parades around the house in front of the child.

- *Disrobing.* The adult or older child disrobes in front of the child, generally when the child and the older person are alone.

- *Observation of the child.* The adult or older child surreptitiously or overtly watches the child undress, bathe, excrete, or urinate.

- *Inappropriate comments.* The adult or older child makes inappropriate comments about the child's body. This can include making comments about the child's developing body (e.g., comments about the size of a boy's penis or the size of a girl's breasts). It can also include asking a teenager to share intimate details about her or his dating life.

- *Back rubs or tickling.* Even these acts can have a sexual aspect to them if the person doing it has a sexual agenda.

- *Emotional incest.* When a parent "romanticizes" the relationship between himself and his child, treats the child as if he or she were his intimate partner, or is seductive with his child. This can also include a parent "confiding" in a child about his or her adult sexual relationships and sharing intimate sexual details with a child or adolescent.

- *Approach behavior.* Any indirect or direct sexual suggestion made by an adult or older child toward a child. This can include sexual looks, innuendos, or suggestive gestures. Even if the older person never engages in touching or takes any overt sexual action, the sexual feelings they're projecting are picked up on by the child.

The above lists have hopefully helped to further educate you as to what constitutes sexual child abuse. Although you may be aware of many forms of abuse, you may be surprised to discover that behaviors you thought were normal are actually considered abusive and can cause considerable, lasting damage to a child's psyche.

The Special Problem of Incest

Incest is sexual contact between family members. Laws vary from state to state and country to country regarding what exactly constitutes incest, but regardless of what the law says, incest will have a lasting psychological and emotional effect on the victim.

According to RAINN, incest is far more common than you might think: over one-third of perpetrators in cases of sexual abuse are family members.

Perhaps the lack of awareness about this is due to the fact that incest is often more difficult to talk about than child sexual abuse by non-family members. This is because many victims tend to protect the perpetrator because they have either loving feelings toward him or her or because they feel sorry for him or her. Victims may be concerned about what would happen to their family member—or their larger family dynamic—if the perpetrator were accused. If a parent is the perpetrator, many victims worry about their parents getting a divorce or the family being unable to manage financially if the perpetrator is put in jail. Other victims keep quiet because they are afraid of what will happen to them if they tell. It is common practice for perpetrators of incest to threaten to kill their victims, their loved ones, or their pets.

Your Reactions to This Information

It is highly likely that the above descriptions induced some rather strong reactions in you. You may feel triggered, and may even have been catapulted back into the past by flashbacks. This is the case for you, practice the grounding procedure ("How to Cope with a Flashback") located toward the end of Chapter 1.

You may feel shocked at how much you have been in denial about your own abuse experiences. If this is the case, it is important for you to know that your level of denial was once necessary for you to keep going and may have even been necessary to your very survival or sanity. If you can, have compassion for yourself for needing to be in denial instead of criticizing yourself for something you couldn't help at the time.

Exercise: The Ways You Were Abused

When you are ready, please take the time to write out all the types of sexual abuse you experienced as a child, even the more subtle types. Recall the feelings you had then; take the time to determine which emotions you're feeling now. As you remember, write about each incident.

Go back over your list and describe how each incident has affected your life. Generally speaking, child sexual abuse causes the same aftereffects as adult sexual assault (refer to the list in Chapter 3). Pay particular attention to how the abuse affected your image of yourself and your ability to defend yourself in the future.

This will obviously take some time, and you will no doubt need to work on this in more than one sitting. Save this information, because we will be referring to it in later chapters.

This is what my client Ronetta wrote about her experience of being sexually abused by her brother, starting when she was seven:

"When my brother started touching my vagina I didn't understand that he was abusing me. He told me that this is what brothers and sisters did with each other—that it was normal. And because it felt good at times, I believed him. But as the years went by he did more and more things to me, until we eventually were having intercourse. By this time I didn't want it, but I was afraid to tell my brother 'no.' He had become very mean to me, and he threatened that if I ever told, he'd kill me. I never put the two things together—why I didn't tell anyone when I was raped in college. I was afraid of the guy like I was my brother. I saw the guy on campus and I was afraid if I told he'd kill me like my brother had threatened to do!"

Goals of Chapter 4

This chapter's intent is twofold: to help those of you who haven't faced the fact that you were sexually abused as a child to come out of denial, and to help those of you who were sexually abused to recognize how the abuse has affected you, especially concerning your desire and ability to protect yourself and your ability to stand up for yourself.

No! Exercise

Learning to say "No!" is especially important for those who were sexually abused as a child. This is because you felt powerless when you tried to resist the abuser, or because your "No!" was not heard or respected at the time. Former victims of CSA, especially those who experienced abuse over a long period of time, often come to believe that saying no is useless and therefore they have given up trying. But even though you weren't heard in the past, this is your chance to say "No" now.

To begin with, imagine yourself saying "No!" to your perpetrator(s).

Picture the person sitting in a chair in front of you. Now imagine saying "No" to him, just in your mind. Notice how this feels.

Many former victims feel afraid to even imagine doing this, let alone actually doing it. If this is your situation, imagine the following, depending on what you think will help you the most:

1. Imagine the person being tied up so he can't get to you to hurt you

2. Imagine he is gagged so he can't say anything or talk back to you

3. Imagine he is blindfolded so you don't have to look in his eyes.

If you can't imagine your perpetrator, try putting a picture of him or her in front of you. If you don't have a picture, create an image of some sort that represents your perpetrator.

Say "No!" out loud to this person. Say it several times and notice how it feels to do this.

Now scream "No!" as loud as you can at this person.

Notice how you feel after you have done this. Give yourself permission to have your feelings.

Write about all your feelings, no matter what they are. It is okay for you to feel afraid, sad, or angry.

If you need to, practice a grounding exercise to center yourself.

Chapter 5
Shame—The Most Damaging Effect of Sexual Violations

We teach girls shame. Close your legs. Cover yourself. We make them feel as though by being born female, they are already guilty of something. And so girls grow up to be women who cannot say they have desire. Who silence themselves. Who cannot say what they truly think. Who have turned pretense into an art form.

—*Chimamanda Ngozi Adichie*

Since shame is the most damaging aspect of any sexual violation and is the number one risk factor for being revictimized, it is important that we spend an entire chapter on this debilitating emotion. If you are like most women and girls in our culture, you have experienced shame around your body and your sexuality ever since you were a little girl. Starting when you first began to develop, you were no doubt heckled by boys or men on the street—and you no doubt felt shame because of it. You also likely felt shame when boys or men made fun of your body or made disparaging remarks about the size of your breasts or behind. You felt shame when your entire being was reduced to how attractive or unattractive a boy or a man found you. You felt shame because others, including other women, made fun of you or criticized you for being too fat, or too thin, or for not meeting the ideal thrust upon all of us by the media.

Most women are overwhelmed with shame. They feel shame because they were sexually abused in childhood. They feel shame because they were blamed for being sexually assaulted as an adult. It is absolutely unbelievable that even today, women are accused of causing their own victimization with comments like, "Why was she walking all alone at night?"; "What did she expect when she dresses like she does?" and "She shouldn't have had so much to drink."

In order to be truly empowered, women and girls need to acknowledge their shame at having been sexually violated in a multitude of ways. *Sexual violations do more damage to a woman's self-esteem, body image, and sexual self-esteem than anything else.* Shame is the primary reason why women blame themselves when they are violated and why more women do not report sexual assault or harassment. It even explains why some women aren't more careful about protecting themselves against sexual assault and why so many women are critical and judgmental toward other women who are sexually violated or who do not report.

Shame is at the core of the intense emotional wounding women experience when they are sexually violated. Shame is a natural reaction to being violated or abused. In fact, child sexual abuse and adult sexual assault are, by their very nature, humiliating and dehumanizing. The victim feels invaded and defiled, and experiences the indignity of being helpless and at the mercy of another person.

Below are some of the things clients who have been sexually abused as a child or sexually assaulted as an adult have shared with me:

"I felt so humiliated when I was raped. I felt dirty and disgusting. The thought of this horrible man being inside me made me want to vomit. I felt contaminated. I didn't want to see anyone. I was afraid to look anyone in the eyes because I felt so much shame."

—Sylvia, age 24

"After I was sexually abused at eight years old I thought everyone could see what a horrible person I was. I thought everyone knew what terrible things I'd done with my uncle and how ugly I was inside."

—Michelle, age 30

To make matters worse, former victims tend to blame themselves for the sexual misconduct of men.

"I was ashamed of myself for going home with that guy. I felt so stupid. Why did I risk my safety in that way? He completely fooled me. I thought he seemed like a nice guy, someone I could trust. He was so mild-mannered, so sweet. Man, was I fooled. That guy was a monster. Once he started coming on to me it was like he became a different person. He was hard and cold and wouldn't listen when I pleaded for him to stop. I tried to fight him off but I couldn't."

—Riley, age 27

Former victims also feel shame because as human beings we want to believe that we have control over what happens to us. When that personal power is challenged by a victimization of any kind, we believe we "should have" been able to defend ourselves. And because we weren't able to do so, we feel helpless and powerless. This powerlessness causes us to feel humiliated— which leads to shame.

This is what my client Monica shared with me after she was brutally raped: "I felt so powerless and that was one of the worst parts of it. I like to believe I'm a strong woman who can take care of myself but I'm obviously not."

The Overwhelming Shame of "Not Fighting Back"

There is still another source of shame for former victims of sexual assault: they blame themselves for not fighting back. Time after time, clients have told me about how ashamed they are because "I should have fought more" or "I just lay there and let him do it." My former client Ramona told me, "I felt so ashamed of myself because I couldn't defend myself. I didn't fight back, I didn't even try to scream. I was just frozen in fear and I just let him do whatever he wanted to do to me. He had a knife and he told me he would kill me if I moved or made a sound and I believed him. I felt so weak, like such a victim. I should have tried to fight him off. I should have screamed. Maybe someone would have heard me and come to my rescue."

Clients like Ramona usually don't consider the possibility that if they had fought back, they might have been harmed even worse. Most women have heard that rape is about power and control. But few understand that in order to maintain control, a rapist will use a level of aggression that exceeds any resistance he receives from his victim. That means that the more a woman resists, the more danger she may be in.

And there is still another factor that may help those of you who feel shame for not resisting more: During a sexual assault the body's sympathetic nervous system takes over, instinctively regulating your responses for the sake of survival. That means your conscious mind stops choosing what to do, and your physical systems take control, producing one of three basic responses: *flight*, *flee*, or *freeze*.

Each of these three instincts have both helpful and harmful aspects to them; they may either increase or decrease your safety. Contrary to what we see in movies or what we read in material written by the self-defense industry, the "fight instinct" is actually rather rare in both women and men. By far the most common instinct we all default to is the "freeze instinct," which causes the body to become very still, rigid, and silent—the "deer in the headlights" response. This is called "tonic immobility," and it is a simple but powerful survival behavior. During rape, temporary paralysis is very common; in fact it occurs in up to 88 percent of rape victims. (Finn 2003)

If you did not fight back or scream during your assault, please stop berating and chastising yourself. Your behavior wasn't *passive*, it was a biologically driven form of *resistance*! It is very important that you understand this. In fact, one study found that the link between this "temporary paralysis" during the rape and later feelings of guilt and self-blame are directly related to increased depression, anxiety, and PTSD. (Heidt & Forsyth 2005)

The bottom line: while tonic immobility is often a source of shame for former victims, it is actually a common self-preservation aid and a basic response to threatening situations. So if you are one of the many women who blames herself (or is blamed by others) for not "fighting back," be reassured that freezing—entirely or partially—is a natural human response to a threatening situation.

Compliance versus Consent

You may also feel shame because you "went along" with an attacker's requests or demands. But the truth is, in most rapes where the victim is conscious, there is some degree of compliance with the rapist simply because it is a reasonable way to protect yourself from further harm.

Nevertheless, women tend to blame themselves for being raped if they complied with the rapist's requests or demands. It is common for women to report things like:

- "When he told me to remove my underpants, I did what he said. That means I gave him permission to have sex with me."

- "The fact that I stopped struggling when he ordered me to means I essentially permitted the rape."

- "He told me I'd be sorry if I screamed, so I remained silent. That means I wasn't really raped, right?"

Most people will do anything to avoid being killed. As a way of illustrating this instinct, rape counselors in training are given the example of a man being mugged. The man cooperatively hands over his wallet and does anything else demanded of him out of a desperate hope that the assault will end without further injury or death. No one questions this cooperation: police even *advise* it. People who hear about the episode later will support the man and assure him that he did the right thing. No one will blame him for carrying money. No one will claim the incident was probably a cash transaction that "got out of hand."

Yet when the crime becomes sexual, people lose all these same insights about the importance of compliance to reduce harm. Suddenly the victim starts to question herself: *Why didn't I fight back? What would have happened if I had resisted him?*

Self-Blame

By continuing to blame yourself for being sexually abused as a child or sexually assaulted as an adult, you are actually delaying your recovery. You need to forgive yourself for whatever actions you took in order to survive. You need to stop blaming yourself for being attacked. You did nothing to cause it. Absolutely nothing.

As Matt Atkinson wrote in his book, *Resurrection after Rape: A Guide to Transforming from Victim to Survivor*, "Self-blame is by far, the most devastating after effect of being sexually violated. This is particularly true for former victims of child sexual abuse and adult victims of sexual assault. In fact, ninety percent of rape trauma recovery is undoing a victim's tendency to self-blame. Ten percent is everything else. But the ten percent has to come after the end of self-blame: it can't happen while the former victim is still ashamed and guilty."

Exercise: How Did You "Ask For It?"

List all the ways you believe you "asked for it" or put yourself in the position to be raped. Don't censor yourself, just write down everything that comes to your mind. For example: "I shouldn't have worn that dress," "I shouldn't have gone to that bar," "I should have had a friend with me."

Now ask yourself: If your rapist hadn't been there, would you have been raped while doing all the same things you did? The reality is that no sequence of behaviors on your part would have caused a rape to happen if a rapist hadn't been present. Every rape that happens is determined 100 percent by the choice made by a rapist to commit rape. Nothing a woman does would cause rape to occur without the man's decision to perpetuate it.

Adding Shame to Shame

Being victimized is in itself a shaming experience, given the humiliation that comes from being violated and the loss of control experienced because of it.

Then we add to this the shame that often surrounds the exposure of the victimization—in particular in the case of rape. As shaming as the experience of rape can be, the exposure of that event can be just as shaming for the victim, depending upon the reactions of loved ones, friends and authorities. Others' negative reactions tend to fall into three major categories:

1. Blaming the victim

2. Reacting so strongly that the victim's feelings are overshadowed

3. Not believing the victim

Blaming the Victim

As we have been discussing, this is by far the most common reaction people have when a woman tells others that she was sexually assaulted and is, by far, the most damaging. The idea is that the victim "put herself in that position" or was "asking for it." Not only does the victim not receive the comfort and support she needs, she is also further shamed by being blamed for her own victimization. As one client told me: "My boyfriend got so angry with me. He yelled at me for going to that party in the first place. 'I told you those guys were trouble! You should have never been there.' "And then he yelled at me for not leaving the party earlier: 'And why didn't you leave when Linda did? That was so stupid of you to stay there all alone! And you were probably drunk, weren't you? Dammit Gina, what did you expect?'"

It is fairly common for boyfriends and husbands to blame the victim. Men are extremely tribal. They identify with one another so intensely that some feel personally attacked whenever another man is being accused of something like rape. Because of this some will defend the man and blame the victim. Other men have the belief that women are the ones who bear the duty to prevent rape. But women are guilty of blaming the victim as well. This can be a way of convincing themselves that they will never be raped because *they* would never put themselves in that position.

In fact, our entire culture is guilty of victim blaming. At its core, this tendency to blame the victim comes from our cultural intolerance of weakness in any form. We can't tolerate weakness in others because it reminds us of our own weakness and vulnerability. What better way to avoid this than by blaming the victim for her own victimization?

We blame the woman who was raped for wearing sexy clothes, or for drinking too much, or for being at the wrong place at the wrong time because we want to hold onto the fantasy that we all have choices—that we are in control. We don't want to admit to ourselves that sometimes we don't have a choice—that sometimes we are not in control.

Even some misguided therapists sometimes believe that their job is to help their client see how she participated in the rape by "putting herself in that position." Others focus on what the victim can do differently next time to prevent being raped again, implying that she had something to do with her own victimization. These therapists seem to believe the old line, "Nobody can abuse you without your consent."

The truth is, you did not cause yourself to be raped. People can and frequently do abuse and rape others "without their permission," and people can and do control others against their will. *There is only one thing that causes a woman to be raped: a rapist.*

Reacting So Strongly that the Victim's Feelings Are Overshadowed

This actually occurs more often than you would expect. Many clients have told me that their boyfriend or their father's reaction to the news that they had been raped was so powerful that it frightened them and caused them to put their own feelings aside.

Other clients knew ahead of time that telling their boyfriend, husband, father, or brother could be dangerous. As my client Tara explained to me, "I was afraid to tell my boyfriend because I was afraid he'd blow a gasket. I was afraid of what he'd do to the perpetrator, someone he knew. Sure enough, as soon as the words were out of my mouth he grabbed his car keys and sped out of the driveway. I knew he was going to look for the guy and I knew that if he found him he'd probably beat him to death."

Tara was left all alone with her feelings about being raped—and worse yet, she now had to worry about what her boyfriend would do.

Still others have had the experience of telling their mother or father or another loved one that they were raped and witnessing the person becoming overwhelmed with pain. My client Katherine told me, "When I told my mother she became so distraught that I became worried about her. She started crying and had to go to bed. I felt bad for her but then I thought, *"Hey, wait a minute, I'm the one who was raped, not you!"*

Not Believing the Victim

Friends and family usually believe a woman when she tells them she was sexually assaulted, but when it comes to reporting the crime, it is another story. Women have to jump through hoops in order to be believed and often the perpetrator's word is taken over hers, especially when the rape has occurred on a college campus or the perpetrator is a popular guy on campus, such as a star football player.

This was the situation with my client Courtney: "I was raped at a party by a popular football player," she told me. "When I reported it to the police it ended up being my word against his. And I became the town pariah. Everyone at school hated me and constantly made comments like, 'How could you accuse Randy of doing such a thing!' 'You're ugly—he can get any girl he wants, why would he chose you?' 'You're just trying to hurt him—why would you do such a thing?' "It got so bad I had to drop out of school. But Randy just kept on playing football. By the time the case went to court I couldn't even step outside my house. There was a mistrial because half of the people on the jury supported Randy. My family had to move out of town so I could get a new start."

In the case of child sexual abuse, it is common for the child to be shamed by the reactions of those to whom they make their outcry. Not being believed can add to the victim's shame, especially if the person interrogates the child or gets angry at the child for telling. When I first told my mother about Steve, a friend of the family, molesting me, she didn't believe me. Since she had already decided I was a liar, she assumed I was making it up to "get attention." This added to the shame and humiliation I already felt as the result of the abuse. As a result of my mother not believing me, I felt horribly alone and humiliated.

Some parents or other significant caretakers shame abused children by saying that they have "falsely accused" the perpetrator—in essence, making the child feel as if they are now the offender, victimizing an innocent person.

This is what happened with my client Celeste. Celeste was sexually abused by her grandfather from the age of four to age nine, when she finally got up enough nerve to tell her parents about it. But instead of believing her and wanting to protect her, her parents sided with her grandfather. "How dare you accuse your dear old grandfather of such a thing!" her mother exclaimed when Celeste first revealed her secret. "Your grandfather loves you. He would never hurt you. He's just a sweet old man who wants to be affectionate toward you. What's wrong with you?"

Celeste felt horribly shamed. She knew that what she was telling her mother was the truth, but she was silenced by her mother's accusations and denial.

Her father's response was even harsher. "You're just trying to get attention," he chastised her. "But what a terrible way to do it—to accuse an innocent old man of such a thing. You ought to be ashamed of yourself."

"I felt like such a horrible person," Celeste told me. "I even began to doubt myself. Maybe it didn't really happen after all. Maybe I made it up to get attention, like they said."

Celeste's parents' denial just added to her shame. Now not only was she carrying the shame of the abuse, she was also carrying the shame of being accused of being a liar and of trying to hurt her grandfather, who supposedly had done nothing but be good to her.

More Ways Shame Manifests for Victims

Still others experience horrible shame when they have to talk to police and other authorities, some more than others. And of course, if a victim ends up going to court, there can be still further shame.

An important aspect of shame is that it makes us feel *exposed*—seen in a painfully diminished way. The more a victim has to tell the story of their abuse, the more exposed she can feel, especially if she is being forced to tell it. (On the other hand, some victims feel relieved of the burden of shame when they make an outcry, since holding secrets can add to our shame).

There is still another important type of shaming that often occurs in both childhood sexual abuse and adult sexual assault, and that is the element of *projection*. Most abusers are projecting their own shame onto their victim when they abuse them. In fact, in many cases, that is their motivation, however unconscious, as no doubt was the situation for my client Selena's father. This is how she described her abuse:

"Each time my father molested me I felt overwhelmed with shame. I felt so dirty inside and out. I always ran to the bathroom to take a shower, trying to wash away his filth and the filth I felt inside. I felt like the lowest of the low. I knew no man would ever want me. I knew I was spoiled, rotten. It was not just the fact that my own father was using me in this way but the things he said to me while he was doing it. He called me 'slut,' 'whore,' 'garbage.' And I felt he was right, I was garbage. Why would my own father treat me like this if I wasn't?"

As I was to discover in later sessions, Selena's father was projecting onto his daughter the shame he suffered due to his own horrendous experiences with sadistic sexual abuse. In other words, he could not contain the amount of shame he felt, so it spilled out onto his daughter.

Finally, there is the shame that victims experience due to the ways in which they've tried to cope with their abuse in the past. Many children who are sexually abused end up passing on the abuse to other children, either by introducing them to sex or by coercing them to engage in sexual activities.

This is how my client Ellie described her situation: "One of the reasons I had such a difficult time coming out of denial about having been sexually abused by my brother is that I sexually abused my younger sister. If I remembered my own abuse, I would have remembered abusing my sister. So I just put it all behind me—or at least I did for many, many years. But when I was raped it all came flooding back to me. All the shame and all the disgust of myself. Since then I've felt horrible shame about harming my sister in that way. I've chastised myself and hated myself for months now."

Other ways that former victims deal with their shame is by becoming self-destructive or by becoming addicted to alcohol, drugs, or sex and this can add to their shame. Brenda's shame caused her to get involved with abusive men: "I hated myself so much that I thought I deserved to be mistreated by men. I got involved with men who abused me verbally, emotionally, and even physically. I put up with it because

I thought that a good guy would never want me. I was too damaged."
Another client, Amanda, expressed her shame by pushing away every person
who had been good to her—and sometimes in a cruel way: "My last boyfriend
seemed to really love me," she said. "But I felt so much shame that I didn't
believe anyone could love me. I didn't believe I deserved love. So I started
criticizing him. I was relentless. I really tore him down. Eventually he ended
up breaking up with me because he couldn't take it anymore."

As you can see, childhood sexual abuse and adult sexual assault are
extremely shaming experiences, as can be the ways in which we cope with the
traumas. To summarize, victims feel shamed by any and all of the following
aspects of abuse or assault:

1. The shame and humiliation that comes from the violation itself and feeling helpless and powerless.

2. The shame that comes from blaming themselves for "asking for it."

3. The shame over failing to "fight back."

4. The shame of feeling exposed when the abuse or assault is reported.

5. The shame the victim takes on when the abuser projects his shame onto
   them.

6. The shame that comes from the victim's attempts to cope with the abuse
   (sexual acting out, alcohol or drug abuse).

Exercise: What Do You Feel Shame About?

Write about the reasons why you feel shame regarding each
act of sexual violation you've experienced in your life, both
as a child and an adult. For example:

- "I feel shame because *I put myself in the situation.*"

- "I feel shame because *I wasn't able to push him away. I
  couldn't defend myself.*"

- "I feel shame because *I couldn't say no.*"

- "I feel shame because *I didn't tell anyone.*"

Make a list of the ways you believe you acted out your shame over having been violated, whether it was from child sexual abuse, from sexual assault as an adult, or from any other sexual violation you've suffered that has caused you great shame.

Exercise: Giving Back Your Abuser's Shame

Giving back the abuser's shame, the shame he or she put on you, can be very empowering. The following exercise will help you do this.

First, ground yourself by placing your feet flat on the floor, taking some deep breaths and clearing your eyes.

Imagine that you are able to look inside your body. Scan your body and see if you can locate where the shame surrounding the abuse is located. Find any shame or feelings that you are "bad" inside your body.

Imagine that you are reaching inside your body and pulling out that dark, ugly stuff.

Now imagine that you are throwing all that dark ugliness at your abuser, where it belongs.

Open your eyes and make a throwing motion with your arms. Say out loud as you do it, "There, take back your shame. It's yours, not mine."

This exercise may bring up anger or it may bring up sadness. Whatever emotions arise, allow yourself to express them freely.

Tell Someone

In addition to completing exercises like "Giving Back Your Abuser's Shame," you can reduce your shame by disclosing your abuse or assault to someone—whether it be a friend, a loved one, or a therapist. If you aren't ready, willing, or able to report child sexual abuse or adult sexual assault to the authorities, that is fine. We will discuss this aspect of the process throughout the book and perhaps you will change your mind later on. But for now, it is important that you tell a trusted friend, family member, or other loved one—someone you can trust, someone who will likely understand and be compassionate.

You've no doubt heard that secrets make us sick. This is true in the case of abuse and assault because the more you keep your truth to yourself, the more shame you will continue to feel and the more your shame will fester. But bringing the secret out into the open—out of the darkness and into the light—will reduce your shame about being abused or assaulted. As much as it is understandable that you would be afraid or reluctant to tell anyone about your sexual abuse or assault for fear of being judged or not being believed, it is vitally important that you tell someone.

There are many benefits to telling someone about your experiences with sexual abuse or sexual assault:

- Telling is the best way to relieve yourself of feelings of shame. Telling the secret brings the abuse or assault out of the darkness and into the light. Although it may be embarrassing to disclose the abuse to others, it will eventually make you feel less ashamed.

- You may have been able to hide your abuse or assault from others, but you can't hide it from yourself. The secret of your abuse has kept you isolated and feeling alone. Only by telling a trusted friend or loved one can your wounds start to heal. And once you tell someone, you won't feel as much like an outcast of society, which in turn will help you to feel less shame.

- Keeping quiet about the abuse or assault can make you feel like you've done something wrong and can keep you alienated from others. In sharing your experience with others, you assert to yourself and others that it is not your fault and that you were an innocent victim.

- Telling can provide closure. You are no longer the abuser's victim. You are on the road to recovery.

- As long as you continue to keep your abuse or assault a secret, you will remain captive to the perpetrator. When you talk to others about it, you will help set yourself free from your abuser's clutches.

- There is a lot of power in telling your story. Women report feeling empowered after opening up with someone they trust.

- If you tell a counselor about your abuse or assault, you'll increase your chances of receiving the help and support you so desperately need.

- Telling the authorities about your abuse or assault will make it harder for the perpetrator to continue to abuse other children or rape any other women, and possibly stop them from doing so altogether.

It will take *courage, strength,* and *determination* to speak your truth aloud—*courage* to allow those difficult words to come out of your mouth and risk the reaction you receive; *strength* to withstand even the slightest hint of disbelief and to answer what may be hurtful or embarrassing questions; and *determination* to face whatever doubts and questions come your way, hold onto your truth, and not allow anyone to cause you to doubt yourself.

I promise you, telling your secret, bringing it out into the light, will be worth the pain, the fear, and the shame of the disclosure. When you relieve yourself of the burden of your secret you will feel less alone, more connected to others, less like an outcast of society, and more like a member of the human race. I can promise you this because the majority of my clients who did tell have found this to be true.

It is only in telling your story that you can begin to heal. When you talk about the abuse you've suffered, you not only feel unburdened, you also take away some of its power. You come to realize that you already survived the trauma, and that as much as it still hurts to think about what you suffered, it is, after all, in the past. It happened, but it is over.

Talking about your abuse can be the most loving, caring thing you can do for yourself. It is essentially telling yourself, "I have a right to talk about what happened to me. My story needs to be heard and I deserve to be heard. I've held in this secret and this pain for far too long, and now I need to get it out of me—I need to release it so it doesn't continue to poison my body, mind, and spirit." You're also telling yourself, "I deserve to begin to put this pain and shame and fear behind me, so I'm choosing to take this first step toward healing. This secret has kept me in the darkness, disconnected from others, feeling lost and alone. Telling my secret will bring me out of that darkness and help me feel closer to others."

Remember, *you* were the victim, and so you have no reason to feel ashamed about what happened to you. Just as you would not feel ashamed to tell someone that your car was stolen, or your house was broken into, there is no reason for you to feel ashamed about having been a sexual abuse or assault victim. Most people don't blame someone for being robbed; such an event is, after all, a crime, and they were an innocent victim. The same is true of childhood sexual abuse or adult assault: You were an innocent victim of a terrible *crime*. It was not your fault.

There are two other major ways of overcoming your shame: 1) having compassion for your suffering, and 2) connecting to and releasing your anger. In the next two chapters, we will focus on both of these strategies.

Goals of Chapter 5:

The purpose of this chapter was to educate you about how shame is the most damaging after-effect of any sexual violation, how that shame is exacerbated by the reactions of others, and how the shame of sexual abuse and sexual assault is often manifested in our lives. The exercises and strategies included were designed to help you begin to purge yourself of this undeserved shame.

No! Exercise

Think about what you need to say "No!" to regarding any sexual violation you have experienced. For example, many former victims need to stop blaming themselves for the sexual violation when it is clearly the perpetrator's fault.

Write a list of the things you need to say "No!" to regarding the shame you carry about child sexual abuse. For example:

Saying "No!" to the shame of child sexual abuse:

- No!—It's your shame, not mine!

- No!—I didn't do anything wrong

- No!—It wasn't my fault

- No!—I was just an innocent child

- No!—I didn't want it!

- No!—I didn't make you do it!

- No!—I didn't enjoy it!

Now make another list—this time about the shame you carry concerning any sexual violation you experienced as an adult. What do you need to say "No!" to? For example:

Saying "No!" to sexual violations as an adult:

- No! I didn't ask for it.

- No! I have a right to walk on the streets at night and not be raped.

- No! It doesn't matter whether I drank too much, I didn't deserve to be raped!

- No! I wasn't wrong for not fighting back. I was saving my life!

- No! I don't care whether you believe me or not, I know the truth—I was raped!

Part II

Out With the Old, In With the New

Chapter 6
Compassion for Your Suffering

Self-compassion is approaching ourselves, our inner experience, with spaciousness, with the quality of allowing which has a quality of gentleness. Instead of our usual tendency to want to get over something, to fix it, to make it go away, the path of compassion is totally different. Compassion allows.

—Robert Gonzales

In tandem with learning the skills and mindset of saying "No!" and becoming comfortable with them, another key component to empowerment is learning the practice of self-compassion. Learning to provide yourself self-compassion will help you to acknowledge the damage you have already experienced due to sexual violations. Once you have done this, once you have come out of denial about your pain and suffering, you will be on your way to true empowerment.

Why is this? *Because we can't heal what we don't face.* And we can't fight when we don't know what we are fighting against.

Whereas compassion is the ability to feel and connect with the suffering of another human being, self-compassion is the ability to feel and connect with *your own suffering.* More specifically, for our purposes, self-compassion is the act of extending compassion to yourself in instances of suffering or perceived inadequacy and failure.

When someone else shows us compassion it may take the form of an all-knowing look, a sigh, or a comforting touch. It can be anything that communicates to you that the other person hears your pain and that he or she is *with you in your pain.* In fact, the word *compassion* comes from the Latin roots *com* (with) and *pati* (suffer); in other words, it means to "suffer with." When a person offers genuine compassion, they join us in our suffering.

Generally speaking, women have the capacity for great compassion when it comes to other people's suffering—yet we have alarmingly very little compassion for our own. But it is very important for you to understand this: *In order for you to come to believe that you deserve to be treated with respect by others, particularly men, you need to learn how to recognize and then tend to your own suffering. And before you can teach others to treat you with kindness and respect, you will need to learn to treat yourself with kindness and respect.*

Self-compassion encourages you to begin to treat yourself and talk to yourself with the same kindness, caring, and compassion you would show a good friend or a beloved child. Just as connecting with the suffering of others has actually been shown to comfort and even help heal others of their ailments or problems, connecting with your own suffering will do the same for you.

If you fall down and scrape your knee, you know that you need to cleanse the wound and apply medicine to it in order for it to heal. But time after time, women get hurt by the sexual misconduct of men (and sometimes women) and instead of tending to the wound, we minimize how much it hurts or we ignore it completely. I don't know about you, but when I was a kid I fell down all the time, and I didn't have anyone around to cleanse the wound or put medicine on it—so my scrapes almost always got infected and I ended up with a red, raw, infected sore.

As women, we often ignore our wounds surrounding sexual violations. Left untended in this way, our wounds fester and get worse. Giving ourselves compassion, in contrast, is like applying a healing salve to our wounds.

Unfortunately, even if you are willing to acknowledge your wound, you may not know how to apply the soothing salve of compassion to it. This will help: Think about the most compassionate person you have known—someone who has been kind, understanding, and supportive of you. It may have been a teacher, a friend, or perhaps a friend's parent. Think about how this person conveyed their compassion toward you and how you felt in this person's presence. If you can't think of someone in your life who has been compassionate toward you, think of a compassionate public figure or even a fictional character from a book, film, or television. Now imagine that you have the ability to become as compassionate toward yourself as this person has been toward you (or you imagine this person would be toward you). How would you treat yourself? What kinds of words would you use when you talk to yourself?

This is the goal of self-compassion: to treat yourself in the same way the most compassionate person you know would treat you—to talk to yourself in the same loving, kind, and supportive ways that this compassionate person would talk to you.

The Practice of Self-Compassion

Practicing self-compassion will help you heal the trauma of having been a victim of sexual violation in any form—and believe me, I mean trauma. It is traumatic to have your boundaries violated, to be forced to do things you do not want to do, to feel trapped and unable to get away, and to feel as helpless and out of control as sexual violations make women feel.

Another benefit of learning how to practice self-compassion is that it is the antidote to shame. You need to offer yourself the healing benefits of self-compassion in order to rid yourself of the overwhelming shame you likely feel—at being sexually violated in the past, at being objectified and disrespected, at being blamed for your own sexual assault, and, most important, for blaming yourself. Self-compassion will help heal the immense amount of shame you no doubt have regarding your body and your sexuality in particular. *Shame has to be brought out, examined, and then healed by self-compassion: only then can you be empowered.*

By following the strategies outlined in this chapter, you can begin to rid yourself of the belief that you are worthless, defective, bad, or unlovable. Instead of trying to ignore these false yet powerful beliefs, instead of denying your shame and the feelings it engenders, you need to bring your shame out into the light of day.

Recent research in the neurobiology of compassion as it relates to shame has revealed new information about the neural plasticity of the brain—the capacity of our brains to grow new neurons and new synaptic connections.

According to these studies, *we can proactively repair (and re-pair) old shame memories with new experiences of self-empathy and self-compassion.* (Longe, et al 2010).

Having Compassion for All Women Who Have Suffered

Women want to be brave and strong. We want people to see us as competent and independent. But time after time, we have experiences that tear down our self-esteem and challenge our competency. By the time a young girl reaches adolescence she has likely experienced sexual bullying, street harassment, and inappropriate sexual behavior including being grabbed at school by boys in her class, confronted by exhibitionists, and even child sexual abuse. Instead of recognizing our suffering, however, girls and women tend to try to just move on and forget these things ever happened. Unfortunately, the shame and pain and fear that these experiences elicit don't just go away.

Because it is often easier for us to feel compassion for others before we can begin to feel compassion for ourselves, let's start there. When you read earlier in this book about our rape culture and how so many women have suffered from sexual violations ranging from street harassment to indecent exposure to sexual assault, how did you feel? Did you feel sad for all the women who have suffered? If you didn't before, please take the time now to acknowledge all that we women are subjected to on a regular basis, and let yourself feel it.

Let yourself feel the suffering of the thousands of women who struggle every day because they are being sexually harassed and sexually assaulted. Think about the single mothers who work as servers for minimum wage, who depend on their tips to make a living. Think about how often they have to smile whenever a male customer makes an inappropriate remark about their body or pats them on the behind when they walk by. Think about the female office workers who have controlling, misogynistic bosses who constantly make lewd, inappropriate comments, or who insist on sexual favors in exchange for letting them keep their job. Think about the married women who are brutally raped by abusive husbands who treat them like property, women who don't even know enough to call it rape, women who will never report their husbands, or leave them. Feel the pain of the multitudes of children all over the world who continue to be sexually abused, all the children who are afraid to break their silence, who can't stand up for themselves.

Allow yourself to feel compassion for all the suffering of all these women and girls. Notice how it feels to have compassion for others. It hurts, but in a strange way it also connects us all, right? It helps us to feel less alone. In opening our hearts in compassion for others, we open our hearts to our own suffering.

Our Resistance to Giving Ourselves Compassion

When you hear about a friend or acquaintance being sexually violated, what do you feel? Do you feel badly for her? Do you try to comfort her? What about when a friend or family member tells you she has been raped? Do you have compassion for her? As women we are compassionate beings, and we tend to offer compassionate understanding and comfort to other women. The problem is, we don't tend to offer the same compassion to ourselves. If we are harassed on the street we make excuses like, "Oh, it wasn't that bad." Even if we were date-raped, we say things like, "I was lucky. Other women have had it a lot worse. At least he didn't have a weapon."

This kind of thinking may seem like a positive way to cope with sexual violations, but it's not. *Diminishing your experiences of being sexually violated is a form of diminishing yourself.* Saying "it wasn't that bad" is like saying "I'm not that important" or "My feelings aren't that important." And thinking "it wasn't that bad" sets you up to accept less-than-appropriate ways of being treated by men. It causes you to set the bar far too low in terms of what you will accept from men.

Telling yourself that "it wasn't that bad" also causes you to be hard on yourself for not "getting over it" sooner. After all, if it wasn't that bad, why are you still suffering from the effects of it? Why are you still carrying so much hurt and anger and shame? Why are you being invaded with memories?

Don't continue to minimize and diminish the sexual violations you have suffered. They *are that bad*. They were painful, frightening, humiliating and just plain horrible.

Other common excuses we make for not feeling compassionate toward ourselves include:

- "I asked for it." (We blame the fact that we were wearing something sexy or we went into a dangerous part of town).

- "I was so stupid, what did I expect?" (Because we went out with a guy who had a reputation for being dangerous).

- "It didn't affect me that much." (Denying how afraid, hurt, or humiliated we felt).

- "I just blocked it out of my mind." (As if that is really possible).

- "It was no big deal. I don't know why women make such a big deal out of it." (Minimizing the damage that street harassment, workplace harassment, or sexual coercion can inflict).

- "Unless a woman is a virgin, being raped on a date is just having sex with someone you don't like." (Minimizing the damage date rape has on a woman).

Many women are afraid to take in compassion from others or offer it to themselves because then they would really have to acknowledge what happened and feel the pain of it. For example, you may be afraid that if you really acknowledge how terrified you were when an acquaintance raped you, you will fall apart or be so terrified of men you won't ever date again.

The truth, however, is that if you don't give yourself compassion for how you have already suffered, if you don't connect with the trauma you experienced on an emotional level, you will find it harder to stand up against further affronts and assaults.

This was the case with my client Rosemary, who told me, "I was date-raped when I was just twenty-one. I'd been dating for a while but I was still pretty naïve. When a guy I liked ended up forcing me to have sex on our first date, I felt so humiliated. I actually thought he liked me too, so when I discovered his intention all along was to rape me I couldn't wrap my mind around it. And I stayed in this confused state for quite a while. Instead of focusing on the fact that I'd been raped, instead of telling anyone, I stayed in my own head. I intellectualized it. I tried to understand why a man would rape a woman. I even talked to other guys about it—from an intellectual place only. Not once did I stop to address how I felt. That didn't seem to be important. Now I know that my feelings of hurt and fear and shame never went away. I just put them in a huge bag that I carried around with me but never opened. I became so tired from carrying around that bag that I just let guys do whatever they wanted to me. I was just too tired to fight them off. I didn't realize the connection for a long time. Now I know I have to open that bag and examine what's inside if I'm ever going to heal and be strong again."

Let It Sink In

Think about how difficult it has been for you to have to live through the sexual violations you've suffered. Ask yourself: *Have I taken the time to acknowledge my own suffering?* Or have you tried to just put it away like Rosemary did?

I want you to take time now to let it really sink in: the dangers you are faced with every day, and especially every night. Allow yourself to feel compassion for what you have endured and for what you will likely continue to endure. Acknowledge how hard it has been to be street harassed, insulted, groped, invaded, and assaulted. Acknowledge all the pain you have endured.

If we don't stop to acknowledge just how bad it really is—not only the sexual assaults and the sexual harassment on the job, but also the everyday intrusions—we run the risk of normalizing this behavior. We need to acknowledge how much the inappropriate sexual comments, how much the creepy stares at our breasts and behinds, how much the grabbing and pinching and rubbing up against us, hurt us, demean us, scare us, humiliate us, and shape who we are. We need to admit the truth—that all of it is bad—so we can take better care of ourselves, honor our bodies, and protect ourselves from further harm.

By learning how to practice self-compassion, you will become more sensitive to your own suffering regarding your interactions with men, as well as the suffering you've felt due to past sexual violations you have experienced. You will gain a deeper understanding of yourself and the way you have interacted with men, and you will become more able to forgive yourself for not taking care of yourself better with men in the past. Most important, you will grow to love and respect yourself more and become more motivated to take care of yourself and protect yourself from harm.

Empowerment through Self-Compassion

At the first Women's March in Washington DC women carried signs that said things like, "A Woman's Place is In the Resistance," "Keep Your Hands Off," and "Keep Your Laws (and Your Paws) Off My Body." I found all these signs to be very empowering. But there was one sign that I was particularly moved by. It read, "To Love Oneself is a Rebellion." This is one of the primary messages of this book: one of the best ways for you to overcome the shame that has been thrust upon you, one of the best ways to resist the current "war on women," is *to love yourself and stand up for yourself.*

Arming yourself with self-compassion is an important step toward learning how to protect yourself. Learning how to practice self-compassion will enable you to stand up to any threat you may encounter and to fight off unwanted sexual advances more than almost anything else you can learn.

Kristin Neff, a professor of psychology at the University of Texas at Austin, is the leading researcher in the growing field of self-compassion. In her ground-breaking book, *Self-Compassion,* she defines self-compassion as "being open to and moved by one's own suffering, experiencing feelings of caring and kindness toward oneself, taking an understanding, nonjudgmental attitude toward one's inadequacies and failures, and recognizing that one's experience is part of the common human experience."

Let's concentrate on "being open to and moved by one's own suffering." Since you can't very well have compassion for your suffering if you aren't clear as to how you have suffered, we will focus on helping you to come further out of denial about how you have been mistreated by men throughout your life and how it has affected you. The truth is, if you are female, you have been sexually mistreated by males, although you may or may not consider the ways you were treated to have been "mistreatment" or "abuse."

Many women have taken on the attitude that sexual coercion, sexual harassment, and sexual assault are just part of every female's experience. They attempt to normalize sexual violations, thinking that since they happen so often and to so many women, they aren't really a big deal. But they are. Sexual assault and abuse are the most damaging of personal violations and can be life-changing, causing a woman to lose faith in her ability to defend herself or even in her *right* to defend herself. Don't continue to deny, minimize, or normalize the sexual intrusions you're constantly experiencing.

If you were sexually abused as a child or raped as an adult, don't ignore the agony, horrific pain, and shame you suffered. Comfort yourself the way you would a beloved friend or loved one.

Exercise: The Words You Wished You Had Heard

You likely did not have anyone to soothe or comfort you right after you were raped or molested. And you surely had no one to acknowledge your pain right after a man exposed himself to you or a man grabbed you on the bus or subway. There was likely no one there to tell you they were sorry it happened or that they felt bad for you. Even if you did tell a girlfriend about what happened, she may not have been able to comfort you in the way you needed.

Think of the words you wished you had heard right after you were sexually abused as a child, raped as an adult, or sexually violated in some other way at any point in your life. Write these words down.

Now say these words to yourself, the words you wished you had heard then. Say things to yourself like:

"I'm so sorry this happened to you."

"No one should have had to endure something like that."

"Oh, how horrible. That must have been so painful, so humiliating."

"I'm sorry you've had to endure this all alone."

Put your arms around your shoulders or across your

stomach, as if someone is hugging you. Let yourself be comforted. Get a cup of hot tea and sit quietly, letting it all sink in—all the pain, all the humiliation. Let your tears flow if you feel sad. Know that what happened to you is not okay. It doesn't matter how many other women have experienced the same thing. It doesn't matter if someone you know had it worse than you. This happened to you and it was horrible. It should never have happened.

Acknowledge how difficult it has been to recover, to move forward from it—to try to not allow the abuse or assault to ruin your life. Acknowledge how much you have continued to suffer, even after many years.

Think about how much the abuse or assault has damaged your self-confidence, self-esteem, and self-concept, how much it has affected your ability to trust, to obtain and maintain a healthy relationship, to experience a fulfilling sexual life. Give yourself credit for how hard you had to work just to maintain your sanity, or perhaps how hard you still have to work. This acknowledgment and compassion for all you've suffered is what will help you to gain the strength and courage to stand up to sexual assault, harassment, and sexual pressure today and in the future.

You've just offered yourself self-compassion. It isn't a complicated process to learn. It is just about acknowledging your suffering and comforting yourself. It is just about treating yourself with the same kindness, understanding, and care you would give to a wounded loved one.

Compassion as a Form of Validation

There is still another benefit that comes from self-compassion: validation.

It is very important for everyone, but especially children, to have their feelings and experiences validated by others. Put simply, to validate is to confirm.

Validation is the recognition and acceptance of another person's internal experience as mattering. When someone validates another's experience, the message they send is, "Your feelings make sense. Not only do I hear you, I also understand why you feel as you do. You are not bad or wrong or crazy for feeling the way you do."

It is often lack of validation that contributes to the development of feelings of guilt and shame as a reaction to negative experiences. For example, if you are like so many other women who were sexually abused as a child, you likely did not tell anyone about the abuse. Because of this, your experience of the abuse itself was likely never validated. In order to heal from the abuse and the shame surrounding it, it is important that you receive validation now—from yourself and others. The same is true if you were sexually assaulted or harassed as an adult.

Instead of receiving validation, most victims are ignored, rejected, or judged. Instead of being encouraged to express their feelings, most are shamed into silence. Worse yet, many of you have actually had your feelings and perceptions invalidated.

To invalidate means to attack or question the foundation or reality of a person's feelings. This can be done through denying, ridiculing, ignoring, or judging another person's feelings. Regardless of the method, the effect is clear: the person feels "wrong." Because of this it is vitally important that your perceptions and your feelings are validated today. Having compassion for someone can be a form of validation. And having self-compassion, connecting to one's own suffering, is a way of validating yourself, your feelings, your perception, and your experience.

Self-compassion will help you give yourself the nurturance, understanding and validation you so desperately need in order to feel worthy of care and acceptance.

Exercise: The Compassionate Letter

I asked my client Valerie to write a "compassion letter" to herself in which she offered herself compassion for all she'd suffered as a result of sexual violations perpetuated against her. This is what she wrote:

"When I read the list of all the sexual violations you experienced as a child and as an adult I feel so sad. I am sorry you have suffered so much. You suffered from so many terrible things and I wish they wouldn't have happened to you. And I wish there had been someone there to comfort you after each and every one of these traumas. You suffered from depression and self-blame afterwards and you became more and more numb. You became more and more afraid in the world and this affected your confidence. You didn't deserve any of these things to happen and there should have been adults around to protect you. It must have been so frightening to suffer all alone and even more frightening to imagine that more terrible things could happen to you in the future."

As you will notice, not only did Valerie offer herself comfort and understanding for her suffering in this letter, she also *validated* her feelings.

Two researchers, Leah B. Shapira and Myriam Mongrain, found in one study they conducted that adults who wrote a compassionate letter to themselves once a day for a week about the distressing events they had experienced showed significant reductions in depression over three months and significant increases in happiness over six months, compared with a control group that was asked to write about early memories.

Other Benefits and Research

In addition to self-compassion being the antidote to shame, it can also act as an antidote to self-criticism—a major tendency of those who experience intense shame. Research has found that self-compassion is a powerful trigger for the release of oxytocin, the hormone that increases feelings of trust, calm, safety, generosity, and connectedness. (Gilbert, 2005). Self-criticism, on the other hand, has a very different effect on our body. The amygdala, the oldest part of the brain, is designed to quickly detect threats in the environment. When we experience a threatening situation, the fight-or-flight response is triggered and the amygdala sends signals that increase blood pressure, adrenaline, and the hormone cortisol, mobilizing the strength and energy we need to confront or avoid the threat. Although our bodies created this system to deal with physical attacks, it is activated just as readily by emotional attacks—from within and without. Over time, increased cortisol levels lead to depression, because they deplete the various neurotransmitters that allow us to experience pleasure. (Longe, etal, 2010).

There is also neurological evidence showing that self-kindness (a major component of self-compassion) and self-criticism operate quite differently in terms of brain function. A recent study found that self-criticism was associated with activity in the lateral prefrontal cortex and dorsal anterior cingulated—areas of the brain associated with error processing and problem solving. Being kind and reassuring toward oneself, on the other hand, was associated with left temporal pole and insula activation—areas of the brain associated with positive emotions and compassion. (Longe, etal 2010). Instead of seeing ourselves as a problem to be fixed, therefore, self-kindness allows us to see ourselves as valuable human beings who are worthy of care.

Obstacles to Self-Compassion

Even when women come to understand how they have been mistreated by men, they can still have a difficult time having compassion for themselves. The following is a list of the many obstacles in the way of women providing self-compassion toward themselves:

- *The belief that self-compassion is self-indulgent.* This is the most common obstacle to learning and practicing self-compassion. Many people view self-kindness, an important aspect of self-compassion, as being soft or self-indulgent. Many have a strong belief that to stop to acknowledge their pain and suffering is to "feel sorry for themselves" or "have a pity party." This is a reflection of our culture's tendency to discourage people from acknowledging and/or talking about their suffering and viewing it as a sign of weakness.

- *The fear that you will seem selfish.* Some people feel guilty when they focus on their suffering. This is especially true for women. They compare themselves with others who seem to have it worse than they do and they feel that they don't have a right to complain. Yes, there will always be someone who has it worse than you—but that doesn't mean you shouldn't take the time to acknowledge your own suffering. Comparing your problems with others can also be a convenient way to deny and avoid your own pain.

- *Blaming yourself.* As we have discussed, believing you are to blame for your own victimization can give you a sense of control, however illusory. If you believe that what happened to you occurred because of something you did or did not do, then you don't have to face the reality that you were a helpless victim. It doesn't help that we have a victim-blaming mentality in our culture today. There are even those whose spiritual beliefs (such as those espoused by some New Age theologies) teach that if something bad happens to you, it is because of your own negative thoughts or attitude. Cultural influences like this actually serve to segregate and blame victims rather than encourage a self-compassionate acknowledgment of suffering.

Stopping to acknowledge your suffering is not the same as whining or feeling sorry for yourself. Self-compassionate statements come from a more nurturing place inside of us and can be comforting and validating. For example, see if you can sense a difference between the following two examples:

- "I can't even walk down the street without some creep yelling obscenities at me! And there's absolutely nothing I can do about it."

- "I hate it when a guy yells obscenities at me when I walk down the street. It makes me feel so angry but also afraid. I'm never quite sure whether the guy is dangerous or not. It's understandable that I am afraid and angry. I feel so out of control. I've got to find some better ways to deal with the situation."

In the first example, the woman is complaining (which is still okay) but she isn't really expressing her emotions. She is also expressing hopelessness (which is okay too) instead of recognizing that there may be something she can do about the problem. In the second example, the women is expressing her emotions (anger and fear) and she is validating her experience by acknowledging that *it is understandable* that she would feel this way. Just as important, she is saying that she needs to find better ways to deal with the problem.

Self-compassion can actually lead to proactive behavior. Once you have *validated* your feelings and your experience, you may feel more motivated to improve your situation. I often find this to be the case with people who are currently being either emotionally or physically abused. Once they acknowledge their suffering and allow themselves to feel and express their emotions because of it, they often feel more impetus to leave the relationship.

Having compassion for your past and present suffering will help you come out of denial about what you have been through and how you have suffered. It will help heal the multitude of wounds associated with sexual violations. It will provide you with *self-understanding*, an important aspect of self-compassion, thereby helping you to better comprehend why you have behaved as you have (being reckless with yourself, freezing when a man touches you, giving yourself away to men).

Exercise: It is Understandable

Make a list of the ways you have coped with the fact that you were sexually violated. For example, maybe you isolated yourself from others for months after you were date raped, perhaps you pushed your boyfriend away, or maybe you went wild for a while—drinking, drinking too much, going out too often, being reckless with yourself.

The way to practice self-compassion concerning the ways you coped, no matter how seemingly reckless or unhealthy, is to tell yourself that *it is understandable* that you needed to comfort yourself or protect yourself or distract yourself in these ways.

For each of the coping mechanisms you used, tell yourself, "It is understandable." For example: "It is understandable that I pushed my boyfriend away. I felt so much shame, I couldn't imagine that he could still love me."

Self-Care

Another important aspect of self-compassion is self-care. Practicing self-compassion will motivate you to take better care of yourself, including making sure you are safe and not doing anything that will jeopardize your safety and integrity. Practicing self-compassion will help you make wiser and healthier choices. It doesn't just make you feel better, it will make you act in healthier ways, including protecting yourself from sexual assault.

Feeling you have permission to say no is rooted in self-compassion. If you don't love yourself and have a deep desire to honor yourself and your values, then saying "no!" can and will be very difficult in every situation—you will continue to be passive when you don't want to be. But when you can put your need to be safe and to be treated with respect ahead of other less important needs, such as giving into a man's sexual demands, you will find that you'll respect yourself far more and that you'll be better able to honor your body and your integrity.

There is significant research-based evidence that girls and women who say "no" firmly, yell, or physically fight back have a greater chance of escaping a sexually coercive situation without being raped compared to those who freeze, cry, apologize, or politely resist (SMU Research News). This does not imply that women are responsible for stopping rape or that preventing rape is up to women, but knowing that it's okay to fight back can help women feel more empowered.

In summary, practicing self-compassion will:

- Help you come out of denial about how you have suffered in the past.

- Provide you a way to comfort yourself and to validate your feelings.

- Help you to stop shaming and blaming yourself for things other people have done to you.

- Help you to forgive yourself for not being able to protect yourself or treat yourself well in the past.

- Help empower you to stand up for yourself today. Research shows that self-compassion and empowerment are positively related. For example, a 2012 study of 205 undergraduate students at a southwestern university identified a significant positive relationship between self-compassion and empowerment. (Stevenson & Bates Allen, 2012).

- Encourage you to have more compassion toward other women. It will help you to stop judging those who have been sexually violated, including those who don't report it; it will encourage you to support other women instead of seeing them as competition; and it will discourage you from fat shaming and slut-shaming other women.

The Price We Pay for Not Practicing Self-Compassion

I've discussed all the reasons why it is important to practice self-compassion—all the benefits it offers you. But it is also important to recognize that there is also a downside when it comes to *not* offering yourself self-compassion. Below is a list of many of the pitfalls to refusing to offer yourself the healing benefits of self-compassion:

- Disconnecting from your pain and other feelings related to sexual violation will likely cause you to feel more and more out of touch with yourself.

- Not practicing self-compassion will encourage you to become hard on yourself and to have unreasonable expectations of yourself.

- Your inability to show compassion for yourself may destroy your ability to have compassion for others. You will expect others to "move on" the way you think you have done, and become insensitive to their pain.

- You may start making excuses for your own inappropriate or abusive behavior and to not recognize when you are being hurtful to others.

- Rejecting self-compassion can cause you to feel envious of others who have seemingly escaped the pain you have experienced because of sexual violations. Sadly, this can even include feeling resentful of your own children.

- By not acknowledging your suffering, you may continue to put yourself in dangerous situations and to continue to minimize or deny further sexual violations.

- You will likely channel your shame into an unhealthy avenue (alcohol, drugs, sex).

- You will likely find unhealthy avenues for your anger, such as becoming abusive toward others.

Remember: You can't become self-compassionate if you don't recognize your own suffering. We can't be moved by our pain if we don't even acknowledge that it exists. So don't dismiss your suffering, don't insult its legacy. Allow it to motivate you to take better care of yourself, protect yourself, and speak out for yourself. Trade your self-blame for self-compassion, your self-criticism for self-acknowledgment and self-encouragement, and your shame for pride—pride that you survived, pride that you endured.

True strength, true empowerment comes from being connected to yourself—your feelings and your needs. It doesn't come from denying your feelings or becoming numb in an attempt to avoid your pain and suffering. Address your wounds; heal them with the soothing balm of compassion and learn from them. As the famous quote from Ernest Hemingway attests, "The world breaks everyone and afterward many are strong at the broken places." Be one of those who becomes stronger at the broken places.

Stop pretending to be strong. Stop denying your pain. Become truly strong with the power of self-compassion. Let yourself feel compassion for the amount of suffering you have endured due to being sexually violated from the time you were a young child in the form of catcalls, derogatory comments about your body, and having sexual obscenities yelled at you. Let self-compassion help you to heal the pain, fear, humiliation, and, most of all, shame you carry around due to childhood sexual abuse or sexual assault as an adult. Let it help you learn how to be kinder to yourself and more forgiving of your shortcomings (imagined or real). This will encourage you to take better care of yourself in every situation you encounter.

Goals of Chapter 6

The primary goal of this chapter is to introduce the concept and practice of self-compassion, which is the antidote to shame. By practicing self-compassion you will strengthen your resolve to take better care of yourself in the sexual arena and come to believe on an even deeper level that you deserve to be treated with respect by the men around you.

No! Exercise

The optimal way of doing this exercise is to find a comfortable place to sit or curl up. Make sure it is a private place where you won't be disturbed and make sure you are not too hot or too cold. You may want to comfort yourself by having a quilt or comforter around you.

Repeat the following or some version of the following to yourself—either out loud or silently to yourself:

- No—I'm not going to continue to blame myself for the sexual violence I have experienced.

- No—I'm not going to shame myself for the way I reacted (or didn't react) to the assault.

- No—I'm not going to shame and blame myself for the way I have coped with the sexual violations I have suffered. It is understandable that I would react as I have.

Yes! Exercise

Now we are going to add "Yes!" to your repertoire.

Again, say silently to yourself or out loud, some version of the following:

- Yes! I deserve to comfort myself about the sexual violations I've experienced.

- Yes! I deserve to take in the compassion of others regarding my suffering.

- Yes! I am going to provide for myself the self-compassion I deserve.

- Yes! I deserve to be treated with kindness, consideration, and respect by men.

Chapter 7
Connecting With and Releasing Your Anger

Bitterness is like cancer. It eats upon the host. But anger is like fire. It burns it all clean.

—Maya Angelou

Anger is one of the most empowering emotions we have. When we allow ourselves to connect with and release our anger, we get in touch with our strength and our power. We release the fierce warrior within.

Connecting with and releasing your anger is also important because it will help you to find your voice and help you to say "No!" Finding your voice involves being able to speak some of the things inside you that you haven't been able to say, the words that wait to be said. This is particularly true for former victims of childhood sexual abuse or rape as an adult.

Former victims of child sexual abuse or sexual assault as an adult were often told to keep quiet, to never tell anyone about what happened. Many were threatened with, "No one will believe you if you tell," and even, "I'll kill you if you tell." If you continue to silence the voices of your own emotions, you are effectively saying to your attacker, "I agree with you. I don't deserve to be heard and no one will believe me," or "I need to continue to remain silent about this or I will be endangered."

Connecting with your righteous anger helps you to bypass those unhelpful warnings and connect with the truth. The truth is that you need to tell your story and express your righteous anger *even if you are not believed.*

Unfortunately, many women have difficulties connecting with their anger, and even more difficulty giving themselves permission to express their righteous anger. Some are afraid of their anger--afraid that if they start expressing it, they will lose control and harm someone. Those who were raised in violent households may be repulsed by any show of anger and may be so afraid of becoming like their abusive parent that they completely repress their own anger. And many girls are raised to believe that it is not okay for girls to get angry. It is common for girls to be taught that it is okay to cry, but not to yell, while boys are raised to believe the opposite. Girls are taught early on that if we express our anger we will not be taken seriously. We will sound "childlike," "too emotional," or "hysterical" and thus undercut the points we want to make.

If you are afraid that if you were to really get angry and let it all out, you would lose control, or if you feel that anger is a disgusting thing and you don't want anything to do with it, this chapter will help you get over these false, unrealistic, and unhealthy beliefs. And this is vitally important, because becoming comfortable with your own anger is a major step toward empowerment. Turning your fear into anger will help you stand up for yourself. Turning your feelings of helplessness and hopelessness into anger will motivate you to continue to value yourself enough to say "No!" to anything or anyone that will undercut your value and worth. Turning your shame into anger will help you stop blaming yourself for your experiences of sexual violation and put the responsibility for it squarely at the feet of your abusers.

Allowing yourself to express your anger and learning to say no are inextricably bound together. In order to be able to say "No!" to unwanted touch or to sexual pressure, you have to be able to connect with your inner power. You have to believe you have the right to say "No!" And anger can help you to do this. When we feel our anger, we connect with our power. It is similar to igniting a flame inside. If you don't light that match, you will never see the flame. You will never feel the heat. You will never feel the power of a bonfire inside of you.

In this chapter, we will focus on encouraging you to turn your fear and helplessness and hopelessness into action—action in the form of standing up and saying "No!" No to unwanted sexual pressure; no to sexual harassment; no to sexual assault. Give yourself permission to turn your fear and anxiety into righteous anger—anger that will motivate you to refuse to be mistreated any further.

Anger—Positive or Negative?

Anger can be either positive or negative. It is positive when you release your anger in constructive, safe ways. It can be positive when you use it to fuel your fury at the outrageous treatment women must endure every day. It can be healing when you find the courage to confront your past abusers by writing them letters (that you will likely not send) or by pretending you are speaking to them. Venting your righteous anger in healthy ways can mobilize, empower you, and motivate you to become a stronger woman around men, stand up for your rights, and become involved in women's causes.

We cannot feel fear and anger at the same time. Anger tells our fear to go rest in the corner. It tells our fear that it is going to take over and protect us.

A perfect example of how you can turn fear into anger is the students at Marjory Stoneman Douglas High School in Florida. After losing seventeen of their fellow students to gun violence, those kids could have cowered in fear and remained silent about the tragedy. And they would have every right to do so. But instead they chose to connect with their righteous anger. Anger at the loss of their friends by senseless gun violence. Anger at the adults around them who did not protect them. Anger when they asked, "When is this going to change?"

We all felt the power of these students' words of anger. We were all moved by their strength and determination. I want you to have that same power and strength and determination when it comes to connecting with and naming the reasons for your anger.

We former victims of sexual violence, we who walk around in fear of becoming another victim, we who have watched while women continue to be treated like sex objects and while men believe they have the right to treat us anyway they choose—we have more power than we realize. We who feel endangered every time we go to a bar or a party, who expect to be catcalled every time we walk down the street—we have a right to stand up and express our rage at the way we are being treated. This kind of anger is empowering and can create change, both inside us and in the world.

Anger can also be a negative force, of course. This is true when we take our anger out on innocent people. The shooter of the seventeen students at Marjory Stoneman Douglas is a good example of this. The young man was certainly angry—at who or at what we cannot know, but I am certain that his fellow students were not the source of his anger. He, like most bullies, like most abusers—was taking his deep-seated anger out on innocent people. So taking your anger out on your boyfriend, or your girlfriends, or on the innocent men around you is not the way to go. Your anger needs to be directed at the source—at the men who have sexually violated you in the past. The man who sexually abused you as a child. The guy who forced sex on you when you went out with him. The guys who grab your breasts or butt as they pass by you. The guys who yell obscenities as you walk by a construction site. These are the appropriate targets of your anger.

Anger is also negative when you bury it deep inside yourself where you can hardly find it rather than expressing it. Repressed anger (anger you unconsciously bury) or suppressed anger (anger you put aside consciously) can cause depression and self-hatred. It can make you feel hopeless and helpless.

Anger can hide out inside us for decades, primarily because it can feel like the riskiest emotion to express. This is especially true for women who were raised to never acknowledge or express anger. It is also true for those who sense on an unconscious level, that if they ever acknowledge their anger they will have to come out of denial—denial about just how deeply the sexual violations they've experienced have damaged them or how other sexual violations they have yet to face have impacted their lives.

Most important, anger is negative when you turn it against yourself. It is not only negative but also unhealthy when you blame yourself for being sexually abused as a kid or sexually assaulted as an adult. It is negative if you blame yourself for going out with a "bad boy" when you think you should have known better. It is negative when you blame yourself for wearing sexy or provocative clothes, telling yourself that you were "asking for it."

Anger is especially negative when you turn it into debilitating shame.

Debilitating shame robs you of your power, your sense of efficacy and agency, your belief that you can, in fact, change your circumstances. Women need to be encouraged to push away this internalized shame with anger. We need to learn how to give the shame back to our abusers, our hecklers, our bullies.

Some women are aware of their anger. They know they are angry at the men who accuse them of "asking for it" when they dress provocatively. They are angry at the men who seem to think that if they allow them to kiss them or touch them in a sexual way it means they are obligated to have intercourse with him. They are angry because they are so often blamed for their own sexual assault. They are angry because men's unacceptable behavior is still excused with the attitude that "boys will be boys." They are angry because time after time, people choose to rally around the popular football player or fraternity brother or boss without taking the time to get the facts straight. They are angry because they are still accused of lying. And they are angry because men have a built-in weapon—their penis—that they can use against them anytime they want. They are angry, but they don't know how to release this anger in healthy ways.

Exercise: What Are You Angry About?

Create a list of all the things you are angry about when it comes to the way women and girls are treated. Begin each sentence with, "I feel angry because" or "I feel angry about." For example, "I feel angry about _____."

Continue writing your list until you can't think of any more responses. Notice how it feels to acknowledge your anger in this way.

Now write about how angry you are about what has happened to you personally—the sexual violations you've endured. You can either complete the sentence "I feel angry that _____," or just write freely about the anger you feel about having been sexually violated.

Notice how this writing makes you feel. Hopefully you

feel a sense of relief acknowledging your anger and naming the offenses you've had to endure. For some of you this can feel liberating, empowering. For others, however, it may have been a difficult exercise. Even though you certainly have many good reasons to be angry, you may have felt at a loss for words; you may even have experienced a "brain freeze" in which you "forgot" how you've been mistreated or abused. Others may have felt like they were doing something wrong.

If you experienced any of these things while performing this exercise, spend some time writing about these feelings. Write about your fear of anger or your discomfort with it. Write about how you feel like you're doing something wrong.

Facing the Obstacles to Releasing Your Anger

My client Raven had been having a difficult time admitting that she was angry at her father, who had sexually abused her starting when she was five and continuing until she was nine. She kept making excuses for him, kept telling me that he was an alcoholic and didn't even know what he had done. But avoiding her anger wasn't getting Raven anywhere in terms of her recovery. She remained passive, especially with men. She often complained that men used her for sex, that she wasn't able to say no to men, and that she hated herself for being so passive.

I suspected that the main reason Raven was resisting connecting with her anger was that she didn't want to connect with the pain underneath her denial. This is often the case with former victims. She didn't want to connect with the reality that her father, whom she loved dearly, had betrayed her, taken advantage of her, and let her down in an essential way by not being the father she deserved—a father who would protect her, (even from himself), a father who would never put his selfish needs ahead of his own, a father who would take responsibility for putting his daughter at risk by being around her when he was drunk and by not seeking help for his drinking problem.

Exercise: What Are Your Obstacles?

Write down all your reasons for not wanting to acknowledge your anger. Maybe you are afraid of losing control; maybe you are fearful of facing other feelings, like sadness. Perhaps you were raised to be a "good girl" and to never express anger. Whatever your reasons are, put them down on paper.

Think about your childhood and try to discover your reasons for being afraid of your anger or for your belief that anger is not supposed to be expressed. For example:

- How did your parents express their anger?

- Were you frightened when one or both of your parents expressed anger?

- Did one or both of your parents become verbally, emotionally, or physically abusive when he or she expressed anger?

- Are you frightened to see or feel someone's anger?

- As a child, did you come to believe that anger was a precursor to someone hurting you?

- Were you given permission or encouragement to express your dislike of unfair situations, or were you given the message that you needed to keep quiet?

Now write about your beliefs about anger. For example:

- Do you believe it's wrong to express your anger or for girls and women to express their anger?

- Do you believe expressing anger is unsafe?

- Do you believe expressing anger is a sign of weakness?

Write about the changes you need to make or beliefs you need to reject in order to give yourself permission to release your anger in healthy ways. For example:

- I need to stop feeling guilty about releasing my anger.

- I need to begin to believe I have a right to release my anger in healthy ways.

- I need to find ways to express my anger in safe ways that don't hurt or damage myself or anyone else.

Write about whether you think there is such a thing as "healthy anger." If so, what is your definition of "healthy anger"? How does your anger expression need to change in order for you to become healthier?

Connecting With and Releasing Your Anger

Continue to tell yourself that you have a right to your righteous anger at having been mistreated, disrespected, or abused by sexual violations and sexual violence. If discovering that the treatment you've experienced was actually sexual assault, abuse, harassment, or some other form of sexual violation makes you feel angry, give yourself permission to express your righteous anger. If you are angry because you were sexually abused as an adult, let out that anger. If you are angry about the countless times that you have been treated with disrespect by the men around you, tell yourself that it's okay to be angry.

At the beginning of the healing journey, grief, fear, and anxiety are often the dominant feelings for former victims of sexual violation. But as time passes and they come to know that they were not to blame for their traumas, former victims often begin to feel stronger, and their anger and rage begin to emerge. They begin to feel the urge to hit, kick, or scream. If this is where you are, it is important that you find some healthy, constructive ways to vent your anger.

Anger Release Techniques

- Write down your angry feelings. Don't hold back; let all your feelings of anger and hurt come out on the page. If you find it difficult to connect with your feelings or to write your feelings down, use this sentence completion: "I'm angry that _____."

- Write a letter to your abuser(s) that you do not plan to send. Let him or her (or them) know how you feel about what was done to you and how the abuse has subsequently affected you.

- Walk around your house (assuming you are alone) and talk out loud to yourself, expressing all the angry feelings you are having. Don't censor yourself; say exactly what is on your mind and use any language you choose, including swear words.

- Imagine that you are sitting across from one of your abusers. Tell him or her exactly how you feel about what he or she did to you. Again, don't hold back and don't censor yourself. If you notice that you are afraid to confront your abuser in this way, imagine that he or she is tied to the chair. If you don't want to see his or her eyes for fear of becoming intimidated, imagine that he or she is blindfolded. And if you are afraid of what he or she might say to you in response to your anger, imagine that he or she is gagged.

- Put your head in a pillow and scream.

- If you feel like you need to release your anger physically, ask your body what it needs to do. You might get the sense that you need to hit, kick, push, break things, or tear things up. Honor that intuitive feeling by finding a way to release your anger in a safe, but satisfying way. For example, it is safe to kneel down next to your bed and hit the bed with your fists. If you are alone and no one is around, you can let out sounds as you hit. You can lie on your bed and kick your legs or you can stomp on egg cartons or other packaging. You can tear up old telephone books or go to a deserted place and throw rocks or bottles.

Notice how you feel after releasing your anger in any of these ways. As my client Teresa expressed to me, "I noticed that my rage felt cleansing. Like it burned away my shame and self-blame. I noticed that I had more and more energy the more I released my anger."

Releasing your anger, in addition to empowering you, will help you recognize that any sexual violation you've suffered was not your fault, and that you did not deserve the abuse. Although you may know on an *intellectual* level that you did not cause the person who sexually violated you to act as he or she did, expressing your anger at having been violated can help you to come to know these truths on a much deeper level. In expressing your righteous anger, you will be drowning out the voices of shame inside you.

It is especially important for those who have *internalized* their anger (i.e., blamed themselves) to redirect that anger toward their abuser. After all, he or she is the appropriate target for your anger. By allowing yourself to get angry at your abuser, the vital force of anger will be moving in the right direction: outward instead of inward.

Internalizing your anger and blame not only makes you feel guilty and ashamed but can also cause you to punish yourself with negative relationships or self-destructive behavior (such as alcohol or drug abuse, starving yourself, overeating, or performing self-mutilation with razors, knives, pins, or cigarettes). Let all that self-hatred become righteous anger toward your abuser. Stop taking your anger out *on* yourself and start taking it out *of* yourself.

If you are still having difficulty giving yourself permission to get angry or fear that you will lose control if you were to get angry, please refer to my book, *Honor Your Anger*. I also write extensively about getting past your resistance to releasing anger in my book, *The Right to Innocence: Healing the Trauma of Childhood Sexual Abuse*. Both these books will help you to work past your fears and resistance and offer you many more suggestions on how to release anger in constructive, safe ways.

What If I Don't Feel Angry?

Not everyone finds it easy to connect with their anger, even when they know they "should" be feeling it. If this is your situation, here are some suggestions that might help you.

- Notice where your body holds anger on the occasion that you do feel angry. Is your jaw tight? Do you clench your jaw or grind your teeth? Do you tend to clench your hands into fists? Are your muscles tight? Now see if there are times where you don't consciously feel angry, but you're experiencing at least one of these things. These body signals are telling you that even though you might not be aware of your anger, it is there, hiding in your body.

- Notice if you are often irritated with others around you. This can also be an indication that you are angry without realizing it. Being consistently irritated, frustrated, or impatient with others is a sign that you are feeling a low level of anger almost all the time.

- Notice if you are often angry or impatient with yourself. Do you have a powerful inner critic who is constantly finding fault in the things you do? Are you consistently disappointed in yourself? These are signs that you are in fact angry, and your anger is not really at yourself.

Exercise: Priming the Pump

I recommend the following exercise for everyone reading this chapter, but especially for those of you who have been sexually abused in childhood or sexually assaulted as an adult. Even if you are not aware that you're angry about these acts of sexual violence, believe me, you are. It may be buried deep inside and covered over with fear or shame; it may be hidden behind a façade of being a "nice girl"; but it is there. Doing the following exercise can be like "priming the pump," in the sense that it might touch off your buried or hidden anger.

First, find a private place where you won't be disturbed and where you will feel free to make noises without disturbing others or drawing attention to yourself. Ideal places can be your home (if no one is within earshot) or in your car, if you can drive to a secluded area.

Think of one of your experiences with sexual violation. Say "No!" out loud while you continue to think about how you were violated. Gradually increase the volume of your *No!*s until you are yelling "No!" at the top of your lungs. Let yourself really feel your "No." Let your voice get louder and louder.

Now chose one the following sentences to say, again thinking of one of the sexual violations you experienced. Go with the sentence that has the most meaning to you. Allow your voice to get louder and louder:

- "Get out!"

- "Leave me alone!"

- "Stop touching me!"

- "I said, 'No!'"

- "Get off me!"

- "Get away from me!"

- "I hate you!"

Repeat the phrase you chose over and over. Let your voice get louder and louder. Don't hold back; let yourself express your righteous anger. If a memory comes up, go with it and use it to fuel your anger and rage.

If you get in touch with some deep, unexpressed anger—brava! That's what we're aiming for. Notice how it feels to release this anger. If you really let yourself go and you yelled loudly and for a long time, you might end up feeling exhausted, but you may also feel a sense of relief. If you start to feel scared of your anger, remind yourself that you are safe, and that you are not hurting anyone. If releasing your anger uncovers more pain, let the tears flow. Tears don't weaken or diminish your anger—or power.

The Controversy Over Anger Release

Some researchers, and some therapists, believe that it isn't healthy to reinforce angry and violent behaviors (such as hitting your bed with a tennis racket, hitting a punching bag, or yelling). If you have a history of being violent, like hitting, pushing, or kicking people, I encourage you to release your anger in other ways, such as writing down your feelings or using art to express your rage. But for most women, expressing their anger, even doing so physically, doesn't make them violent. Instead, it empowers them to say "No!" and to be more assertive, especially with men. It also helps them release years of pent-up anger—anger they never before felt they had permission to express. Since most women did not get the chance to express their feelings of anger when they were being abused or assaulted, doing so now is extremely healthy.

Other people may tell you that you shouldn't express your anger, that it is somehow more spiritual or moral to let your past go instead of releasing your anger. You ultimately need to be the one to decide whether this is true for you. But in my experience, our past experiences with being sexually violated don't just "go away" and I don't believe you can truly "forgive" until you've released your anger. In any case, let your body and emotions determine what is right for you and your healing process.

My client Deborah shared with me, "I was raised a Catholic and trained to believe we should forgive those who harmed us. After I was raped I tried to put my beliefs into practice. I prayed and prayed for help in being able to forgive my attacker, but my anger just continued to come up. It wasn't just anger, it was rage.

"I finally went to a woman's rape support group and was encouraged to express my rage. We practiced stomping our feet and screaming, and it felt so good! They had a punching bag there, and after watching other women get their anger out on it I took my turn. My hands weren't strong enough, so I used the wooden dowel they had there and I began hitting that punching bag over and over, imagining my attacker's face on the bag. I could feel the amount of rage I had been holding in. I felt it streaming out of my arms and hands as I hit his face over and over.

"After it was over I felt exhausted, but also invigorated. I felt strength in my heart that I've never felt before. I felt strong and determined to do everything within my power to never let that happen to me again. My rage didn't all go away in that one session, but after several times of working on the punching bag, I felt my rage was spent. After that I did feel more like forgiving the rapist."

Fight, Flight, or Freeze

Peter Levine, the author of *Waking the Tiger*, has studied stress and trauma for thirty-five years. He has found that when a situation is perceived to be life-threatening, as in the case of sexual abuse or assault, both our mind and our body mobilize a vast amount of energy in preparation to fight or escape, often referred to as the "fight or flight" response. This is the same energy that can enable a mother to lift a car off her son's legs when he is trapped under a car. This kind of strength is created by a large increase in blood to the muscles and the release of stress hormones, such as cortisol and adrenaline.

In the act of lifting the 2,000-pound car, the mother discharges most of the excess chemicals and energy she has mobilized in order to deal with the threat to her child. This discharge of energy from the body, when complete, informs the brain that the threat is over, and it is time to reduce the levels of stress hormones in the body.

If the message to normalize is not given, however, the brain just continues to release high levels of adrenaline and cortisol, and the body remains in a high-energy, ramped-up state. Unlike his mother, this is the situation the son faces. Unless he can find a way to discharge the excess energy brought on by the crisis, his body will continue responding as it did when he was helpless and his body was in pain.

Unfortunately, human beings don't know how to "blow off the stress" of a near-death experience the way animals do. For example, a captured bear that has been shot with a tranquilizer dart, will come out of its state of shock once the tranquilizer wears off. It does this by beginning to tremble—lightly at first, and then at a steadily intensifying level until it peaks into a near-convulsive shaking, its limbs flailing seemingly at random. After the shaking stops, the animal takes deep, organic breaths that spread throughout its body.

What is even more interesting is that when the bear's response is viewed in slow motion, it becomes obvious that the seemingly random gyrations it is doing during this process are actually coordinated running movements. It is as if the bear is completing its escape by actively finishing the running movements that were interrupted when it was tranquilized by the dart. Then the bear shakes off the "frozen energy" as it surrenders in spontaneous, full-body breaths.

Researchers like Levine explain that people do, in fact, possess the same built-in ability to shake off threat the way animals do—many of us have simply forgotten how to use it. Given the appropriate guidance, human beings can and do shake off the effects of overwhelming events like sexual assault using exactly the same procedures that animals use.

Levine says that the reason his program works is that trauma is primarily physiological. Trauma happens initially to our bodies and our instincts. Only afterward do its effects spread to our minds, emotions, and spirits.

Another reason why anger release is so important is that it helps former victims release the frozen energy trapped in their body after a physical attack. In other words, if you were sexually assaulted, you may have tried to fight off your attacker; you may have tried to escape. But in the end, he overpowered you. Now you likely have that unspent rage and fear trapped in your body. Discharging this energy informs the brain that it is time to reduce the levels of stress hormones in the body—that the threat is no longer present. Until the message to normalize is given, the brain just continues to release high levels of adrenaline and cortisol, the body holds on to its high-energy state, and you continue to feel pain and helplessness.

Releasing your anger in any of the following ways can help you "shake off" the stress associated with the attack. (Please note: Doing any of these exercises can act as a trigger, catapulting you back to the sexual assault. This is okay if you are imagining pushing, shoving, or kicking your attacker away and feeling empowered, but if you slip into feeling fear and helplessness, ground yourself (refer to the exercise near the end of Chapter 1) and bring yourself back to the present. Stop doing the exercise until you are completely back in the present.

- Lie flat on your back on your bed, bend your knees, and place your feet flat on the bed. Now stomp your feet as hard as you can. You can also do this exercise by keeping your legs straight and alternating lifting each leg up and slamming it down hard on the bed. Say "No!" as you do this.

- Lie flat on your back on the floor, perpendicular to your bed. Place both your legs up against your mattress and push as hard as you can. Imagine you are pushing your attacker away with the power of your legs. Say "Get away from me!" or "Get off!"

- Stand in front of a sturdy door in your house. Put both arms out and place your palms flat against the door. As you push against the door as hard as you can, say "Get away!" or "Get out of here!"

Confronting Your Abuser(s)

If you feel like confronting your abuser or attacker in person, I encourage you to continue releasing your anger in healthy, constructive ways first so that you do not put yourself or the other person in danger. I also encourage you to carefully consider whether it is safe for you (emotionally and physically) to confront this person. Aside from the safety concerns of confronting a man with a history of violence, there is a chance that you will sustain psychological damage from the encounter. Just being in his presence may cause you to be re-victimized. And child molesters and rapists seldom, if ever, acknowledge their crime. Instead, he is likely to deny that he did anything wrong, insist that it was consensual, accuse you of lying, or, if he does admit any wrongdoing, blame you for his actions. This could cause you to once again begin to doubt yourself. (For more information on the pros and cons of direct confrontations, consider reading my books *Breaking the Cycle of Abuse* and *The Right to Innocence*.)

If you feel trapped by a continuous pattern of being used and abused by men, anger is your way out. It will strengthen your resolve to break your patterns and empower you to begin to behave in healthier ways with men—as their equal instead of their victim.

Let your anger motivate you to take up the warrior mantle—to become a woman who fights against the continual onslaught of men who want to stop us from progressing, men who want to use their power to control us. Think about the power Ana Maria Archila and Maria Gallagner—the two women who confronted Senator Jeff Flake outside the elevator—had when they voiced their anger. Although we can't be certain, it seems that these women speaking up in anger, insisting on being heard and being looked at, caused him to have a change of heart.

Goals of Chapter 7

The main goal of this chapter has been to educate you about the benefits of releasing anger in healthy ways and to provide you with helpful suggestions as to how you can go about it. Another goal is to help you work past your resistance to owning and releasing your righteous anger over having been sexually violated in the past. And finally, it is about helping you turn your fear and helplessness and hopelessness into action.

No! Exercise

Even though it is usually not safe or recommended to actually confront your attacker, you can still have the experience of confronting him in your imagination. Many former victims report that imagining confronting their abuser or attacker felt almost as good as they imagined it would if they had done it in reality.

- Find words for what you want to say to your attacker. Examples: "I hate you!" "Don't touch me!" "Get the hell away from me!" "You disgust me!"

- Walk around your house and say these words out loud or imagine you are facing the confronter as he sits in a chair across from you (again, tie him up, blindfold him, and gag him if you need to in order to feel safe).

- Notice how it feels to confront your abuser(s) like this. If you still have too much fear of your attacker to confront him, think about all the men who have harassed you, pressured you, thrown insults at you, or violated you in any way sexually. Tell them how you feel about them! Say "No!"

Chapter 8
Body-Esteem: A New Way of Viewing Your Body and Your Sexuality

To be beautiful means to be yourself. You don't need to be accepted by others. You need to accept yourself.

—Thich Nhat Hanh

Most people are critical of their bodies, but women tend to be especially so. This is primarily due to our culture's preoccupation with bodily perfection, especially for women and girls. This causes most women and girls to judge themselves by unreasonable standards. In addition, most girls grow up experiencing body shaming from their peers. The end result: body hatred runs rampant in our culture.

Why am I discussing body image in a book about learning how to stand up to sexual assault, harassment, and pressure? The sad truth is, if you are constantly critical of what you see in the mirror, or if you hate your body, you are less likely to care what happens to your body. You are less likely to protect it from being mistreated or sexually violated. This is especially true for women and girls who have previously been sexually abused or assaulted. Former victims tend to feel a great deal of shame around their bodies and are often angry with their body for betraying them. Those who felt some pleasure during the sexual violation can be particularly angry with their body.

Those who hate their bodies tend not to stand up for themselves by saying

"No!" to unwanted sexual advances. They simply don't care what happens to their body. It's like the difference between hearing a good friend be berated by someone and hearing someone you hate being berated. If it's a good friend, you probably want to step in and defend her or him; if it is an enemy, you probably don't feel compelled to help. The same is true for your body. If you make your body your friend, you will be more likely to want to protect it, whereas if you perceive your body as your enemy, you won't care what happens to it.

Many women, even those who have not experienced sexual violations, don't give their body or their sexuality the respect and consideration it deserves. But if you don't respect and honor your body and your sexuality, how can you expect others to do so? One of the reasons so many women get into sexual situations where the other person goes too far is because of a reasoning process that goes something like this: "It's no big deal if he touches my breasts (or vagina). He likes it and it doesn't hurt me."

It may seem like it doesn't hurt you if you allow someone to do things to your body that you don't really want him to do, but the truth is, *it does hurt you*. It lowers your self-esteem, because it causes you to begin to *lose respect* for yourself. And it can *humiliate* you and add to the shame you already feel about your body or your sexuality.

In this chapter, we are going to focus on the importance of respecting and honoring your body, and I will show you ways you can accomplish these tasks. By doing this you will begin to gain what I call *body*-esteem—the ability to value and respect your body just as it is. When you gain body esteem, you will be more inclined to set boundaries around who can touch you and in what ways, and you will be more motivated to stand up for yourself and say "No!" when someone tries to violate your boundaries.

Most people are aware of the problems women and girls frequently experience concerning low self-esteem and poor body image. In this chapter, I will connect the dots between the consequences of these two issues and the sexual assault and other sexual violations of women.

Many women are not only critical of their body but are also disconnected from it. This is especially true for those of you who have experienced prior sexual abuse or assault. It is a common phenomenon for former victims of sexual invasion to dissociate from their body and become numb. In addition to raising your sense of body esteem, in this chapter I will teach you techniques that will help you stay in the present *and* become more aware of your body and what it is experiencing.

Most important, I will encourage you to continue to offer yourself self-compassion for the pain and embarrassment you experience due to our body-shaming society. Research has shown that self-compassion reduces body dissatisfaction and body shame and improves body appreciation (Albertson et al. 2014).

Let's start by finding out how you feel about your body. The following quiz will help you do this.

Body-Esteem Quiz

Answer "Never," "Seldom," "Often," or "Always" to each question.

1. I respect my body

2. I feel good about my body

3. I feel that my body has at least some good qualities

4. I take a positive attitude towards my body

5. I am attentive to my body's needs

6. I feel love for my body

7. I appreciate the different and unique characteristics of my body

8. My behavior reflects my positive attitude toward my body: for example, I hold my head up high and smile

9. I am comfortable in my body

10. I feel like I am beautiful even if I am different from media images of attractive people (e.g., models, actresses)

If you answered most or many of these questions with a "Seldom" or "Never," you have a very unhealthy body image and low body esteem. On the other hand, if you answered "Often" or "Always" to most of the questions, you have a positive body image and high body esteem.

Self-Esteem and Body Image

Much has been written about modern society's focus on body image, especially regarding women and girls. We now know that girls and women are socialized to worry about their appearance. And we know that one of the main reasons so many women perceive their bodies as problems is that we live in a culture that dictates that women must be beautiful in order to be worthwhile, and then sets up standards of female beauty that are not only impossible for most women to live up to, but are also unhealthy. Many diets and all surgeries to control weight, for example, are physically dangerous.

Getting and staying thin have become major pastimes for women, consuming a significant amount of our time, energy, and money. The entertainment and advertising media not only promote certain ideals in terms of how women's bodies should look but often, in the absence of other sources of information, tell us that a "normal" and "healthy" body should look a certain way. By trying to conform to our culture's ridiculous ideas, we women place ourselves in a no-win situation where we will never be satisfied with our bodies.

An acquaintance of mine, Ellie, is constantly worried about what other people think of how she looks. She always wants to make a good impression, so she spends a lot of time on her wardrobe, makeup, and hair. "It's almost a full-time job making myself look beautiful," she shared during a luncheon I attended one day with a group of women. "You won't believe what I went through to get ready for today." She laughed, and several of the other women at the table nodded in agreement.

Most people are concerned about their public image but women tend to focus on "what other people think" a lot more than most men. Some of this is due to the amount of pressure put on girls and women to be attractive to boys and men. To make matters worse, girls and women are constantly "body shamed" and "fat shamed" and expected to meet certain prescribed physical standards, whether it be the size of their breasts, waists, or butts. Given all this, it's no wonder that girls and women feel insecure and inadequate. Body shaming, fat shaming, and slut shaming all negatively affect the way a woman views her body, her sexual attractiveness, and her self-worth.

The sad truth is, when a girl or woman feels insecure about her looks, she is more likely to put up with unacceptable sexual behavior from boys and men. This is partly due to her desire to be accepted or popular and partly due to the fact that she lacks the confidence it takes to say "No!" and stand up for herself.

As much as some men objectify sexually attractive women and girls, the women and girls they seem to disrespect and take advantage of most often are less traditionally sexually attractive females. They assume they can disrespect or mistreat these females and get away with it. Often, males will pursue girls who lack self-confidence precisely because they know this type of girl will allow them to go further sexually than a more self-confident girl will.

My client Lucy, a freshman in college, was invited to a fraternity party by one of the most popular boys at school. She couldn't believe her good fortune. But unbeknownst to Lucy, there was a tradition at this particular fraternity to invite the most unattractive, unpopular freshman girls to a party where the frat brothers would see how much they could get away with and how much they could shame the unsuspecting girls. They plied Lucy with alcohol and then, one by one, asked her to dance. While they danced with her they rubbed up against her in lewd, overtly sexual ways while the rest of the brothers looked on. This progressed to the guys grabbing her breasts and butt while they danced with her and then to getting her to go into a bedroom where they had sex with her, one by one, while the other guys looked on.

Lucy came to see me because she was devastated about what had happened to her and because she blamed herself for letting it happen. "I hadn't even been in college a month before I was slut shamed all over campus," she told me. "I don't know why I wasn't more suspicious about such a good-looking, popular guy asking me out. After all, I know I'm not attractive. But I foolishly wanted to believe that he was able to look past my appearance and see something in me that he genuinely liked . . . What an idiot!"

At this, I immediately called Lucy on her self-blaming and self-deprecating talk and started encouraging her to have self-compassion for what she had gone through. But Lucy wasn't buying it.

"I wanted those guys to like me so much that I let them do whatever they wanted to me," she said. "I thought I was the life of the party since they were all asking me to dance. I'd never had so much attention from guys before, and it felt great. I can't believe I just let my better judgment fly out the window."

It took some time for Lucy recognize that her low self-esteem and poor body image had set her up for this debacle. Eventually, she was able to understand her own behavior—and that of the frat boys.

"Now I see that I feel so bad about myself—about the way I look—that it made me vulnerable to those guys and what they were up to," Lucy told me in a later session. "I was so needy for attention and validation from them that I was desirable, that I was sexy, I ended up betraying myself. And who could imagine that guys would actually think like that—that they could stoop so low to shame a girl like me? It wasn't my fault that I wasn't aware that there are guys like that. I didn't deserve any of it. But I do need to honor myself and my body more. I need to make sure I don't give myself away like that."

It is important that like Lucy, you learn, as Lucy has, to respect and honor your body and stop defining yourself strictly based on your physical attributes. The following body-image exercises will encourage you to stop criticizing your weaknesses or limitations. They will also encourage you to focus on the positive aspects of your body and the many wonderful things it allows you to do.

Exercise: Your Imperfections and Your Assets

Make a list of your physical attributes that you dislike the most—for example, your large nose, your large hips, your small breasts.

Now make a list of the physical attributes that you like the most. If you think you don't have any positive physical features, think harder. Ask other people to tell you what your good physical attributes are.

If you are being fair, once you have your two lists completed you will see that the two lists are about the same length—you probably have as many positive physical attributes as negative ones. It is just a matter of which ones you choose to focus on.

If, on the other hand, your list of negative physical attributes is far longer than your list of positive attributes, set a goal for yourself for the next two weeks to shorten the list about what you *dislike* about your body and increase the list of what you *like*.

Distorted Images of Self

Most people have a negative body image not because they have an unattractive body but because they see themselves inaccurately. Their image of their physical self is distorted, either because they see their overall size and shape inaccurately (seeing themselves as much fatter, thinner, taller, or shorter than they actually are) or because they see specific body parts in a distorted way. When the latter situation occurs, not only do they perceive their long nose, acne, wide hips, sagging breasts, or large behinds as more grotesque than they are, they also see these "flaws" as dominating their entire physical selves. This is the case for my client Britany, who once told me: "Everyone tells me that I am pretty but I know I'm really not. They don't know that I have these huge hips and thighs. That's because I do such a good job of hiding them. All I see when I look in the mirror are my hips and thighs. They disgust me so much that I know they would disgust other people if they saw them."

Unfortunately, Britany has been blinded to her other physical attributes—her beautiful skin and hair, her lovely shoulders and breasts, her striking facial features. All these beautiful parts of her are overshadowed by her dislike for her hips and thighs. Most people, especially women, are far more attractive than they think. About one-third of people, particularly women, report being strongly dissatisfied with their bodies. And women are more likely to have a negative self-image than men. In fact, studies have shown that relatively few women look in the mirror without focusing on all the things they'd like to change, whereas men tend to be more accepting of what they see. Women tend to distort their perceptions of their bodies negatively, while men—just as unrealistically—distort their perceptions in a positive, self-aggrandizing way. (Fix 2018).

Mirror Exercise

Most people take a look at themselves in the mirror while they are getting ready to go out and many take a final glance just before leaving, a kind of "sizing themselves up" action.

- For the next couple of weeks, make a concerted effort to focus on your positive attributes as you go out the door—*only your positive attributes*.

- Say something positive about the way you look and say it out loud. It can be something like, "Your eyes look beautiful today" or "You're looking sharp today, that new bra really accentuates your great breasts!"

Body Hatred

Far too many of you don't just fail to see your beauty, you actually hate yourself. And you especially hate your body.

One of the reasons some women and girls hate their body is because they feel it draws too much attention from men—attention they don't want. As my client Sabrina told me, "I hate my breasts because they are so big. I can't walk down the street without some man making a comment as he walks by or some men calling to me across the street. I feel so mortified. I just want to dig a hole in the ground and disappear. I've ended up wearing really baggy clothes or carrying something in front of my breasts to hide them."

Those who were sexually abused in childhood often hate their body because they feel so much shame over having been abused. It is not uncommon for former victims of sexual abuse to have the following beliefs:

- My body is disgusting.

- Certain parts of my body are particularly disgusting.

- I am inferior to others because of my sexual past.

- No one can ever love me because of what happened to me.

- I am dirty and rotten inside.

- There are some things I have done sexually that I can never forgive myself for.

Later on in this book, we will focus on helping those of you who hate your body due to prior sexual abuse to forgive your body. For now, continue with the other exercises in this chapter.

Exercise: I Hate My Body

You may hate your body but not be exactly clear as to why. Completing the following sentence may provide you with some answers. Complete this sentence until no more responses come to mind.

"I hate my body because _____."

You Are Beautiful

How do you feel when you read those words? Do you think, "Yeah, right"? Or do you feel warm inside? Some women are triggered by the words "You are beautiful" because they are often used as a pickup line or as a manipulation to get them into bed. If this is your situation, you may feel angry reading these words. Some women even hate these words because they hate their body or think they are ugly.

In one of his songs, Joe Cocker sings, "You are so beautiful to me." I once had someone sing those words to me on the phone, and it made me feel very uncomfortable because I didn't feel the least bit beautiful. It was only after the person who sang the song to me explained what he meant by the song that I understood its true meaning. He said, "I experience all of you—your heart, your mind, your very essence—as beautiful." Only then did I finally understand what the singer was saying. He was saying, "You are so beautiful to *me*." The man I was seeing was saying that he saw my whole being and found me beautiful. Isn't that what we all want? To be really seen and accepted? Not just for our body but also our heart, mind, and spirit?

Almost all women say there is something they don't like about their bodies. They put an overemphasis on the way their bodies look and assume that men are attracted to them solely or primarily because of their bodies. They don't believe the opposite sex is also taking into account their personality, their mind, their sense of humor, their sensitivity, their ability to relate to others, or, most important, their ability to love.

Exercise: The Things that Make You Beautiful

Make a list of your best attributes—your *non-physical* attributes, like your personality, your emotional strengths, and the things other people appreciate about you. Again, if you are having difficulty thinking of these things, ask your friends what they like and value most about you.

Now write about qualities of character you admire most in yourself, like your honesty, your loyalty, your perseverance, etc. If you can't think of anything, ask your friends what they admire about you or think about the compliments you get, the things people have told you they like or admire about you.

Take a good look at these two lists. These are the things that make you beautiful—not how fat or thin you are, not whether you look sexy or not. Look at your lists whenever you are feeling insecure or critical about how you look. Hopefully doing so will remind you that you are so much more than the size of your clothes, how much you weigh, or how big your nose is.

Developing a New Perspective on Your Body

In spite of the negative messages women receive about their bodies every day, in spite of the fat shaming, the slut shaming, and the expectation of perfection, it is possible to develop a new, healthier relationship with your body—a relationship in which you honor and appreciate your body just the way it is.

Let's start with what you like most about your body.

Exercise: What Your Body Provides For You

What body part do you like the most? Write, in detail, about what you like most about this part of your body—not how it looks, but how it allows you to pleasantly experience some aspect of life. For example, "I like my hands the most because they give me so much pleasure. I love working with clay and I love working in my garden. Both of these activities allow me to connect with myself and with nature."

Spend some time considering how different parts of your body help you—all the things various parts of your body allow you to do. Now write about your experience, being very specific. For example: "My legs help me to stand." "My stomach processes my food." "My eyes make it possible for me to see the beauty all around me."

Next, let's focus further on what you can do and experience with your body.

- Go for a walk in nature—to a park, the ocean, a forest. Mindfully pay attention to all your senses: notice the smells in the air, the textures beneath your feet, the views along your route, the taste on your lips, the ever-changing sounds all around you.

- Spend some time thinking about all the amazing things your body does for you. Allow yourself to really celebrate these things and celebrate your body!

Forgiving Your Body If You Were Previously Abused or Assaulted

As I mentioned earlier, former victims of child abuse and adult sexual assault typically have a very negative relationship with their body. They may hate their genitals or consider them filthy or contaminated. It is not unusual for former victims to refuse to touch their genitals or to abuse them in some way. Some don't keep their genitals clean; some mutilate them by pinching them or having them pierced. Others punish their body by starving themselves, eating unhealthy food, smoking, or engaging self-mutilation practices such as burning or cutting themselves.

Some former victims hate their body for the way it responded during the abuse. Many feel as if their body betrayed them because it became aroused while they were being sexually abused or assaulted. If this applies to you, it is important to know that our body responds to being touched—no matter who is doing the touching, and no matter how much our *mind* fights it or feels repulsed by it. Some victims have experienced orgasms even though they were being traumatized, hated the perpetrator, or were terrified. This kind of experience can make you feel like your body betrayed you and is sometimes the hardest thing to forgive. A child does not know that her body can respond without her consent, or even that it can respond in such a way at all. You may have felt that you must have wanted the sexual act, otherwise, why would your body feel pleasure? In addition, the perpetrator may have used the fact that your body responded to manipulate you into believing that you wanted what he did to you.

As odd as it may sound, you need to forgive your body for responding. It is especially important to forgive those parts of your body that were directly involved in the sexual acts and the parts of your body that felt any pleasure. For example, forgive your hands for touching his penis; forgive your breasts for responding to his touch; forgive your genitals for becoming stimulated.

Just as you were innocent in this situation, so was your body. Stop punishing and hating your body for doing what it was made to do—react to stimuli, respond to touch, give you pleasure when touched. Stop hating it when it is a perfectly good and normal body. Your body did not betray you. It was tricked, just as you were.

Self-Healing and Cleansing

In addition to and connected with the overwhelming feeling of shame a victim feels, they also feel dirty, tainted, spoiled, polluted, "ruined." This is what one client shared with me about how she felt about her body after she was abused. "After I was sexually abused by my uncle," she told me, "I felt horribly ugly and dirty inside. I took dozens of baths hoping that I could wash away the dirtiness I felt, but it didn't work. I started becoming obsessed with washing my hands—the hands that touched his dirty, filthy penis. I brushed my teeth constantly, trying to get the taste of his penis and his ejaculate out of my mouth. I changed my underwear several times a day because it always smelled like him."

When a child is sexually abused or a woman is sexually assaulted, she often feels dirty inside. She feels as if her body is contaminated. These feelings are not only present at the time of the violation, they can also remain with a person for years. This can lead to problems with self-esteem and body image, relationship troubles, and behavioral issues such as obsessive washing.

Former victims can also feel that their genitals are "gross" and need to be cleaned. Some former victims continue to clean their genitals obsessively, often washing them several times a day. This is what my client Annette shared with me: "I wash my vagina several times a day but it always feels dirty to me. It feels like the man who raped me left traces of himself in my body and I need to get them out of me."

A recent study cited in *Behavior Modification* discusses a treatment that can help relieve these intrusive feelings. This treatment appeals to both logic and emotion, via mental imagery.

Psychologists at Goethe University Frankfurt in Germany tested a brief treatment consisting of one session and a follow-up "booster" meeting. First, therapists and participants discussed the details of the participants' contamination thoughts—what it felt like, when and where it occurred, and how it affected their daily life. Then participants were instructed to research online how often human skin cells are rebuilt. They also calculated how many times the cells in their trauma-related body regions have been replaced since their last contact with their abusers. (Skin cells rebuild every four to six weeks; mucous membranes more often.) The subjects discussed with the therapists what these facts mean—for instance, "not one of the dermal cells that cover my body now has been in contact with my abuser." Finally, they performed an exercise in which they imagined shedding their contaminated skin.

The researchers who conducted this study found that this treatment significantly decreased participants' feelings of being contaminated and also—to their surprise—their overall post-traumatic distress scores. Study author Kerstin Jung says the combination of factual information with mental imagery is key, because the information alone can leave a patient knowing the facts but not feeling they are true on an emotional level. At that point, "we introduce the imagery technique as a vehicle to transport the rational information from the head to the heart," she says. "Images are much more powerful to change emotions than verbal information."

Exercise: Cleansing Your Body

Soak yourself in a hot bath or Jacuzzi. Imagine that all the residue of the abuse or assault, especially your feelings of shame and self-blame, are being soaked *out* of you through your skin. Visualize the shame and impurities flowing out of your genitals, breasts, lips, mouth, anus—any part of your body that was "contaminated" by the abuser. Image all this residue going down the drain.

Now imagine pouring compassion and loving energy *into* your body. Visualize yourself being reborn into a body that is wholesome, pure, and free of shame. Emerge from the water feeling cleansed, inside and out.

Self-healing rituals can bring you a sense of being reborn, cleaned, and refreshed. Combining them with this writing exercise can be a powerful way of working on forgiving your body:

For each part of your body that was involved in the sexual abuse, assault or that you feel betrayed you, complete the following sentence: *I forgive you, _____,* *for _____.*

Changing Your Relationship with Your Body

Several years ago, I traveled to Bali. I went with the purpose of getting some much-needed rest and to work on developing a healthier relationship with my body, which I had been neglecting.

The Balinese people are noted for several things: how much their spirituality infuses most aspects of their lives, their incredible kindness and caring, and their ability to give wonderful, healing body massages. I experienced the first two qualities every day by just being around these people. But in the middle of my trip, I gave myself the gift of experiencing the third: I dedicated three days to receiving massage.

Each morning I got up and went to the same person for a two-hour massage. I chose this young man because of his demeanor. He exuded kindness and compassion. I was able to choose everything from the scent of the oil used to the tempo and type of music I preferred. I chose the traditional Balinese massage, which was a combination of palm pressure and stretching to achieve relaxation and increased blood flow.

The young man massaged my body in a very kind and loving way. Unlike some other massage experiences I've had in the US, I could tell he was focusing all his attention on me. He treated my body as if it were precious.

After the three days I came to the surprising conclusion: this man, this total stranger, had taken better care of my body than I did. He had respected and honored my body. He had communicated loving acceptance of it. He had touched me in a way that communicated kindness and compassion. In essence, he cared more about my body than I did. I became determined to change my relationship with my body. I wish the same for you. Let's start with the following exercise.

Body Acceptance Exercise

Light candles all around your bathroom or bedroom. If you have a bathtub, you may choose to do this exercise in the bathroom. If you don't, you may choose to do this exercise on your bed.

Lie naked, or as naked as you are comfortable with. Notice how the candlelight makes your skin look—how it glistens and takes on a dreamy quality. Choose a part of your body that you feel most comfortable with, a part that you like.

Tell this part of your body how much you appreciate it, how grateful you are for it, or how much you like how it looks or feels.

Now move to a part of your body that you like but aren't completely comfortable with. Once again, tell this part of your body that you appreciate it and are grateful for it. Find something about this body part that you like. Notice that uncomfortable feelings may arise in you. You may hear a critical voice telling you reasons why you don't like this part of your body. Move past this voice by focusing on connecting with your body and finding loving, kind, or compassionate things to say to it. For example, you could say, "Thank you, legs. You are strong and you carry me everywhere I want to go."

Now progress to another part of your body—a part you actually dislike—and do the same routine: find some reason to be grateful for it, tell it how much you appreciate it, and even find something about it that you like. Notice any critical thoughts and be compassionate with yourself as uncomfortable feelings and thoughts come up. Don't focus on all the reasons why you don't like this part of your body. Just continue connecting with it in a positive way.

Eventually, make your way through your entire body, even those parts of your body you absolutely hate. Lovingly touch each part of your body and, if need be, forgive that part of your body. Think of ways this part of your body helps you. Find something about it that you like—the shape, the smoothness. Find things to appreciate and feel grateful for.

Once you have addressed all your body parts, think of your body as a whole. Admire your body in the candlelight, focusing on loving, kind, and compassionate thoughts.

Be aware that at many points in this exercise, negative thoughts are likely to pop into your head. Just notice them, thank them for sharing, and then shift your attention back to appreciating your body and focusing on compassionate thoughts. Don't get hooked into the negativity.

If the negativity is persistent, take a break to get in touch with what you are actually feeling. Try to identify the feelings behind your thoughts and get in touch with those feelings so you will know what hooked you. This practice is about reconnecting with your body, and your feelings are a part of that. For example, if you hear an internal voice say, "I hate my thighs," ask yourself, "What am I feeling?" Always start by asking, "Am I feeling angry?"—then move to sadness, fear, and finally guilt, shame, or regret. Check to see if something happened recently to make you feel this way. If you can't identify anything, think about whether you have been triggered; does something negative from your past come up when you look at or touch this part of your body? It can be difficult to identify feelings associated with automatic negative body-image thoughts and feelings. A therapist can help you work on this at a deeper level if you're feeling overwhelmed or stuck.

You may need to do this exercise several times before you notice any real change in the way you view your body. But by doing it, you can change the story you carry around in your head about your body. As Dr. Christine Northrup states, "The body is self-renewing. We turn over every cell in our body within seven years, but you can almost make your body over completely in three months. It begins with the story you tell yourself in your head."

If your story is, "I hate my body. I hate the way it looks and I wish I had a different body," that message will permeate everything you do. But if it can become, "I love my body for what it does for me, I am grateful for it, and I appreciate how much it helps me," that will infuse everything you do with an attitude of gratitude and self-respect.

Take time to regularly practice body acceptance by reconnecting with your body. Commit to regularly working on one of these body image exercises to make peace with and build love toward your hard-working body. Work on slowly replacing negative thinking with compassionate thinking, and over time, you will begin to feel differently about your body.

Creating a New Image of Your Genitals

They have a lot of orchids and other exotic flowers in Bali. This reminded me of a workshop I attended many years ago. The workshop was for those who had been sexually abused or assaulted, and its purpose was to help former victims create a more positive image of their genitals.

The workshop leader had a table filled with orchids, and she asked us all to go up and pick one out. Then she asked us to draw our orchid, not paying so much attention to our drawing skills but to capturing the essence of the flower. Next she asked us to think of our vulva (the outside portion of our vagina) and our vagina (the inside portion) as a beautiful orchid. She noted that our outside lips gradually unfold to reveal inside lips that lead to our opening, just like a flower.

Many famous artists have focused on painting orchids, the most notable being Georgia O'Keefe. I urge you to check out her paintings by going online and typing the phrase "Flower images by Georgia O'Keefe" in your search bar. You will find dozens of orchid paintings and you will no doubt notice their similarity to the female vulva and vagina.

I'd like you to begin to perceive your vulva and vagina as a beautiful orchid. Replace whatever negative image you have of your vulva and vagina with the beautiful image of an orchid.

Floating Exercise

Imagine your body floating in water or on a cloud. Notice that your body is surrounded by beautiful orchids or lotus flowers.

Feel the weightlessness, the lightness of your body as it floats.

Now imagine a cool breeze wafting across your body—a cleansing wind that blows all your aches and pains and negative body memories away. Feel your body in its lightness and purity.

Now imagine a beautiful ray of sunshine streaming down onto your body. Let the light surrounding your body bathe it in more cleansing magic.

Become one with the water, the wind, the sunlight. Become one with nature. Know that you are being loved and held by nature.

Your body is precious, beautiful, and magnificent. It deserves to be nurtured, cared for, cherished, and protected. It deserves to be touched gently, lovingly, by people who see you, accept you, cherish you, and love you. It doesn't deserve to be disrespected or mistreated by people who aim to harm you, have power over you, use or misuse you. It is your job and your responsibility to determine who can touch you. It is your choice, and your choice alone, who you allow to touch you and how you want to be touched.

Goals of Chapter 8

I have many goals for this chapter, and they are lofty ones. One is encouraging you to become more connected to your body and less critical of it. Another is helping you begin to understand that the way you feel about your body affects not only how you treat it but also how you allow others to treat it. Yet another is to help you begin to appreciate your body for what it provides you and forgive your body if you feel it betrayed you. The last is nudging you to take ownership of your body and protect it from anyone who wants to harm it. I hope that I have accomplished at least one of my goals here.

No! Exercise

Think of a situation in which someone recently disrespected, invaded or abused your body.

Imagine that you are saying "No!" to this person.

Now say it out loud. Say "No!" as many times as you feel like it. Notice how good it feels to say it.

If you'd like, in addition to saying "No!" to the way the person mistreated your body, add any other words you feel like saying. For example, "No! You can't do those things to me." "No! I'm not going to let you treat my body like that!" "No! I don't want you to touch me like that!"

Commitment

Write several statements expressing your commitment to caring for, honoring, and respecting your body. You can either make "No!" statements or "Yes!" statements.

"No" Example:

- "I'm saying 'No!' to hating and neglecting my body."

- "I'm saying 'No!' to allowing my body to be used, abused, or mistreated in any way."

- "I'm saying 'No!' to 'giving my body away' to anyone who doesn't appreciate me and care for me."

"Yes!" Examples:

- "I'm saying 'Yes!' To loving my body and caring for it."

- "I'm saying 'Yes!' to protecting my precious body from those who wish to mistreat it."

Chapter 9
Another Key to Empowerment—
No More Ms. Nice Girl

The most common way for people to give up their power is by thinking they don't have any.

—Alice Walker

Hopefully at this point you recognize the dangers all around you, you have gained compassion for the ways you have suffered due to being sexually mistreated or assaulted in the past, and you've acknowledged your anger at having been victimized in the past. But there is still one more thing you need to do in order to protect yourself from further mistreatment or abuse. You need to become further empowered by giving up any vestiges of "Nice Girl" behavior you still cling to.

We began to discuss the "Nice Girl" phenomenon in Chapter 2 as one of the reasons why women are afraid to say "No!" In this chapter, we will expand on the Nice Girl discussion in terms of how maintaining this stance prevents you from protecting and defending yourself in the sexual arena.

Who are Nice Girls? Nice Girls have several things in common: 1) They are more concerned about what others think of them than about what they think of themselves; 2) They are more concerned about other people's feelings than they are about their own; and 3) They believe in giving people the benefit of the doubt more than they do in trusting their own instincts and perceptions.

What is Nice Girl behavior, exactly? Nice Girl behavior includes the following:

- *Being compliant.* Nice girls tend to do what they are told. They've learned that it is easier to just do what someone asks than to risk an argument or confrontation.

- *Being passive.* Nice girls tend to just let things happen. They are too afraid to stand up for themselves.

- *Being easily manipulated and controlled.* Nice girls get talked into things because they don't trust their intuition and don't believe they have a right to say no.

The bottom line: You may be too nice for your own good. This "niceness" attracts the wrong kind of people and sends the message that you are an easy target to be taken advantage of, controlled, emotionally, physically or sexually abused, sexually violated, and harassed. It also prevents you from standing up for yourself and saying "No!" to unwanted sexual advances and keeps you in relationships that are unhealthy or abusive.

The reality is that women today cannot afford to be Nice Girls. It simply is not safe. Nice Girl behavior can cause us to bypass our instincts and our intuition. It can cause us to put aside our own needs and our own best interests.

Nice Girls are far more likely to become victimized—emotionally, physically, and sexually—than those who are not so nice. Being too nice sends a strong message to those who already have a tendency to use and abuse. The message is, "My need to be seen as nice (or sweet, or innocent) is more powerful than my instinct to protect myself."

This chapter is for all women who have yet to learn that if they don't take care of themselves, no one else will. It is for every woman who puts her own needs aside on a regular basis in order to either attract or keep a man. And it is for all the women who are beginning to learn that being "nice" doesn't pay off in the long run. It is for all the women who have been sexually assaulted, sexually harassed, or emotionally, verbally, or physically abused and who want to prevent such abuse from happening in the future. Most especially, it is for all women who need to learn the myriad of ways that being nice prevents them from protecting themselves from predators and being manipulated by romantic partners.

Nice Girl behavior is especially dangerous when it comes to protecting yourself from sexual predators, as well as being able to stand up and say "No!" to sexual advances from acquaintances and even partners. Examples of Nice Girl behavior in the sexual arena include:

- *Going along with sexual activities and practices that you are not interested in being involved with just to please your partner.* For example, my client Rene shared with me, "My boyfriend wanted to have a three-way with me and one of my friends. I didn't want to do it at all. I knew I would feel jealous when he was with my friend and I was even afraid that my friend would end up taking my boyfriend away from me. But I went along with it because I knew he wanted it so much and I wanted to please him. Sure enough, I was extremely jealous seeing my boyfriend and my friend together sexually, and sure enough, he did end up leaving me for her. Now I realize what an idiot I was for not seeing that he set the whole thing up because he was attracted to her!"

- *Giving the person "the benefit of the doubt."* My client Rebecca learned the hard way how this can become a problem. "There was a guy at work who was a real ladies' man," she told me. "He was very attractive and charming and he constantly flirted with women in the office. But several women told me to stay clear of this guy—that he was bad news. We had an office picnic and I got to work late that morning and missed the bus to the country. He also arrived late and asked me if I wanted a ride. I said yes and we had a nice chat on the way. I thought to myself, *Why is everyone so critical of this guy, he's really nice.* As we were leaving town he said he forgot something and had to stop off at his apartment. When we got there he asked if I'd like to see his apartment. That was my mistake. I should have never agreed to go inside his place. As soon as we got inside he started coming on to me. I was attracted to him but I didn't want to have sex with him—it was just too soon. He really turned on the charm and I ended up having sex with him, against my better judgment. I thought, *Why are all the women turned off to him—he's not so bad after all.* But I was wrong. He practically raped me. Even though I'd agreed to have sex, I didn't agree to him being so rough with me and I certainly didn't agree to anal sex. He was a lot bigger than me and he was able to maneuver me around like a rag doll. By the time he was finished with me I was a complete emotional and physical wreck. I wished I had heeded everyone's warning and stayed clear of this guy."

- *Feeling sorry for someone.* My client Jan told me the story of how she was brutally raped by a fellow student because she felt sorry for him. "There was a guy at school that everyone kind of steered clear of. He was awkward socially and he dressed in a really sloppy way. After class one night he asked me if I could give him a ride home. It was raining really hard and he looked so pathetic that I felt sorry for him. When we got to where he said he lived he moved over to my side of the seat and started groping me. I pushed him away and he got really angry. He ended up hitting me in the head with something and raping me."

Questionnaire: Are You a Nice Girl?

1. Do you get talked into things because you can't say no?

2. Are you overly concerned about what people think of you?

3. Is it overly important to you that people like you?

4. Are you afraid to say how you really feel out of fear of making someone angry?

5. Do you apologize too much or too often?

6. Do you have friends or acquaintances you don't really like or have much in common with but feel obligated to continue seeing?

7. Do you often say yes to invitations because you don't want the person to feel rejected?

8. Do you tend to give in because it makes you feel selfish if you refuse to help someone?

9. Are you afraid people will dislike you if you're not cooperative?

10. Do you have trouble speaking up as soon as something or someone is unfair to you?

11. Do you hesitate telling someone that he has hurt your feelings or made you angry because you don't want him to feel bad?

12. Do you avoid telling someone he or she has upset you because you don't think it will do any good or will only cause a big problem between you?

13. Do you have people in your life who take advantage of you?

14. Do you tend to take the blame for things just to avoid an argument or to avoid rejection or abandonment?

15. Do you often make excuses for people's poor behavior, telling yourself that they didn't mean it or they didn't know better?

16. Do you avoid conflict or confrontation at all costs?

17. Do you get a terrible feeling when someone is angry with you?

18. Do you give people the benefit of the doubt even when others tell you this person is trouble?

19. Do you continue to give people another chance even when they continue to exhibit the same hurtful or inappropriate behavior?

20. Do you tell yourself that you don't have a right to complain about a person's behavior if you've ever been guilty of the same behavior?

21. Are you attracted to bad boys or people with a large dark side?

22. Do you strongly believe in being fair even when other people are treating you unfairly?

If you answered yes to two or more of these questions, you still have some Nice Girl in you, no matter how assertive, successful, or self-actualized you think you are. This chapter will help you to shed whatever vestiges of "niceness" you still have.

If you answered in the affirmative to more than five of these questions, you have some work to do in terms of changing the way you view yourself in the world.

If you answered yes to more than ten of these questions, you have an extreme version of the Nice Girl Syndrome and will need to do some serious work on ridding yourself of the negative and false beliefs that are basically dictating your life.

In this chapter, we will focus on how to identify and change the Nice Girl behavior that can set you up to be manipulated, misused, and abused. You will learn that you can be kind without sacrificing your soul and you can remain feminine without giving up your power. While not every Nice Girl gets raped or is emotionally, verbally, or physically abused in her relationships, every Nice Girl is putting herself at risk by continuing to believe and act as she does. Nice Girls tend to put up with inappropriate or abusive behavior, minimize the damage they are experiencing, and make excuses for their partner. Extinguishing Nice Girl behavior will help you to stop being nice and start being strong, stand up for yourself, and refuse to be treated in abusive ways.

How Big of a Problem is the Nice Girl Syndrome?

Surely, in this day and age, we must be talking about only a small number of women, right? Unfortunately, no. There are far more Nice Girls out there than you can imagine. And even the most empowered women still have some Nice Girl in them.

Most women have tolerated unacceptable behavior from friends, family, or lovers for far too long in their attempts to be understanding, tolerant, and compassionate. And we've all known women who are too nice for their own good. When someone does something to them that is inconsiderate, or offensive, they try to "understand" the other person instead of getting angry. They spend more time asking "why" the person did what they did than they do telling the other person how unacceptable his or her actions were.

If there weren't so many Nice Girls in the world, the rate of domestic violence and emotional abuse would not continue to be so high. We would not have so many women who stand by while their children are being emotionally, physically, or even sexually abused by their husbands and boyfriends. We would not have so many women staying in relationships where they are being manipulated and taken advantage of. And most important, we would not have so many women remaining silent when they are sexually assaulted, sexually harassed, or sexually pressured.

False Beliefs

For many, letting go of the need to be seen as "fair," "understanding," or even "selfless" can sometimes be a painful process. Others have a fear of confrontation, most often brought about from having experienced constant conflict in their childhood home or having been emotionally or physically abused as a child. More than simply becoming more assertive or learning to establish boundaries, the process of letting go of niceness involves unearthing and then discarding deeply buried false beliefs and replacing them with healthy ways of thinking about yourself and others.

Below is a list of some of the most damaging beliefs and attitudes common to Nice Girls. As you read the list, notice which false beliefs you identify with:

1. Other people's feelings and needs are far more important than my own.

2. If I am nice (and fair) to other people they will be nice (and fair) to me.

3. What other people think about me is more important than my self-esteem, my health, or even my safety.

4. If I am good and perfect I will be accepted and loved.

5. I don't have the right to stand up for myself or act on my own behalf.

6. Anger is a destructive emotion and shouldn't be expressed, especially directly to those with whom you are angry.

7. It is better to avoid conflict at all costs.

8. There is good in everyone, and if you give someone enough chances he or she will eventually show you his or her good side.

Exercise: Your False Beliefs

List which of the false beliefs listed above you still adhere to.

Now think about where you got these beliefs. (Refer to Chapter 2 to review where Nice Girl beliefs come from).

Based on how much and in what ways you have been hurt in your relationships, which of these false beliefs are the most important for you to work on letting go of, especially as they relate to protecting yourself from sexual assault or harassment? These will be the false beliefs you will need to exorcise out of your mind and heart.

As you read over your list, you may notice that there is a ring of truth to some of these false beliefs. For example, while there certainly is good in everyone, we don't have to get burned over and over again by waiting around for it to finally emerge. Kindness and tolerance can often soften even the hardest heart, but they can also be an open invitation for others to continue manipulating and taking advantage of us.

Nice Girls need to learn that these beliefs and attitudes are simply not working for them. For example, it is true that anger can be a destructive emotion and many people cause a great deal of harm to others because they are out of control with their anger. But this is generally not true of Nice Girls, who tend to have the opposite problem: repressing and suppressing their anger. They usually need to give themselves permission to acknowledge, feel, and express their anger in constructive ways; otherwise, they'll just keep on ignoring or denying their righteous anger.

How Do We Reverse This Brainwashing?

In many cases women have been "brainwashed" to believe these false beliefs, often starting when they were small children. Sometimes this brainwashing has come from society at large and other times it has come from specific messages or behavior from parents or other authority figures.

Needless to say, it can sometimes be difficult to reverse this brainwashing and begin to face the truth. For this reason, I offer "remedies" specifically designed to counter false beliefs and help install beliefs that are more conducive to becoming a Strong Woman instead of a Nice Girl.

Let's examine each false belief more closely in order to help you: 1) Recognize exactly why it is a false belief; 2) Help you begin to recognize where this false belief comes from in you; 3) Recognize how each false belief contributes to the Nice Girl Syndrome.

False Belief #1: Other people's feelings and needs are more important than my own.

It is extremely difficult to prove to most women that this is actually a false belief. *What do you mean?* you might be thinking, *Of course we need to think of others first. Otherwise we are just being selfish.*

One of the main reasons why women believe that thinking of their own needs first is selfish is that women are biologically hard-wired to be mothers and nurturers. Until very recently, girls and women have always been considered to be the caretakers of the family. (Nature has an investment in women being unselfish when it comes to their children—otherwise, children would be left to their own devices and likely starve or be killed.)

You may think that every human being is taught when they are young that they should put others' feelings and needs first. That's how we teach children to be kind, considerate, and generous, right? No, this simply isn't true. Girls are taught it much more than boys. And in some families, parents teach their children that they should always look out for number one first. Girls are repeatedly taught that they should put the needs of others before their own and that they are selfish if they think of their own needs first. Boys, in contrast, are not generally taught to consider other people's feelings at the expense of their own.

For many girls, the message of putting others' needs ahead of their own is conveyed more by the example their mother sets than it is by actual words. Many girls grew up observing their mother sacrificing her own needs and desires for those of her husband. In some homes, particularly homes in which there is rampant misogyny, girls are taught that the feelings and needs of males are more important than those of females. (The definition of misogyny is a distrust, fear, dislike, or hatred of females. Inherent in misogynistic beliefs is that males are superior to females). As antiquated as misogyny may seem to be, it is a powerful force in many cultures and religions today—both in the US and in the rest of the world.

In other families, particularly those with parents who are self-absorbed or even narcissistic, the message is, "*My* needs are more important than yours, or anyone else's for that matter." Self-absorbed and narcissistic parents teach their children that their own needs do not matter. Instead of meeting their child's needs, self-absorbed and narcissistic parents expect their child to cater to them. A child raised in this environment often comes to believe that her happiness lies in fulfilling the needs of others.

False Belief #2: If I am nice (or fair) to other people they will be nice (or fair) to me.

At the core of this belief is the assumption that by being nice you can avoid painful experiences, such as someone getting angry with you, being disapproved of, or being rejected or abandoned. But this belief borders on superstition. You might as well throw salt over your shoulder to ward off evil spirits as believe that being nice to other people will guarantee their being nice to you.

On the surface, this belief makes sense. Doing unto others as we would have them do unto us elicits positive responses from people. And generally speaking, this is what happens. But there are four major flaws to this belief:

1. Being nice to someone doesn't guarantee they will be nice to you, because everyone has their own issues. There are people who will not be nice to you (or like you) no matter how nice you are to them. This may be because they are prejudiced against you (you are a woman, you have a dark complexion, you are "too fat" or "too thin" or "too short"), because they are envious of you, or because you remind them of someone else that they dislike. There are many reasons why people may not return your niceness, and they often have nothing to do with how you act or who you are.

2. There are people who can and will cause you harm even if you are nice. There are people who are, by their very nature, short-tempered, impatient, demanding, controlling, or abusive.

3. Sometimes Nice Girls are so nice that it turns people off. This may be because they sense that your niceness is not genuine, or because your

niceness seems to have a price tag on it. Or it may be that they don't respect you because you are too nice. Nice Girls are often viewed as being too compliant or too ingratiating, and this can turn some people off.

4. There are people in the world who will take advantage of your niceness or who interpret niceness as an open invitation to be cruel or abusive. This is particularly true of sexual predators or sexual opportunists.

Bad things do, indeed, happen to good people. Nice Girls get hurt, rejected, and disliked by others all the time—not because of what they have done, but just because.

False Belief #3: What other people think of me is more important than almost anything else—including my self-esteem, my health or even my safety.

Like many false beliefs, this one is not something that women consciously think about and "decide" to believe. If you were to ask them, most women might even say that they don't really believe this. But their behavior belies this. They show by their actions, especially their behavior with men, that what others think of them is indeed more important than nearly anything else in their life.

Time after time, I have worked with female clients who have put aside their own safety and integrity to be accepted by a man or by their social group. My client Willow, for example, became involved with a man who was polyamorous (the practice of, or desire for, intimate relationships with more than one partner, with the knowledge of all partners involved). He told her he loved her very much but wasn't willing to give up his lifestyle (or his other partners) in order to be with her. If she wanted to be with him, she needed to embrace the polyamorous lifestyle.

Willow thought about it seriously and came to the conclusion that she didn't want to lose Max, so she'd give his lifestyle a try. Two years later she came into therapy because she felt horrible about herself, "I can't believe I put myself through that ordeal," she told me. "I wanted to impress Max with my 'openness,' so in addition to Max, I got involved with two other men. I told myself that I could have sex with all three men and become involved with all three emotionally, but the truth was, I was just lying to myself. I became confused and even disoriented. I didn't know what end was up. I ended up feeling like my whole life was about these men and I completely neglected my career and my friends. And I was constantly jealous of the other women that Max was involved with. I actually think I came close to going over the edge emotionally."

As Carol Gilligan, a pioneer in the study of women's development, writes in her book *In a Different Voice: Psychological Theory and Women's Development*, relationships play an unusually important role in girls' social development. They care deeply about what others think about them; in fact, much of their self-esteem centers on whether others perceive them in a positive or negative light. For this reason, girls and women have been known to do embarrassing, hurtful, and even dangerous things in order to garner the approval of others.

Think about this a moment: What have you done in your life in order to get the approval of others? Have you "gone along" with the crowd, even when your instincts told you that what they were doing was unhealthy or even dangerous? This might include taking drugs because everyone else was doing it, driving too fast because your friends told you to "go faster," or sleeping with a guy because you thought he would dump you if you didn't. How many times have you put your own best interests aside in order to gain the acceptance of a group or individual, to be part of the group, or to "look good" to your group or to the public?

False Belief #4: I need to be good and perfect in order to be accepted and loved.

For many years, girls were raised to believe that if they were "good"—if they minded their parents and did what was expected of them at school—they would in turn be accepted and loved by others. This "sugar and spice and everything nice" mindset continues into the present in some circles (e.g., conservative or deeply religious homes). In these environments, girls are supposed to be sweet and caring, little caregivers in training.

After talking to hundreds of girls for her research project on girls and aggression, Rachel Simmons, the author of *Odd Girls Out*, found that many expressed exasperation at being expected to be nice all the time and to be nice to everyone. One girl expressed her frustration like this: "They expect you to be perfect . . . When boys do bad things, they all know they're going to do bad stuff. When girls do it, they yell at them." Still another said, "They expect you to be perfect angels and then sometimes we don't want to be considered a perfect angel."

Some parents also instill in their children the belief that they have to be perfect. While she was alive, my mother sometimes told me this story: One day, as she dropped me off at the babysitter's and gave me her usual admonishment—"Now you be good for Mrs. Jones today"—I turned to her and said, "I have to be good for Mrs. Jones, I have to be good for you, I have to be good for my teachers, I have to be good at church. When can I be bad?"

My mother always laughed when she told this story, since in many ways she loved my being precocious. But I doubt that she truly appreciated what I was trying to tell her—that I felt too much pressure to be good and perfect.

False Belief #5: I don't have the right to stand up for myself.

Hopefully, since we've been focusing on why women have a difficult time standing up for themselves throughout the book, you already have a good idea why you took on this particular false belief. As we have been discussing, women have good reasons for not being able to stand up for ourselves. We have been conditioned to be passive, especially when it comes to our relationships with men. As mentioned earlier, it was not so long ago that girls and women were completely dominated by their fathers and husbands. It was unheard of for a woman to stand up to a man, no matter how abusive he might be. It simply was not safe. For many women today, this is unfortunately still true.

We also need to remember that women have had to fight for the rights they now have—these rights were not given to us freely. It wasn't all that long ago that women couldn't vote. Suffragists like Susan B. Anthony met in the 1840s to organize the American women's movement for the primary purpose of securing the right to vote. So the false belief that women do not have a right to stand up for themselves is a powerful remnant of our history as females.

For some women, this false belief also comes from their personal experiences of being dominated and or abused. Although much has changed regarding the reporting of child abuse, countless girls are still dominated and abused in their homes. Standing up to an abusive parent is almost impossible for a child—and not usually a smart thing to do. And many girls learn by example—from their mother who is being verbally, emotionally, or physically abused by their father, for instance—that standing up only gets you in more trouble.

False Belief #6: Anger is a destructive emotion and shouldn't be expressed directly, especially to those with whom you are angry.

We discussed the difficulty women have expressing their anger in a previous chapter. While both males and females have difficulties with expressing anger, research tells us that parents and teachers discourage the expression of physical and direct aggression in girls early on, while anger in boys is either encouraged or ignored. There is still a double standard when it comes to aggression—it is seen as unfeminine, and displays of aggression in females are punished with social rejection.

Girls and women are socialized to avoid expressing their anger in direct or outward ways. In fact, "good girls" are not expected to experience anger at all. This is primarily because aggression imperils a girl's ability to be caring and "nice"—in other words, it undermines who girls and women have been raised to become. And since girls are raised to be the caretakers and nurturers in relationships, they are taught that aggression endangers relationships and thereby discouraged from ever showing it.

This false belief is a very common and powerful one for many people, not just women. Those who were raised in an environment where there was one or more angry and/or violent adults tend to grow up believing that anger is dangerous and should be avoided at all costs. This was the case with Vanna, who grew up with a father who had frequent, unexpected rages that he directed at whomever was around. Throughout her childhood, without much warning at all, her father would suddenly start screaming and throwing objects around the room.

Vanna grew up to be an extremely mild-mannered woman who never got angry. She had a string of boyfriends in her twenties, mostly men who were very controlling. She seldom, if ever, stood up to any of them, even when they were being unreasonable or cruel. Because she was so used to her father's anger and because she felt she had no right to her own, each of her relationships became more and more abusive. By the time she was thirty, she had graduated to being involved with a man who beat her—and each time it happened, she would make excuses for him. Finally, after more than a year of this, Vanna escaped one night because she was afraid for her life. She ended up at a local shelter. She stayed there for only one week before going back to him. Everyone at the shelter was afraid Vanna would end up being killed by her boyfriend and wished they could talk her out of going back, but she was terribly afraid of being alone.

The good news is that one of the counselors at the shelter gave Vanna my book *Honoring Your Anger*—and she ended up reading the book and contacting the counselor to ask her if she could come in for therapy sessions with her. She continued seeing the counselor, and together they worked on her ability to express her anger in constructive, healthy ways. This was the final impetus for Vanna being able to leave her abusive boyfriend.

False Belief #7: It is better to avoid conflict at any cost.

Girls are encouraged to identify with the nurturing behavior of their mothers, and many spend their childhood practicing caretaking and nurturing each other. Because they are expected to be caring and nurturing and to have "perfect relationships" with one another, girls are unprepared to negotiate conflict.

In a normal conflict, two people use language, their voice, or even their bodies to settle their dispute. The relationship they have with each other is considered secondary to the issue being worked out. But with girls and women, the relationship is primary. They will do anything to preserve it— even if that means remaining silent and not expressing their hurt or anger. And because most girls and women have been discouraged, if not forbidden, to express anger, it goes underground. When anger cannot be voiced and the skills to handle a conflict are absent, the problem is never brought up.

There are several other possible reasons for the difficulties girls and women have with conflict:

- Researcher Carol Gilligan has found that girls perceive isolation as dangerous. Most girls and women will do anything to avoid isolation, including not speaking up when they disagree and avoiding conflict at all costs.

- Sociologist Anne Campbell, in her interviews with adults, found that whereas men viewed aggression as a means to control their environment and integrity, women believed it would terminate their relationships.

- From her conversations with girls, Rachel Simmons discovered this identical attitude: "Expressing fear that even everyday acts of conflict, not to mention severe aggressive outbursts, would result in the loss of the people they most cared about, they refused to engage in even the most basic acts of conflict. Their equation was simple: conflict = loss."

As Rachel Simmons explains it, "In a world that socializes girls to prize relationships and care above all else, the fear of isolation and loss casts a long shadow over girls' decisions around conflicts, driving them away from direct confrontation." Many of the girls she interviewed expressed the fear that even everyday acts of conflict would result in the loss of the people they most cared about. One sixth grader told her, "You don't want to express it [whatever is bothering you] to them and if you do, it's like, well, you might as well just walk off because they're not going to want to be your friend." A seventh grader explained, "If I tell my friends I'm angry with them, I'll have another enemy. It's a vicious cycle."

False Belief #8: There is good in everyone, and if you give someone enough chances they will show it to you.

Women, far more than men, give people too many chances. This is often due to the fact that girls and women are expected to be compassionate and forgiving; as nurturers and mothers, furthermore, we are supposed to have infinite patience and tolerance. We are biologically programmed to have these very qualities when it comes to our own children. When you think about it, the qualities of a good mother (or parent) include patience, tolerance, unconditional love, and forgiveness. So it is within our very nature to give people a second chance—to believe someone when he tells us he won't do it again, or at the very least will try not to. But we need to rein in this tendency. Giving someone a second chance is a good idea if the person has shown us in the past that he or she deserves it or if there is reason to believe he or she will, in fact, change. Otherwise, giving a second chance is usually a bad idea, especially when it comes to abusive behavior.

Action Steps

Once you have examined your beliefs and attitudes and have come to recognize how they add to your risk of being sexually assaulted, harassed, or coerced, you will need to take action. We already discussed some of these action steps in earlier chapters, but there are some additional ones to consider now. Some of the action steps you will need to take are:

- Learn to put your own needs first, even at the risk of being called selfish or a bitch. Your need for safety should be at the top of the list.

- Stop playing sweet, gullible, and naïve. It's outdated and it invites people, especially men, to take advantage of you.

- Learn that setting limits and boundaries and expecting others to take care of their own needs can be the greatest "act of kindness" you can perform when it comes to personal relationships. You don't do anyone a favor by allowing them to take advantage of you.

- Let others know when they have hurt or angered you. By not speaking up when someone disrespects, insults, or mistreats you, you are inadvertently giving them permission to continue to mistreat you in the same way in the future or to treat you in even more hurtful and disrespectful ways.

- Confront your own anger. Sometimes under all that niceness lies a huge storage bin of repressed and suppressed anger. Find constructive ways to release pent-up and repressed anger (refer to Chapter 7 for suggestions for healthy anger release).

- Stop giving people second (and third and fourth) chances. If someone shows you who he or she is, pay attention and act accordingly.

- Stop being "fair" and start being strong. Women's need for fairness often gets them into trouble. Their tendency to want to look at both sides of a situation often blurs the real issue, making it too easy for others to manipulate them. Gavin de Becker wrote about this phenomenon in his book, *The Gift of Fear,* which we will discuss in Chapter 10.

- Be honest with yourself about your real reasons for being a Nice Girl. When we look for the motive for our "niceness," we often find guilt, shame, fear of confrontation, fear of rejection, and an intense fear of being alone.

- Allow yourself to be bad sometimes. It's not only okay to be bad once in a while, it's also healthy. In fact, if you don't allow yourself to be bad at times you will continue to attract people into your life who will act out your "badness" for you.

Pauline is always attracted to "bad boys." This is how she explained it: "I like them because they're so sexy and they're so much fun. Nice guys are boring." But Pauline gets hurt a lot too. Many of her "bad boy" boyfriends have cheated on her and some have become physically abusive.

Pauline is not alone. Many women are attracted to bad boys, though dating them goes against their better judgment. This is especially true of Nice Girls. Nice Girls like bad boys because they do all the things Nice Girls wish they could do, but can't. It isn't a coincidence that girls who are raised by strict parents or in deeply religious families are often the ones who get involved with bad boys. It's their way of rebelling against all the rules and "being bad" without having to take responsibility for it.

For a much more comprehensive discussion about Nice Girls and more tips on how to change your attitude and behavior around this subject, refer to my book, *The Nice Girl Syndrome: Stop Being Manipulated and Abused—and Start Standing Up for Yourself.*

Goals of Chapter 9

The goal of this chapter was to introduce you to "Nice Girl" behavior and beliefs and show how they can put you at risk of being abused in your relationships, as well as sexually assaulted, harassed, and coerced by men in general. Although some of you may have more work to do in terms of extinguishing these beliefs and behaviors, this chapter is a good beginning to discovering your patterns.

No! Exercise

Think about a recent situation in which you should have said "No!" but didn't. Perhaps it was an unattractive or obnoxious guy coming on to you or your boyfriend or husband pushing you to engage in sexual acts that you find disgusting.

Think about the reasons you gave yourself for not saying "No!" Be honest here. Was it because you were afraid of conflict? Was it because you didn't want to hurt his feelings? Try to find the false belief that corresponds to your reason for not saying "No!"

Now imagine that you are saying "No!" to this person. Picture him in front of you and say the word "No!" out loud. Say it over and over until you can say it with conviction.

Notice how you feel afterwards. You might feel a little shaky—that's normal. After all, you are probably not used to saying "No" to this person or to this kind of person. That shaky feeling will eventually go away the more you practice saying "No!"

Perhaps you felt strong rather than fearful. You might even feel empowered. If that's the case, that is great. You deserve to feel empowered; you deserve to speak up and take care of yourself.

Part III

Standing Up and Saying "No!"

Before you continue . . .

At this point you understand the risks you face when it comes to sexual violence. And, hopefully, you now know that you have the right to protect and defend yourself from being sexually coerced, harassed, or assaulted and you believe you deserve to be safe and treated with respect.

This section of the book is devoted to making yourself as safe as possible despite the dangers around you. Although reading about suggestions and strategies for self-protection may make you feel like you will lose your spontaneity or even frighten you, believe me, preparing in these ways will eventually empower you and make standing up for yourself and saying "No!" much easier.

A word of reminder is appropriate here—this book is about learning how to *stand up against* sexual assault, harassment, and pressure. It is not about *prevention* in the way that most people think of the word. Prevention implies that you have total control over the situation and that if you do certain things, you can prevent sexual violations. Unfortunately, this is not the case; no matter what you do, you cannot completely guarantee your own safety from these violations. Nor should you feel that you are totally responsible for doing so. As much as this book is about empowering women to stand up against sexual assault and harassment and say "No!" to unwanted sexual comments, touches, and approaches, the reality is that ultimately, it is up to men, as well as our entire culture, to make the changes that will ultimately make women and girls safe.

We do, however, have some power when it comes to opposing the sexual violation of women and—resisting it at every turn. There is much power in resistance. That is what standing up is all about: resisting.

Chapter 10
Have Your Wits about You—
Strategies that Can Help Prevent
Stranger and Acquaintance Rape

Distrust and caution are the parents of security.

—Benjamin Franklin

I f you aren't present, if you aren't paying attention to your environment and the people around you, you can't protect yourself from danger. Unfortunately, many women walk around being only half present—too distracted checking their cell phone, thinking about what they have to do, fantasizing about a man or an upcoming event, obsessing about something that happened with a friend or lover, or being otherwise "checked out" to be aware of their surroundings.

You need to have all your wits about you in order to protect yourself from the multiple dangers in the world. You need to be present and in your body in order to be safe. And those who have been traumatized in the past will need to work extra hard to stay connected to their body and their feelings, because traumatized individuals often walk around in a dissociated state: disconnected from their body, numb to their feelings.

If you are aware that you tend to "space out" or dissociate, the following grounding exercise will help you to remain in the present. I offered you a more complicated version of a grounding exercise located toward the end of Chapter 1, and I recommend you use that one whenever you find yourself triggered by a past memory or when you find yourself "leaving your body" or dissociating. But many former victims were so traumatized or are traumatized on such a regular basis that they are in the habit of dissociating, even when there is no present danger. If you are one of those who are perpetually "spaced out," I recommend that you practice the "Basic Grounding Exercise" below whenever you catch yourself disconnecting from yourself or your environment. This version of grounding is simpler and can be done in less time. It is extremely effective method of remaining in the present.

Basic Grounding Exercise

1. Find a quiet place where you will not be disturbed or distracted.

2. Sit up in a chair or on the couch. Put your feet flat on the ground. If you are wearing shoes with heels, you will need to take your shoes off so you can have your feet flat on the ground.

3. With your eyes open, take a few deep breaths. Turn your attention once again to feeling the ground under your feet. Continue your breathing and concentrating on the feel of having your feet flat on the ground throughout the exercise.

4. Now, as you continue breathing, clear your eyes and take a look around the room. As you slowly scan the room, notice the colors, shapes, and textures of the objects in the room. If you'd like, turn your neck so you can see a wider view.

5. Bring your focus back to feeling the ground under your feet as you continue to breathe and to notice the different colors, textures, and shape of the objects in the room.

Strategies for Preventing Stranger Rape

While learning to say "No!" will help prevent most types of sexual assault by acquaintances and dates, stranger rape is another story. Some feminists balk at the idea of teaching women how to protect themselves from stranger rape because they don't like the fact that this puts the onus on women instead of holding men accountable for their behavior. But I believe there are some prevention strategies that can protect women from being assaulted by a stranger, so I believe it is worthwhile to offer these here. *This in no way implies that if a woman doesn't practice these strategies, and she is attacked, the attack is her fault.*

Understanding the risks associated with stranger rape allows you to make informed decisions regarding your own safety and self-protection, and helps you be less susceptible to assault.

Awareness and Alertness

In my opinion, having your wits about you at all times is the most important way to prevent rape—either by strangers or acquaintances. If you aren't alert, aware, and present in your body and in the moment, you won't be able to pick up on the important cues that can help you avoid being sexually assaulted. If you are numb or dissociated due to past trauma, you will not notice when you are in danger and won't be able to stand up to a potential abuser. If you are high on drugs or intoxicated with alcohol, your judgment will be impaired and you will not have access to all your faculties.

Here are two of the most important ways of staying alert:

- *Stay focused and stay safe.* An important aspect of awareness is being alert. Always pay attention to your surroundings. No reading or texting while you are walking, no using headphones. Don't break basic safety rules, such as making sure you are looking and listening to what is going on around you. Don't jog alone in the park or down the street at dusk or at night—and if you do, don't wear headphones, since this disables the survival sense most likely to warn you about dangerous approaches: your hearing!

- *Use all your senses.* Don't be afraid to look squarely at strangers who concern you. If you believe you are being followed, don't just take a tentative look, hoping to see if someone is visible in your peripheral vision. It is better to turn completely, take in everything, and look squarely at someone who concerns you. This not only gives you information, but also communicates to him that you are not a tentative, frightened victim-in-waiting. You are an animal of nature, fully endowed with hearing, sight, intellect, and dangerous defenses. You are not easy prey; don't act like you are.

Trust Your Intuition

Another way to keep your wits about you is to trust your intuition. "Women's intuition" gets minimized and made fun of, especially by men. But Gavin de Becker—author of the best-selling book, *The Gift of Fear* and someone who advises many of the world's most prominent media figures, corporations, and law enforcement agencies on predicting violence—believes women's intuition is one of our most important resources when it comes to protecting ourselves. Men often refer to this sense as a "gut-feeling." It's a sensation that appears quickly in our consciousness—noticeable enough to be acted on if we so choose—without us being fully aware of the underlying reasons for its occurrence. It is a reaction that gives us the ability to know something directly without analytic reasoning, bridging the gap between the conscious and unconscious parts of our mind, and also between instinct and reason.

Intuition is our most complex and at the same time our simplest cognitive process. It connects us to the natural world and to our own nature. As humans, we have the distinct advantage of having both instinct and reason at our disposal. According to de Becker, we are innately well equipped to make an accurate evaluation as to whether a situation or a person is safe.

Unfortunately, many of us are uncomfortable with the idea of using our instincts as a guidance tool. In fact, we spend a great deal of time ignoring or dismissing this aspect of ourselves. This can be dangerous, as this case example shows:

My client Wendy was waiting for a bus to go home after work. It started to rain and she hadn't brought an umbrella or raincoat. A car stopped close to her and the man asked if she wanted a ride home. She recognized the man; she had seen him at her workplace. But she had never spoken to him. She approached the car and looked at him in the face to get a sense of whether he was safe or not. He gave her a big smile. He looked like a nice man. The rain was really coming down, so she thanked him and got in his car.

When Wendy gave the man her address, he said they lived quite close to each other. As they drove, he chatted with her about their neighborhood— just small talk, really. It wasn't long before they drove up to her apartment. "Hey, I have an umbrella in my trunk," the man said. "Stay put and I'll get it and walk you to your door."

Wendy sat patiently while he got out of the car, opened his trunk, and opened her car door. Before she knew it, he was pushing a rag over her mouth and nose. When she woke up she was lying on the ground and the man was on top of her, raping her.

Many of my clients who have been sexually assaulted have shared with me that they "sensed" that something was wrong just before they were raped or they suspected something wrong with the guy who sexually assaulted them on a date. These same clients tend to blame themselves for not paying attention to this internal warning. This is what Wendy did. "Why did I agree to get in a strange man's car like that?" she said. "I didn't really know him, he just looked familiar from work."

"How could you have known the man was dangerous?" I responded. "Since you'd seen him at work, you couldn't have imagined he'd do something like this to you."

"Yes," she said, "but you know what? As we were chatting in the car I noticed that he seemed very nervous. In fact, his hand was shaking. I remember wondering why he was so nervous, but then I just let it go."

Wendy's intuition was trying to tell her something. Protect yourself by paying attention to and trusting that silent voice inside you. Trust that what causes you alarm probably should, because when it comes to danger, intuition is always right in at least two important ways, according to de Becker:

- It is always in response to something.

- It always has your best interest at heart.

Rather than making a quick effort to explain intuition's message away or deny the possible danger, it is wiser (and more true to our nature) to make an effort to identify the danger we're sensing.

Perpetrators' Signals

The human violence we fear and abhor the most, says de Becker—that which we call "random" and "senseless"—is neither random nor senseless. It always has purpose and meaning—to the perpetrator, at least. As de Becker explains, every perpetrator sends out certain signals and repeats certain patterns, and if we stay connected to and then trust our intuition, we can spot these signals as the danger signs they are. Unfortunately, most of us don't pay attention to the signals, and even when we do, we often talk ourselves out of trusting them. It is vitally important that we change this tendency, especially when it comes to preventing sexual assault by strangers. These signals include:

- *Forced teaming*. This is what de Becker calls an effective way that perpetrators establish premature trust. In Wendy's case, the man from work made a big thing out of the fact that they worked at the same company and lived in the same neighborhood—like this was supposed to create an instant comradery between them. In reality, as Wendy was to discover later, the man didn't work at the same company at all. The reason his face was familiar was that he routinely "trolled" her company for vulnerable women.

- *Charm and niceness*. The predatory criminal does everything he can think of to put his prey at ease. "He was so nice" is a common comment women who have been attacked make about their predator. But niceness does not mean goodness. Niceness, as we discussed in the chapter on Nice Girls, is a strategy of social interaction, not a character trait. People seeking to control others almost always present a "nice person" image in the beginning.

- *Loan sharking*. This is the term de Becker uses to describe a situation where someone offers to help you so you will be in his debt, or so it will make it difficult to ask him to leave you alone. In Wendy's case, she wanted to get out of the car as soon as she was in front of her apartment building, but when the man told her to stay put while he got an umbrella, she felt obligated to do so. Her defense could have been to remind herself that he'd *offered* to help her; she hadn't asked for his help. But instead she sat patiently, waiting for him to open her car door and offer her his umbrella.

- *Discounting the word "No."* This is perhaps the most important signal, and the most appropriate one for women who want to protect themselves from sexual assault by strangers and acquaintances alike. As we have discussed throughout this book, the ability to say "No!" can be our most powerful asset when it comes to safety. And as de Becker explains, one of the most significant signals that a man is up to no good is if he ignores your "no." Declining to hear "no" is a signal that someone is either seeking control or refusing to relinquish it.

Saying No! In a Strong, Assertive Way

It is important to know that your "No!" must be spoken in a strong voice and with conviction. If it is offered in a tentative way, it cannot be effective. Women are often afraid to say "No!" in a strong and assertive way because they don't want to hurt the other person's feelings. And they don't want to appear to be rude. Remember, these are Nice Girl qualities that must be replaced with a strong sense of self-preservation.

You cannot waffle. If you let someone talk you out of the word "no," you might as well wear a sign that reads: "You are in charge." Also, "no" is a word that must never be negotiated, because the person who chooses not to hear it is trying to control you. If you say "No!" with conviction but then turn around and agree to what you just said no to, it loses all its power.

This is crucial: Someone who declines to hear "No!" is either seeking control or refusing to relinquish it. Otherwise, he would hear your "No!" and respect it. The worst response to a "No!" is to give ever-weakening refusals and then give in.

Negotiating—as in, "I'm really not in the mood tonight, perhaps another night"—is another common response that serves the perpetrator. Negotiations are about *possibilities,* and providing access to someone who makes you feel apprehensive is not a possibility you want to keep on the agenda. As de Becker encourages his readers to remember, "no" is a complete sentence. Remember, in order for "no" to work, you must say it in an assertive way. Don't be passive or tentative. Say it clearly, and with emphasis: "No, I don't need any help,"; "No, I don't want a ride."

The Interview

Perpetrators each have their own process of victim selection, something de Becker calls "the interview." He likens it to a shark circling potential prey. A predatory criminal is looking for someone who is vulnerable, someone who will allow him to be in control. Just as he constantly gives signals of his intention, he reads signals of vulnerability from his potential prey.

Let's say that you are walking toward your apartment with your arms full of grocery bags. A man comes up to you and offers to help you, saying, "Can I carry some of those bags for you?" What would you do? Would you take him up on his offer?

Let's say your instinct is to say no; he is a stranger, and you don't want him knowing where your apartment is. You say, "No, thanks, I've got it."

The man looks a little dejected and says, "Come on, I'm just trying to help you."

What do you do? Do you tell yourself that he is right—that he is just being polite, and you should let him help you? Do you tell yourself, "I'm just being paranoid, he seems like a nice man, why not let him help me"? Or do you decide that no matter how nice he seems to be, he is a stranger and you need to protect yourself?

Let me help you make this decision based on what de Becker advises. If a man refuses to take no for an answer and says something like, "Come on, I'm just trying to help," ask yourself: *Why is this person seeking to control me? What does he want?* It is best to get away from the person altogether, but if that's not practical, the best response is to dramatically raise your insistence, skipping several levels of politeness. "I said, 'No!'"

For those of you who are still worried about being rude, consider this:

Even if the man gets angry and calls you a bitch, paranoid, or crazy, that is far preferable to giving a man the message that he can control you.

As for the worry that you will appear paranoid, think about this:

- Is it really paranoia for a woman to react this way in a country where crimes against women have risen four times faster than any other crime and three out of four women suffer a violent crime in their lifetime?

- Is it really paranoia to worry even though you've heard horror stories from nearly every woman you know?

- Is it fair that women have to consider where they park, where they walk, and whom they date out of fear of being raped or killed?

- Are you paranoid when several times a week someone makes an inappropriate comment, stares at you, harasses you, follows you, or drives alongside your car yelling obscenities at you?

- Are you paranoid to wonder about a strange man's motives when women deal with life-and-death issues that most men know nothing about?

Women, particularly those who live or work in big cities, live with a constant wariness. Their lives are literally on the line in ways that men just don't experience. Ask any man you know, "When is the last time you were concerned or afraid that another person would harm you?" Most men cannot remember an incident in their recent past, if ever. Ask a woman the same question and you are likely to get the answer "last night" or even "every day." So let men try to make you feel foolish for being "too cautious." Let them make you feel like you are paranoid. At least your actions are likely to protect you. Who cares if it hurts their feelings?

The scenario I presented above of the woman with groceries is a real-life example; it's a story from a client of De Becker's. She was so concerned about appearing to be rude or ungrateful that she let the man carry her groceries to her apartment, and she ended up being raped by him.

De Becker gives another example of a woman in an underground parking lot at night. A man approaches her and offers to help her as she puts grocery bags in her car. The man may be a gentleman or he may be conducting an "interview." The woman tenses her shoulders slightly, looks intimidated, and says, "No, thanks, I think I've got it." From de Becker's perspective, this woman is putting herself in a position of possibly becoming that man's next victim. Conversely, if she turns toward the man, raises her hands to a "stop" position, and says directly, "No, I don't want your help," she is less likely to become his victim.

Few of you reading this book would consider being this bold. After all, what if he were a decent guy who really just wanted to help? The answer is, if he were a decent guy he would understand such a reaction from a woman all alone in a parking lot. More likely, he wouldn't approach the woman in the first place, unless she really had some obvious need.

What if the man doesn't understand the reaction and stomps off feeling dejected? Well, that's just fine. In fact, any reaction, even anger, from a decent man who had no sinister intent is preferable to continued attention from a violent man who might have used your concern about being rude to his advantage.

Let's explore some common scenarios that you could experience:

- You've locked yourself out of your car

- You've run out of gas

This is de Becker's advice:

- If you are in a situation in which you need help, such as being locked out of your car with your purse and cell phone inside, it is better if you choose the person you want to help you rather than accept an offer of assistance from someone. The person you choose is nowhere near as likely to attack you as the person who chooses you. The possibility that you will inadvertently select a predatory criminal for whom you are the right victim type is very remote.

- Ask other women for help when you need it. And if you have to accept an offer of help, it's much better to accept it from a woman than from a man.

Another Important Aspect of Keeping Your Wits about You: Booze and Drugs

Another way that women need to stay alert is to not consume too much alcohol or drugs when on a date, at a bar, or at a party. The association between alcohol consumption and sexual assault is an important one, and it's one that women need to be aware of. According to the magazine, *Campus Safety,* in an article entitled, "The Role Alcohol Plays in Sexual Assault on College Campuses," there are some important things to know:

- Because intoxication lowers inhibitions and decreases mental awareness, women using drugs or alcohol are at a much greater risk of being sexually assaulted.

- At least 50 percent of student sexual assaults involve alcohol.

- 43 percent of sexual victimization incidents involve alcohol consumption by victims.

- One study found that 55 percent of those raped by an acquaintance had been using drugs or alcohol immediately prior to the assault.

- A study involving college students revealed that 90 percent of acquaintance rape involved alcohol.

- Women need to not only watch how much alcohol they consume, but how much their date is consuming. One out of three sexual assaults, are perpetrated by those who are intoxicated.

The truth is, if you are drunk or high you cannot be aware of your environment and be alert to the dangers around you. If you consume too much alcohol or drugs when on a date, at a bar, or at a party, you are taking a huge risk.

Women need to stop assuming that their friends will protect them if they drink too much. It used to be much more common for women to stick together when they went out and to make sure that a friend who had drank too much found her way home safely. But this isn't always the case nowadays, especially with younger women and friends who don't know each other well. And what used to be seen as a natural tendency for males to want to protect a female that they see is high or intoxicated no longer exists today; in fact, men at a party are just as likely to take advantage of a high or intoxicated female as they are to attempt to protect her. For example:

- A high school girl in Texas went to a party with her male cousin who was a few years older than she was. When she drank too much, instead of her cousin watching out for her or making sure she got safely home, he stood by while several of the young men at the party raped her. He even participated by videotaping the entire attack, which he then placed on social media for the entire school to see.

- A young woman in California went to a bar with some friends for a "girls' night out." One young man in particular seemed to take an interest in her and she danced with him several times. He kept buying her drinks and she became quite drunk. When her friends told her they were leaving, she told them she wanted to stay. As one friend later reported, "We knew she was drunk and we should have insisted she go with us." Instead, they left, and the man the young woman had been sitting with ended up putting a date-rape drug into one of her drinks. When she regained consciousness she was lying in an alley outside the bar. It was obvious that she had been roughed up and raped.

Fraternity parties and parties made up of football players are particularly dangerous places for young women. Fraternity men have been identified as being more likely to perpetrate sexual violence or sexual aggression than non-fraternity men. For example, research has found that:

- Members of fraternities are more likely to hold rape-supportive beliefs and sexually aggressive attitudes toward women than non-members. They also have been found more likely to use alcohol incapacitation, verbal coercion, threats, and force to obtain sex. (Boyle, 2015).

- Men who participate in organized sports exhibit more aggressive behaviors, including bullying, sexual violence, and physical aggression. Athletes who play sports like football and basketball display high levels of hyper-masculinity and sexual aggression and hold strong beliefs in gender inequality. (Passero, 2015).

- This group also scored higher on attitudinal measures thought to be associated with sexual coercion, such as sexism, acceptance of violence, hostility toward women and rape myth acceptance.(Passero, 2015).

Fraternity parties and even parties made up of high school kids are also dangerous places for young women, who often become prey to young men who constantly grab them, try to talk them into giving them oral sex, or, worse yet, get them drunk with the intention of sexually assaulting them once they have passed out. For example:

- A young woman in California was given a date rape drug at a fraternity party. When she became dizzy, one of the young men suggested she lie down. He took her into a bedroom, where six young men repeatedly sexually assaulted her.

- A high school girl was raped by a popular football player at a party. When she reported the incident to the police, none of her friends supported her. In fact, the entire school turned against her.

I hope the above information, statistics, and real-life stories will make you think twice about drinking too much alcohol when you are on a date, at a bar, or at a party.

The Danger of Date Rape Drugs

Perpetrators are using so-called "date rape" drugs more and more often these days to assist in sexual assault. Often, these drugs have no color, smell, or taste, so you can't tell if you've been drugged. They make you feel weak and confused and can even cause you to pass out. Date rape drugs make it impossible for you to consent to sex.

The three most common date rape drugs are rohypnol, GHB, and ketamine. All three drugs are very powerful. They can affect you very quickly and without your knowing what's happening. The length of time that the effects last varies. It depends on how much of the drug is taken and if it has been mixed with other drugs or alcohol. Alcohol makes the drugs even stronger and can cause serious health problems—even death.

Rohypnol

Rohypnol comes in a pill that dissolves in liquids. Some are small, round, and white. Newer pills are oval and green-gray in color. When slipped into a drink, a dye in these new pills makes clear liquids turn bright blue and make dark liquids turn cloudy. But this color change might be hard to see in a dark drink like cola or dark beer, or in a dark room. Also, the pills with no dye are still available and can be ground up into a powder

The effects of rohypnol can be felt within thirty minutes of its ingestion and can last for several hours. If you are drugged, you might look and act like someone who is drunk. You might have trouble standing. Your speech might be slurred. Or you might pass out. Rohypnol can also cause muscle relaxation or loss of muscle control; difficulty with motor movements; problems talking; nausea; inability to remember what happened while drugged; loss of consciousness; confusion; problems seeing; dizziness; sleepiness; lower blood pressure; stomach problems; and death.

GHB

GHB has a few forms: a liquid with no odor or color, white powder, and pill form. It might give your drink a slightly salty taste. Mixing it with a sweet drink (like fruit punch or fruit juice) can mask the salty taste.

GHB takes effect in about fifteen minutes and can last three or four hours. It is very potent: a very small amount can have a big effect. So it's easy to overdose on GHB. Most GHB is made in home or street "labs," so what is in it and how it will affect a person can vary significantly. GHB can cause relaxation; drowsiness; dizziness; nausea; problems seeing; loss of consciousness; seizures; inability to remember what happened while drugged; problems breathing; tremors; sweating; vomiting; slow heart rate; dream-like feeling; coma; and death.

Ketamine

Ketamine comes as a liquid and a white powder. It is very fast-acting. You might be aware of what is happening to you but unable to move. It also causes memory problems. Later, you might not be able to remember what happened while you were drugged. Ketamine can cause distorted perceptions of sight and sound; lost sense of time and identity; out-of-body experiences; dream-like feeling; feeling out of control; impaired motor functions; problems breathing; convulsions; vomiting; memory problems; numbness; loss of coordination; aggressive or violent behavior; depression; high blood pressure; and slurred speech.

How to Protect Yourself from Becoming a Victim of a Date Rape Drug

- Don't accept drinks from other people.

- Open containers yourself.

- Keep your drink with you at all times, even when you go to the bathroom.

- Watch your drink to make sure no one is putting something in it, even while you are holding it. This is especially true at parties or busy bars.

- Don't share drinks.

- Don't drink from punch bowls or other common open containers. They may already have drugs in them.

- If someone offers to get you a drink from a bar or at a party, go with the person to order your drink. Watch the drink while it's being poured and carry it yourself.

- Don't drink anything that tastes or smells strange. Sometimes GHB tastes salty.

- Bring a non-drinking friend with you when you go out drinking to make sure nothing happens.

- If you realize you left your drink unattended, don't drink it.

- If you feel drunk and haven't drunk any alcohol—or if you feel like the alcohol you've had is affecting you more strongly than usual—get help right away.

What You Should Do If You Think You've Been Drugged and Raped

- Get medical care right away. Call 911 or have a trusted friend take you to a hospital emergency room. Don't urinate, douche, bathe, brush your teeth, wash your hands, change clothes, or eat or drink anything before you go. These things may give evidence of the rape. The hospital will use a "rape kit" to collect evidence.

- Call the police from the hospital. Tell the police exactly what you remember. Be honest about all your activities. Remember, nothing you did—including drinking alcohol or doing drugs—can justify rape.

- Ask the hospital to take a urine sample that can be used to test for date rape drugs. The drugs leave your system quickly. Rohypnol stays in the body for several hours, and can be detected in the urine up to seventy-two hours after you've taken it. GHB leaves the body in twelve hours. (Again, don't urinate before going to the hospital.)

- Don't pick up or clean up where you think the assault might have occurred. There could be evidence left behind—on a drinking glass or on bed sheets, for example.

- Get counseling and treatment. Feelings of shame, guilt, fear, and shock are normal. A counselor can help you work through these emotions and begin the healing process. Calling a crisis center or a hotline is a good place to start. One national hotline is the National Sexual Assault Hotline at 800-656-HOPE.

How You Carry Yourself

Another important aspect of alertness is increasing your awareness of how you present and carry yourself. Many men who rape strangers tend to stalk potential victims and assess the situation before acting, and the way a woman carries herself has been found to be a factor in stranger rape. A woman who walks with a strong presence and purpose and an assertive gait is less likely to be targeted than a woman who walks with her head down, has a tentative gait, or appears to be distracted or passive.

Above all, don't appear to be vulnerable. Keep your head up and always appear as if you know where you are going, even if you do not. Studies suggest that through assertive physical and psychological presence, women convey an element of strength and authority in the eyes of those observing them. Remember, a rapist is looking for a vulnerable victim, not a strong one.

Again, none of this means that if you are raped, it is your fault for not carrying yourself in the right way!

Acquaintance Rape: Remember the Power of "No!"

In addition to staying alert and becoming more educated about the risk of alcohol and drug consumption and date rape drugs, your other primary defense against acquaintance rape is the ability to say "No!" in a clear, assertive way. Acquaintance rape is defined as any unwanted sexual intercourse or sexual contact, however slight, imposed on you by a friend or acquaintance. This kind of behavior includes touching, indecent exposure, and in some states, aggressive, sexually suggestive statements. Sexual contact is considered unwanted if you have not given legal consent to such contact. Saying "No!" clearly establishes a lack of legal consent.

Some men need to actually hear this "No!" in order to understand that you do not want them to continue whatever sexual behavior they are imposing on you. However, saying "No!" or physically resisting sexual contact are not necessary to demonstrate a lack of legal consent. For example, while state laws vary, if you are suffering from certain disabilities or are intoxicated, you are considered by law to be incapable of giving legal consent. That does not mean that you have to be intoxicated to the point of unconsciousness, only intoxicated.

Saying "No!" and continuing to saying it in an assertive way won't deter all male acquaintances, but it will most of them. And remember, when saying "No!" isn't enough, you always have the option of leaving a situation. You never owe anyone an explanation for your decision to not participate in something; you don't have to be afraid of hurting a man's feelings or his ego. And if you decide to leave and a man tries to stop you, at least attempt to physically resist.

It is a myth that compliance is the best strategy if the man tries to forcefully assault you. Department of Justice statistics indicate that women who use some sort of self-protection or resistance early on in an assault are twice as likely to escape. (You do need to trust your instincts on this, however).

Women who are not confident in making their decisions, wishes, or demands known and women who believe they are helpless and powerless against a man's demands are at a greater risk of being sexually assaulted on a date with an acquaintance. For this reason, remember to say "No!" loud and clear.

Strategies for Preventing Acquaintance Rape

When people think about a woman being raped, they usually imagine the perpetrator being a stranger. But in eight out of ten cases of rape, the victim knew the person who sexually assaulted them. And according to the National Institutes of Mental Health, 84 percent of victims of completed rape knew the offender, and of those, 66 percent were on a date. *In fact, acquaintance rape accounts for the largest category of reported sexual crimes.*

Women have a difficult time accepting the fact that someone they know, perhaps even someone they care about, could force them to have sex. But this is one of the hard truths women must face in order to protect themselves.

Most men who rape don't want you to resist. They don't want a fight, they don't want to force you. Instead, they use a strategy such as the one below:

Intrusion phase. In this phase, would-be sexual assaulters will test your boundaries and limits. They will do this both verbally and physically. Examples of verbal testing include: using swear words, talking about other women in sexual or derogatory ways, talking about sex and sexual acts. Examples of physical testing include: putting his hand on your knee, pulling you onto his lap, kissing or licking your face, rubbing his body against yours.

By doing this, the would-be assaulter is testing you to find out how much you will allow. If you allow him to continue, if you dismiss what he says or does as harmless, he will continue.

Desensitization phase. In this phase, the man continues to push boundaries. Because many women are still Nice Girls, they try to ignore such behavior or they minimize it. Their boundaries become blurry. This leaves the door open for the assaulter to continue pushing your limits.

Alcohol is the drug of choice for non-stranger assaulters. Alcohol speeds up the desensitization phase. If you are intoxicated, you are more likely to allow a man to cross your boundaries. You will be more desensitized to his comments. In fact, depending upon how much you have had to drink, you may be basically defenseless.

Isolation phase. In this phase, the assaulter gets you away from others to a place where he can freely push you into having sex with him, even if that includes using force.

Goals of Chapter 10

This chapter is designed to encourage you to make sure you have your wits about you when you are out in the world. This includes trusting your intuition, being smart about so-called "good Samaritans," and making sure you aren't too drunk or too high to protect yourself.

No! Exercise

As a way of protecting yourself from both stranger and acquaintance rape, make a commitment to the ways you can say "No!" regarding the issue of your alcohol consumption. For example:

- "I am saying 'No!' to being raped at a party by making sure I don't drink too much."

- "I am saying 'No!' to being drugged by never leaving my drink and by never accepting a drink from a stranger."

- "I'm saying 'No!' to being raped by a date or acquaintance by practicing saying 'No!' so that I can say it firmly when a guy tries to go too far."

- "I'm saying 'No!' to date or acquaintance rape by putting my own safety first and not worrying about the guy's feelings."

Chapter 11
Setting Boundaries and Limits

Love yourself enough to set boundaries . . . You teach people how to
treat you by deciding what you will and won't accept.

—Anna Taylor

In addition to keeping your wits about you, another essential aspect of creating safety is the setting and enforcing of boundaries. Creating boundaries can be extremely empowering. For some, just knowing they have set them gives them the courage to enforce them. A lack of boundaries on the other hand, is like leaving the door to your home unlocked: anyone, including unwelcome guests, can enter at will.

Boundaries are guidelines, rules, or limits that you create to identify for yourself what reasonable, safe, and permissible ways for other people to behave around you are, as well as how you will respond when someone steps outside those limits. This includes what types of communication, behavior, and interactions are acceptable to you.

It is important to set boundaries as a way of saying "No!" and as a way of practicing self-care and self-respect, communicating your needs in a relationship, and setting limits in a relationship in a way that is healthy.

Physical Boundaries

Physical boundaries define where you end and others begin and are determined by the amount of physical and emotional space you allow between yourself and others. They provide a barrier between you and an intruding force and include your body, your sense of personal space, and your privacy. We all have a "comfort zone," a given space between ourselves and others that enables us to feel safe and unthreatened. Your comfort zone will differ depending on whom you are dealing with. When it is a stranger, you will probably need a great deal more physical space than you do when your lover is near.

You have a right to choose who can touch you and who can't, where you wish to be touched, for how long you want to be touched, and what type of touch is acceptable to you. This does not refer only to sexual touching. If you do not like your coworker putting his arm around you while he is talking to you, move away. This will usually give the person the hint that you don't like this. If he continues this behavior, you have a right to say, "I'd appreciate it if you didn't do that. It makes me feel uncomfortable." If he continues to do it, you also have the right to be firm. No one, under any circumstances, has the right to touch you if you don't want to be touched!

Here is an example of a physical boundary violation: You are at a party, and a man walks up to you and starts a conversation. You notice right away that he is standing too close to you for your personal comfort. Your immediate and automatic reaction is to step back in order to protect your personal space. By doing this, you send a non-verbal message that when this person stood so close, you felt an invasion of your personal space.

Now let's say the person continues to move closer. What do you do? You might verbally protect your boundary by telling him to stop crowding you. You can do this in a humorous way by saying something like, "Hey, back up will you? You're in my space." If the person still refuses to back off, he is refusing to hear the word "no" (recall from Chapter 10—the person who refuses to hear your "no" is trying to control you), and the smartest thing to do may be to walk away. Remember, you don't have to be "nice," you don't have to worry about hurting his feelings. Your needs and your safety are the most important things here.

In addition to your physical comfort zone, you may also need to set boundaries about how much and what kind of casual touch you feel comfortable with. This is especially true for those of you who have been physically or sexually abused. Some people are very "touchy-feely": they like to hug you every time they see you, they enjoy putting their arm around you when they are standing next to you, and they often reach out to touch your arm when they are talking to you. And you may be perfectly comfortable with these casual touches. On the other hand, they may feel invasive to you. If this is the case, you need to communicate this to the other person.

If the person is a total stranger, you haven't had the chance to tell them what your boundaries are. In this case, you need to communicate your preferences via body language. Let's say an acquaintance walks up to you and before you know it, he has reached out to hug you. It is perfectly okay for you to put your hand up to block the hug or to turn your body to the side. Again, don't worry about hurting the other person's feelings. With people who like to put their arm around you, you can wriggle free from their embrace or excuse yourself and leave the area. With a person who likes to touch your arm, you can back up so that part of your body is out of their reach.

You can also put up a boundary verbally. With those you know, even casually, you can say something like "I'm not comfortable with hugging" or "I don't know you well enough for you to put your arm around me." If you know the person quite well, you may wish to share the fact that you are uncomfortable with casual touch.

Other examples of physical boundary invasions by relative strangers include:

- Sitting too close to you when it isn't necessary.

- Putting their hand on your knee when they are sitting next to you.

- Touching your face in an intimate way.

- Inappropriate touching, such as unwanted sexual advances.

What Stops Us From Setting Boundaries?

Since it is important to set boundaries, why do so many women have difficulty enforcing or upholding their boundaries? As we discussed in the Nice Girl chapter, many women are raised to put other people's needs and desires ahead of their own. Others are afraid to make other people angry. Here are some other reasons women have trouble holding firm to boundaries:

- Fear of rejection and, ultimately, abandonment.

- Fear of confrontation.

- We are not taught healthy boundaries.

- A history of abuse. Those who were physically or sexually abused in childhood often have difficulty establishing boundaries. This is because whenever the perpetrator wanted to have access to your body, he just reached out and grabbed. Whenever your parents wanted to, they could hit, push, or grab you. Now, as an adult, you may still behave as if you have no rights over your own body. You may allow others to touch you when you do not want to be touched.

It may take work on your part, but setting healthy physical boundaries can be extremely empowering and will allow you to:

- Protect your self-esteem and self-respect.

- Protect your physical and emotional space from intrusion.

- Send the message that you are not a candidate to be overpowered, manipulated, or abused in any way.

Discovering Your Sexual Boundaries

Discovering and asserting your sexual boundaries is an act of self-care when you are in an intimate relationship. It is an effective way to avoid being sexually pressured or coerced. In a relationship, whether it's a new one or one you've been in for quite some time, it is important to be able to set boundaries around your sexual relationship. This includes communicating to your partner what type of touch and sexual activities you prefer, and which ones you don't. It is especially important for you to convey to your partner what kinds of sexual activities you *absolutely do not want to engage in*. With strangers, boundary setting and verbal assertiveness are the most important defensive measures you can employ.

Part of learning to say "No!" is finding out what you want to say "Yes" to. If you don't know what your specific preferences are, you are likely to get blindsided when someone makes a sexual advance toward you. The same is

true even in an ongoing relationship; if you don't know what kind of intimate sexual interactions you are open to, you won't be as prepared to make
your preferences known to your partner and you will be more vulnerable to
sexual pressure and coercion. Most important, being clear about what you
are open to and what you prefer sexually will help you discover what you
aren't open to and don't want. For example, you may prefer just straight-
forward intercourse to any other type of sexual activity. If you know this,
instead of "going along" with a partner's desire to have oral sex or anal sex,
you can say "No!" to these forms of sex, with the understanding that you
have every right to do so.

This also goes for what are considered "kinky" types of sex, such as sado-
masochism and "butt play" (allowing a partner to put their finger or tongue,
or an object like a vibrator or dildo, inside your anus, or them asking you
to do the same). If you are open to exploring these less conventional types
of sex, more power to you. But if the thought of these types of sex turns you
off, repulses you, or triggers you (meaning they remind you of previous abuse
experiences), you need to be able to say "No!" to them and make it abundantly
clear that you are not open to them.

The following information will help you become clear as to what you like,
what you don't like, what you are open to, and what you are definitely not
open to.

Touches and Intensity: Strong or Gentle?

Let's start with discovering what types of touch you prefer. Here is where not
judging yourself comes in. Some women prefer a gentle, slow touch, whether
it be on their breasts, their butts, or their vaginas. Others prefer a stronger
touch or even a rough touch. Some women prefer intercourse that is slow
and deliberate, with both partners looking into each other's eyes. Others
prefer deep and rapid thrusting and find eye contact to be distracting. And,
of course, you may prefer both slow and gentle and rapid and deliberate,
depending upon your partner, the situation, and your mood. It is all good—
just know what you like and be prepared to tell your partner what that is.
You can also *show* your partner what types of touches you like—demonstrate

them to him or her or by placing your hand over their hand and directing their hand to the places you like to be touched and moving it in the ways you like to be touched.

Exercise: Yes, No, Maybe So

Read through the list below and put a check mark next to each type of sex you find pleasurable, exciting, or fulfilling. Cross out any item that makes you feel uncomfortable. Put an "M" next to items that you may be open to, depending on your partner, how you are feeling at the time, and other circumstances. *Warning: former victims of child sexual abuse or adult sexual assault may be triggered by reading this list.* Deciding whether you are ready for this exercise can be an example of respecting your limits and setting an appropriate boundary.

- Kissing, closed mouth
- Kissing, open mouth
- Being kissed or touched on my neck
- Kissing or touching a partner's neck
- Giving hickeys
- Getting hickeys
- Tickling, doing the tickling
- Tickling, being tickled
- Wrestling or "play fighting"
- General massage, giving
- General massage, receiving
- Having my breasts or nipples touched or rubbed
- Touching or rubbing a partner's chest or nipples

- Frottage (dry humping/clothed body-to body rubbing)

- Tribadism (scissoring, rubbing naked genitals together with a partner)

- A partner putting their mouth or tongue on my breasts or chest

- Putting my mouth or tongue on a partner's breasts or chest

- Masturbating in front of/with a partner

- A partner masturbating in front of/with me

- Manual sex (hands or fingers on vulva—receiving)

- Manual sex (hands or fingers on vulva—giving)

- Manual sex (hands or fingers on penis—giving)

- Manual sex (hands or fingers on testes—giving)

- Manual sex (hands or fingers inside of vagina—receiving)

- Manual sex (hands or fingers inside of vagina—giving)

- Manual sex (hands or fingers around anus—giving)

- Manual sex (hands or fingers around anus—receiving)

- Manual sex (hands or fingers inside rectum—giving)

- Manual sex (hands or fingers inside rectum—receiving)

- Oral stimulation—having a partner kiss or lick your breasts, having him lick other parts of your body (your stomach, your vagina), kissing or licking his penis.

- Vaginal intercourse (receptive partner)

- Vaginal intercourse (insertive partner)

- Anal intercourse (receptive partner)

- Anal intercourse (insertive partner)

- Oral sex (to vulva—receiving)

- Oral sex (to vulva—giving)

- Oral sex (to penis—receiving)

- Oral sex (to penis—giving)

- Oral sex (to testes—receiving)

- Oral sex (to testes—giving)

- Oral sex (to anus—receiving)

- Oral sex (to anus—giving)

It's Okay to Not Reciprocate

It is perfectly okay to enjoy a partner doing certain things to you and yet not want to reciprocate. For example, you may like it if your partner wants to perform oral sex on you but you might not enjoy going down on him or her.

In order to make this clear to your partner, you will need to let go of the idea that you always have to reciprocate or "be fair." And this is where knowing your limits and communicating them to a partner can end up being extremely positive. If you like it when your partner performs oral sex on you but you don't really like going down on your partner, letting them know this ahead of time will allow them to make their own choices. If they want to go down on you just so you will reciprocate they may choose not to do it. On the other hand, some partners really like performing oral sex on women, and if this is the case, your partner may choose to do it and be okay with you not reciprocating. The important thing is that you don't create a situation in which you feel obligated to do something you don't want to do or actually can't do. For example, some women have a strong gag reflex and can't "give head" without gagging, making the whole experience uncomfortable or even painful. Other women were forced to go down on an adult or older child, during child sexual abuse or adult rape, and have an aversion to engaging in this sexual activity.

Making it clear right from the start that you are not into a particular form of sexual activity is a way of honoring your needs and will help prevent the situation of a partner "hounding" or pressuring you to do something you don't want to do. It is also another way for you to determine whether a new partner is going to be able to respect your boundaries or if he or she is the type who won't give up trying to get their way.

Exercise: Other Sexual Activities

As you did with the last list, read the list below, put a check mark next to the items you find pleasurable or fulfilling, and cross out the items that you are not interested in or that frighten or repulse you. Put an "M" beside those items you are curious about and may be open to depending on the circumstances. *Warning: this list may be especially triggering.*

- Bondage (having your movement restricted)
- Bondage (restricting the movement of a partner)
- Wearing a blindfold that covers my eyes
- A partner wearing a blindfold
- Being slapped or spanked by a partner in the context of sexual pleasure
- Slapping or spanking a partner in the context of sexual pleasure
- Pinching or having any kind of clamp used on my body during sex
- Pinching a partner or using any kind of clamp on them during sex
- Three-ways
- Swinging
- Communicating my sexual fantasies to a partner
- Receiving information about a partner's sexual fantasies
- Role-play

- Phone sex

- Cybersex in IM

- Cybersex in chatroom

- Giving sexual images to a partner in their email or on the phone

- Reading pornography or erotica with a partner

- Viewing pornography or erotica with a partner

Especially for Former Victims of Sexual Abuse and Assault

Knowing what your sexual preferences are is especially crucial for those of you who were sexually abused in childhood or sexually assaulted in adulthood—and in many cases, it is important to recognize that all this goes beyond sexual "preferences" to sexual *needs*. For example, if the person who molested you fondled your breasts as a part of the molestation, you may have an aversion to having your breasts touched. This is a common scenario and is completely understandable. On the other hand, if the perpetrator did every thing else *but* touch your breasts, that may be a "safe zone" for you, a place on your body where you are not re-traumatized and from which you can actually derive some pleasure. If the perpetrator did not penetrate your vagina with his finger, his penis, or another object, having vaginal intercourse may be your "safe zone" and may be quite pleasurable. A fairly common scenario is for former victims of child sexual abuse to be able to enjoy having those parts of the body that *were not* touched by the abuser touched by their sexual partner, and enjoy engaging in sexual activities that the abuser did not impose on them.

The same can be true of those who were sexually assaulted as an adult. If there was any part of your body that was not touched or penetrated by the rapist, that part of your body may be your safe zone and thus you may be able to experience pleasure in that area.

There is another important issue we need to focus on here. Although I am not making a judgment about this, there may be certain sexual activities that you may enjoy or find exciting that may not be good for you in the sense that they may be what are referred to as "reenactments." For example, if the person who raped you tied you up and put a blindfold over your eyes, you may actually get excited if a partner does this during the act of lovemaking. If this is the case, I encourage you to seriously think about whether it is healthy for you to continue this practice. Another example may be that you enjoy tying your partner up or blindfolding or gagging him or her. This may be your way of "turning the tables," so to speak, and feeling what it is like to be the one in power. It is understandable that you might want to experience this, but think about whether there might be a healthier way of feeling in control or expressing your anger at having been sexually violated.

Exercise: Your No's—What's Off-Limits

Take another look at the two lists you just spent time on and write out the activities that you are uncomfortable with. I'm asking you to write them out in addition to crossing them out because the action of writing them down will help cement them into your mind. And if you have a partner who is not getting the message, you can actually give him or her the list you have written down.

You can also complete the following sentences:

Some parts of my body are just off-limits. These are:

_____

_____

_____

I am not comfortable looking at, touching, or feeling some parts of another person's body. These are:

_____

_____

I am triggered by (have a post-traumatic response to) certain sex acts. These are:

_____

_____

Communicating Your Preferences

While it is vitally important that you know what you like and don't like, it is equally important to be able to communicate your preferences to your partner(s). Ideally this conversation should be a direct one, with your partner agreeing to listen to you without interrupting you. You can also do this in writing, as was discussed above.

Telling your partner one time what is off-limits should be enough, but it rarely is. He or she can legitimately forget what you've said and make the mistake of touching you in an area of your body or in a way that you find uncomfortable or even threatening. But if he or she continues to "forget," this is more serious. He or she may be the kind of person who can't take a 'no" because he or she needs to be in control (refer Chapter 10).

You may need to set a boundary several times before you make it clear that you are not interested in an activity. Do so clearly, calmly, firmly, and respectfully. And do it in as few words as possible. *Do not justify, get angry about, or apologize for* the boundary you are setting.

You are not responsible for the other person's reaction to the boundary you are setting. You are only responsible for communicating your boundary in a respectful manner. If it upsets them, know that it is their problem. Some people, especially those who are accustomed to controlling, dominating, abusing, or manipulating others, might test you. Plan on it, expect it, and remain firm. Remember, your behavior must match your words. You cannot successfully establish a clear boundary if you send mixed messages by apologizing for being too rigid or for your partner not getting his or her needs met.

It is common to feel selfish, guilty, or embarrassed when you set a boundary, but do it anyway. Remind yourself that your needs are important and that you deserve to protect and care for yourself. Setting boundaries takes practice. Don't let your fear, discomfort, anxiety, or guilt prevent you from taking care of yourself.

A key signal that you have not set a boundary or need to reset it is if you become angry, resentful, or find yourself whining or complaining. Pay attention to these signals and determine what you need to say or do to take better care of yourself.

Learning to set boundaries, to say "No!" in an assertive, strong way takes time and practice. Don't get discouraged and don't become critical of yourself. Just do the best you can and you will see the results you are looking for.

Giving Your Consent in the Moment

Consent is when someone agrees, gives permission, or says "yes" to sexual activity with another person. Consent always needs to be given freely, and all people in a sexual situation must feel that they are able to say "yes" or "no" or stop the sexual activity at any point.

Official definitions of consent include: "A clear and unambiguous agreement, expressed outwardly through mutually understandable words or actions, to engage in a particular activity." Consent can be withdrawn by either party at any point.

Sexual consent is an agreement between participants to engage in sexual activity. There are several ways to give consent. For example, you can:

- Explicitly agree to certain activities, either by saying "yes" or by using another affirmative statement like, "I'm open to trying."

- Use physical cues to let the other person know you're comfortable taking things to the next level. Please note: Relying on physical cues can be risky, as your partner may not note physical cues or may misunderstand them. Consent doesn't have to be verbal, but verbally agreeing to different sexual activities can help both you and your partner respect each other's boundaries.

- Let your partner know ahead of time what your physical boundaries are.

Consent is about communication. And it should happen every time. Giving consent for one activity, one time, does not mean giving consent for increased or recurring sexual contact. For example, kissing someone doesn't give that person permission to remove your clothes. Having sex with someone in the past doesn't give that person permission to have sex with you again in the future. Even in an ongoing relationship, a person should not assume they have consent for sexual activity. Marital rape (which we will focus on in a later chapter) is as serious as any other sexual assault.

A person's silence should not be considered consent. A person who does not respond to attempts to engage in sexual activity, even if they do not verbally say "no" or resist physically, is not clearly agreeing to sexual activity.

It is also important to know that you can withdraw consent at any point if you feel uncomfortable. If this occurs, you need to clearly communicate verbally to your partner that you are no longer comfortable with the activity and wish it to stop.

In order for someone to give consent, they must be of legal age. This is defined by the state in which you live, but generally, the age of consent for any sexual activity is eighteen years old. It is also important to note that in order to give legal consent, the person must not be incapacitated by drugs or alcohol. If you are drunk or stoned, you cannot give legal consent. Alcohol is often used as a weapon to target potential victims and is used by perpetrators to excuse their own actions.

Finally, being pressured into sexual activity by the use of fear or intimidation precludes you from giving legal consent. Consent must be voluntarily given and is not valid if a person is being subjected to actions or behaviors that elicit emotional, psychological, physical, reputational, financial pressure, threat, intimidation, or fear responses.

Setting Boundaries with Complete Strangers

So far we've been discussing setting boundaries with intimate partners or acquaintances. But you also need to set boundaries with strangers when you are at a bar or party, or in any other social situation. Since you don't know this person, you obviously haven't had an opportunity to let him know what your physical and sexual boundaries are. This means you will need to do so in the moment.

Earlier, we discussed your "comfort zone" in terms of the physical distance you need between yourself and another person. It is extremely important for you to respect your comfort zone with a man who is pursuing you, because men will test you by invading your space. For example, if a stranger puts his hand on your knee, he is sending a clear signal that he is interested in having sex with you. If you are not interested, or it is too soon, you need to push his hand away. Otherwise, you are sending the wrong message.

As soon as your boundaries are crossed, speak up. Don't wait until you are more comfortable speaking up—that may not happen.

A word of warning: sexual predators will deliberately try to isolate you from others. This affords them a better opportunity to assault you. So probably the most important boundary you need to set for yourself is this: *Never be in a room alone with a man you don't know*. This gives the man too much opportunity to cross your boundaries and force you into sexual activities you do not want to engage in. For example, sitting in a room alone with a man while at a party gives him the message that you may be open to him touching you or even to having sex with him. If you are not open to these things you need to let him know this right away, preferably by telling him so. You can also push his hand away. But the safest thing is for you to go back to the party.

The following three-part strategy is very effective when communicating your boundaries with strangers.

- State the behavior

- State how it makes you feel

- State what you want or don't want

For example, let's say you have been sitting at a bar with a man and having a great conversation. Earlier, he's put his hand on your knee and you pushed it away. Now, he does it again. This is a good time for you to use the three-part strategy above: "When you touch my knee like that it makes me feel uncomfortable. I'd like you to stop." (Note: you can include all three parts in the same sentence).

Alcohol is the drug of choice for sexual predators and even well-meaning men will tend to ply their dates with alcohol—so you need to be aware if this might be going on. If you think it is, you can say something like, "When you keep offering me drinks, it makes me feel disrespected. I feel like you are trying to get me drunk."

The sooner you set your boundaries, the better. You don't want to lead someone on, and telling his sooner rather than later can save you both time if you aren't interested in getting involved with him sexually.

Other techniques are also effective in setting boundaries. The "broken record" is an excellent way to deal with a man who is not respecting a boundary. What you do is simply repeat the same words to him, over and over. For example, the man you've spent the evening with asks you to come to his apartment and you've told him, "Not tonight." He asks you again several minutes later. The broken record technique works like this: "I told you I'm not going to your apartment." When he asks again, repeat the same words: "I'm not going to your apartment." Repeat the same words to him as many times as you need to for him to stop asking. It may seem silly, but this technique is very effective.

Remember, you have to speak with conviction, using assertive statements, when setting a boundary. If you aren't heard and he continues pushing, don't be too embarrassed to shove him, push past him, or run. Don't worry about his feelings—don't be a Nice Girl. Put yourself and your safety first.

We will continue this discussion about boundaries in Chapter 12, which focuses on saying "No!" to sexual pressure and coercion.

Safety Concerns

This is important: If you are dealing with someone who is physically dangerous or threatening to you, it may not be safe to attempt to set explicit boundaries with them. For example, if you are still associated with someone who has been physically violent with you (such as a romantic partner), setting boundaries may not be safe. The same is true if you have to associate with someone who has a history of being violent toward others. If you are in this situation, it can be helpful to work with a counselor, therapist, or advocate to help you create a safety plan. Boundary setting may or may not be a part of this.

Goals of Chapter 11

The goal of this chapter was to introduce the subject of boundaries and how to set them for optimum effectiveness. For some of you, this may have been new information; for others, it may have been a review. Either way, don't underestimate the importance of setting and enforcing your boundaries.

Your Commitments

The work you have done in this chapter has helped you get clear about what your commitments are concerning sexual boundaries. Try saying those commitments out loud right now. For example:

- "I make a commitment to myself to never engage in any sexual activity that makes me feel uncomfortable."

- "I make the commitment to never get involved with sexual activities that are a reenactment of my experience of being sexually assaulted."

No! Exercise

Practice saying "no" to some of the most common sexual approaches you are likely to experience. For example, "No, you don't get to touch me unless I give you permission or consent" or "No, I just met you and I don't want to have sex with you."

Think about some of the most recent encounters you've had in which you had a difficult time saying "no." It may be that you felt pressured for sex when you didn't feel like it, or it may be that a partner pressured you to engage in a particular sexual act that repulsed you. With the scenario in mind, say "No!" For example:

- "No, I don't want you to tie me up and blindfold me. No!"

- "No, I don't want to have anal sex. Don't keep pressuring me about it. No!"

Yes! Exercise

Practice saying "Yes!" to the changes you want to make or to the behaviors you want to get more comfortable with. For example, "Yes, I have the right to decide what type of sexual activities I want to engage in."

Chapter 12
Saying "No!" to Sexual Pressure and Coercion

It's not consent if you make me afraid to say no.

—*Anonymous*

Women should never feel forced into any type of sexual activity that they are not comfortable with or don't feel like doing. And yet countless women are pressured to have sex every day—by a date, a boyfriend, or a spouse.

Not all sexual assault involves physical attack. Sexual coercion can be extremely unnerving and can result in unwanted sexual interactions without the woman even realizing what has happened. *Sexual coercion* is unwanted sexual activity that occurs after someone is pressured, tricked, or forced in a nonphysical way. Sexual coercion lies on the continuum of sexually aggressive behavior and can include being egged on or persuaded (on one end of the continuum) or being forced to have sexual contact (on the other end of the continuum). It often comes in the form of statements that make you feel pressured, guilty, or ashamed.

Social and emotional pressure to force a woman into sexual activity that she doesn't want to agree to can take many forms—from pressure and flattery, to threats of violence. If a woman has sex because she feels that she cannot say "No!" she has been coerced. If she is pressured to have a type of sex that repels her, she has been coerced. If she has unprotected sex because her partner doesn't want to use a condom, she has been coerced. If she has sex because of a guilt trip her partner has laid on her, she has been coerced.

Like rape, sexual coercion is never okay (some consider coercion to be a subset of rape). Your body is your own, and no one else has a right to it. You don't owe anybody sex, no matter how they feel, what they want, what they've done for you in the past, or if you've had sex with them before. This can be hard to believe, especially if you don't have a healthy sense of self-esteem—but remember, you are the only person with a right over your body and over your decisions concerning whom to share it with. No other person is inherently more worthy than you.

What Sexual Coercion Sounds Like

Below is a list of the ways someone you are dating might use sexual coercion, along with some examples of the tactics and words they might use. For example:

- Making you feel like you owe them ("I spent all this money on you, don't you think you owe me something?")

- Giving you compliments that sound extreme or insincere ("You are the most beautiful woman I have ever seen, I just can't help getting turned on when I am around you.")

- Giving you drugs or alcohol to "loosen you up" ("Here, take this; it will relax you.")

- Making you feel it is too late to say no ("But you've already gotten me all worked up," "You can't just make a guy stop.")

Young women experience sexual pressure in especially painful ways:
- Telling you that not having sex will hurt your relationship ("Everything is perfect. Why do you have to ruin it?" "I'll break up with you if you don't have sex with me.")

- Lying or threatening to spread rumors about you ("Everyone thinks we already have, so you might as well," "I'll just tell everyone you did it anyway.")

And in some situations, sexual pressure actually crosses the line into sexual harassment:

- Threatening your children or other family members ("I'll do this to your daughter [or sister] if you don't do it with me.")

- Threatening your job, home, or school career ("I really respect your work here. I'd hate to have to let you go," "Don't worry about the rent. There are other things you can do," "You work so hard, it'd be a shame for you not to get an A.")

Women deal with sexual pressure not only from dates and acquaintances but also in their ongoing, intimate relationships. Here are some common tactics used to pressure an intimate partner into having sex:

- Wearing you down by asking for sex again and again, or making you feel bad, guilty, or obligated ("If you really loved me, you'd do it," "Come on, it's my birthday.")

- Playing on the fact that you're in a relationship ("Having sex with me is the way to prove your love for me.")

- Threatening to get sex from someone else unless you give in ("If I don't get sex from you, I'll get it somewhere else.")

- Reacting negatively by becoming angry or resentful or depressed if you say no or don't immediately agree to have sex or have sex in a certain way ("I hate it when you reject me like this! It makes me crazy!")

- Trying to normalize his sexual expectations ("I need sex. I'm a man.")

- Making you feel threatened or afraid of what might happen if you say no ("I don't know what I'm going to do if you tell me no one more time.")

Even if your partner isn't forcing you to engage in sexual acts against your will, being made to feel obligated is coercion in itself. Dating someone, being in a relationship, or being married never means that you owe your partner intimacy of any kind.

A coercive partner may feel that consent is ongoing. However, as was discussed in the previous chapter, consenting to something once doesn't make it a "given" each time. Consenting to one action doesn't mean you have given your consent for other actions. In a relationship where sexual coercion is occurring, there is a lack of consent, and the coercive partner doesn't respect the boundaries or wishes of the other.

The following are suggestions as to how to respond in an assertive, empowering way to each type of sexual coercion tactic:

- *If your date or partner tries to appeal to your need to please him.* If your date or partner puts his needs and desires above your own, as in, "Don't you want to make me happy?" you can respond with something like, "Don't you respect my need to say no?" or, "Yes, but I also value my own happiness/comfort/needs."

- *If your date or partner acts as though you owe him sexual favors in exchange for gifts, dinners, and other such things.* Point out that the decision to buy a gift and the decision to have sex are fundamentally different. Your body is not an object, it is a part of you. The exchange is not equal or fair, and his or her expectation is therefore unreasonable.

- *If you notice that someone is particularly eager to supply you with alcohol or drugs.* This person may be trying to take advantage of you. Just be aware that, if you choose to use alcohol or other substances, someone else might see this as an opportunity. Being aware can help you avoid these people and these situations, or take steps to make the situation safer, such as having a sober friend nearby and being moderate with your intake.

- *If you are being threatened with abandonment or cheating.* This can be extremely difficult to respond to in a healthy way. If you care for the person, the thought of him or her not being with you or being intimate with someone else can be very frightening and painful. But the fact is, a person who uses this tactic does not respect or care for you as much as you care for him or her. This is not a healthy relationship, and although it will hurt in the short-term, ending the relationship rather than compromising yourself and your sense of worth is the healthiest decision. (See Chapter 13 for more on intimate partner abuse.)

- *If your partner or date threatens physical violence.* If this happens, you are not safe. Do whatever you can to remove yourself from his or her presence. If you feel safe and comfortable enough to do so, report the person's behavior to someone you trust.

Advice Especially for Young Women

- *If you are being manipulated using cultural expectations and social judgments.* If you're called a prude for not having sex, you can point out that responsibility and prudishness are not the same thing, that your maturity shouldn't be mistaken for a personality flaw. If you're told that everyone else is doing it, you can point out that not everyone *is* doing it, and also say that what others do has no bearing on your personal readiness anyway. You're no follower, and you make your own choices.

- *If your partner makes an emotional appeal for sex.* If he or she claims that you would do it if you loved him or her, one way to respond is to point out that this simply is not true. Your partner may not purposely be manipulating you here: he or she might actually think this is true. But being in love does not necessarily mean a person is ready for sex. Perhaps having sex right now would conflict with your values in some way, or maybe you're not comfortable with your body yet. These are things you can explain to your partner, if you so choose.

When Sexual Coercion Becomes Emotional Abuse

Sometimes sexual pressure or coercion crosses the line into abuse or assault. It becomes emotional abuse when you feel not only pressured but also hurt, humiliated, or frightened. Emotional abuse is any behavior that is done in order to control or humiliate another person. It can include emotional blackmail, gaslighting, domination, verbal assaults, the silent treatment, and sexual harassment.

Sexual pressure or coercion becomes emotional abuse under the following circumstances:

- *If your partner punishes you when he doesn't get sex.* Sex is about being vulnerable and giving yourself to someone. It is a deep expression of trust and love for both yourself and the other person. This type of romantic love is only true if it *is freely given*. If your security—financial, emotional, physical—depends in any way on you complying to perform sexual favors, you have crossed the line from freely giving yourself to coercion. The coercion can be subtle--as simple as knowing that if you want to go shopping for clothes, you'd better give it up tonight, or that if you want him to be nice to your family when you visit them, you should consider taking the initiative in sex tonight. It can also be as well intentioned as helping him "work out his anger" so he doesn't take it out on the kids. Over time, the abuser conditions the other person to believe that his response (anger, violence, indifference) is her responsibility. He delegates his self-control to her, and she falsely believes that she indeed has that kind of control over him. Ultimately, he is always in control of his choices and in control of himself. But instead of putting himself in a "time-out" when he loses control, he punishes her for "provoking" or "not preventing." This is classic behavior of any abuser. Hardly ever does sexual mistreatment exist without other forms of abuse: 70 percent of domestic violence includes rape and sexual abuse. And in marriages, due to the expectation of intimacy, emotional abuse and manipulation almost always get played out in the bedroom.

- *If your partner requires sex in order to engage with you.* If he only pays attention to you when he feels you are sexually appealing, he is emotionally abusing you. The strength of a relationship cannot possibly hinge on meeting all of your spouse's sexual needs. If he is unable or unwilling to engage with you when you are not "in the mood," or if all of his intimate moments with you depend on him reaching an orgasm, your relationship is abusive. You are more than your sexual organs. A man who cannot value the whole woman and engage her mind and spirit as well as her body, is not in love with her.

- *If your partner demands that you do things you are uncomfortable doing.* If you are repeatedly pressured into having sex, you are being emotionally abused. It might not be considered rape in legal terms unless he forces penetration on you, but in marriage it is very possible to be pressured and manipulated into sexual activities you don't want to engage in. If your spouse constantly requests that you perform sexual activities that you dislike (sexual toys, pornography, certain positions, anal intercourse, exhibitionism, filming you, etc.) he is emotionally abusing you. If you know that declining his requests will be followed by more insistence and a backlash, then you are definitely experiencing emotional abuse.

- *If you comply with a sexual request out of fear of the repercussions.* It is not a wife's job to make sure her husband never gets upset. If you are afraid of your partner's anger, you are not in a healthy relationship.

In these situations, saying "No!" and stating your boundaries loudly and clearly are likely to be the only ways to stop your partner from pressuring you for sex. The problem is, if your partner is treating you in any of the above ways, he isn't likely to hear you. And in the meantime, your self-esteem, your libido, and your image of yourself as a good partner are slowly being destroyed. It may be that the only way to really say "No!" is to end the relationship. We'll have more on this in Chapter 13.

Goals of Chapter 12

The goal of this chapter was to define and give examples of sexual coercion and help you to understand, on a deep level, that you do not have to put up with it under any circumstances. By giving you examples of coercive statements, as well as examples of the kinds of responses that are most effective, I hope to arm you with the tools you need to protect yourself from this form of abuse.

No! Exercise

Think about the dynamics in your relationship and look for situations in which you feel pressured for sex. If you find that there are situations when you have been unable to say "No!" to your partner, do so now. Imagine that he or she is pressuring you for sex and say "No!" out loud.

Notice how it feels to say "No!" to your partner. Do you feel guilty? Afraid?

If so, examine the reasons why and make sure you aren't being manipulated. You may also feel guilty because of the belief that you should have sex with your partner whenever he wants it. If this is the case, pay close attention to how you feel when you have given in. How do you feel about yourself? Do you feel angry at yourself? Do you feel shame that you have allowed someone to use you in this way? How do you feel about your partner? Do you feel angry or resentful?

Write about the feelings you have when you give in, when you have been coerced. Now, once again, imagine saying "No!" instead. Write about how that feels.

Chapter 13
When Sexual Pressure Becomes Intimate Partner Abuse or Assault

I had read my share of Kate Millet and Susan Brownmiller but nothing prepared me for how to handle it. Within a marriage, fighting back has consequences. The man who rapes me is not the silhouette in the car park, he is not the masked assaulter, he is not the acquaintance who spikes my drinks. He is someone who wakes up next to me. He is the husband for whom I make coffee the following morning. He is the husband who can shrug it away and tell me to stop imagining things. He is the husband who can blame his action on unbridled passion the next day, while I hobble from room to room.

—Meena Kandasamy

S exual assault by an intimate partner remains a "hidden crime." This is partly due to the fact that many women who experience marital or intimate partner sexual assault do not realize they have been raped.

Marital rape is defined as any unwanted sexual penetration (vaginal, anal, or oral) or contact with the genitals that is the result of actual or threatened physical force or when the woman is unable to give affirmative consent. This includes: being held down while your partner physically forces himself or an object inside you, your partner tying you up or otherwise confining you (without your consent) so that he can have complete control over your body, your partner forcing your head down on his penis and repeatedly pushing your head up and down, and your partner putting you in a doggy position and forcing himself inside you or forcing an object inside you (without your consent and without lubrication). It also includes sexual exploitation involving sexual contact, such as when a husband coerces a wife to engage in sexual acts with someone else.

Intimate partner sexual assault is an assault that is committed by a current or past spouse or boyfriend. This includes cohabiting couples who are not married, since the relevant relationship dynamics of long-term cohabiting couples are similar to those of legally married couples.

Forced intercourse within a marriage is often called "marital rape." Like other forms of domestic violence, marital rape is about exerting power and control over one's partner. Nearly one in ten women has been raped by an intimate partner in her lifetime, including completed forced penetration, attempted forced penetration, or alcohol/drug-facilitated completed penetration. Surprisingly, rape by intimate partners is more common than stranger rape (Bachman & Saltzman, 1995; Finkelhor & Yllo, 1985; Randall & Haskell, 1995).

Marital Rape is Illegal

Historically, marital or intimate partner rape was not considered a crime. In many countries, including the United States, rape was traditionally defined as forced sexual conduct with someone other than one's wife. As a matter of law, rape could not occur within a marital relationship; the wife's consent to the sexual conduct was presumed. In recent years, however, there has been marked progress in removing such marital exemptions from rape statutes (stopvaw.org).

As of 2011, at least 52 countries have explicitly made marital rape a criminal offense, and according to a 2006 report from the UN Secretary-General, at least 104 countries criminalize marital rape—if not under explicit marital rape statutes, then under general rape laws. Yet despite the trend on the books, legal systems in many countries continue to reflect the belief that rape within a marriage is not rape.

Regardless of the extent to which marital rape is defined or recognized by law, in practice, it is rarely reported, prosecuted, or punished. Many women throughout the world do not know that marital rape is illegal, and even those who do are discouraged from reporting by norms and social stigmas. Law enforcement and prosecutors are often unwilling to respond to complaints, and when they do, the burden is placed on the victim to prove the act was illegal, which generally requires visible physical injuries, since it's difficult to prove lack of consent or resistance without them.

When it comes to marital rape, saying "No!" and asserting your boundaries does absolutely no good. In fact, it may make your partner more angry and/or violent. As it is with all kinds of physical abuse, the only way to truly say "No!" if your partner has resorted to raping you is to report the assault or end the relationship.

Why Marital Rape is So Underreported

As you may already know, rape is one of the most underreported crimes in the US (Bachman & Saltzman, 1995). Victims of marital rape are even less willing to report the crime than victims of stranger rape. A number of factors contribute to this underreporting:

- *Loyalty to husband/privacy of family.* Women feel uncomfortable casting their husband in a negative light, and keeping the family secrets is typical in abusive relationships.

- *Unwillingness to accept their own victimization.* It is emotionally painful to acknowledge that one has been betrayed by someone they depend upon for love and support. For many women who lack the economic resources, social support, or job skills that would enable them to leave the relationship, acknowledging rape by a partner would only add to an already painful situation. Instead, they minimize or deny their experiences in order to make their lives bearable.

- *Reluctance to label the experience "rape."* A common thread found in studies of wife rape is the women's avoidance of the words "rape" or "sexual assault" when discussing experiences of forced sex with a husband or intimate partner. Many, who submit to sex out of fear, don't consider themselves rape victims.

I met Mary Ann at a shelter for battered women. She had finally fled her husband after many years of being physically beaten by him. Although she freely talked about her various experiences of being physically abused by her husband, she had answered "no" when asked if she had ever been raped by him. Finally, several weeks after being in the shelter, she opened up about being sexually assaulted by her husband after another woman in the group shared her experiences. It turned out her husband had not only beaten her, he had also demanded sex several times a day. If she did not comply he would hit her, demean her verbally, or throw her out of the house. He also forced her to have sex in front of their children.

When we talked to Mary Ann further, she revealed that the reason she had denied being sexually assaulted by her husband was because her husband had insisted that it was her duty to have sex with him. This had confused her, and made her think his assaults weren't actually rape.

Other women have shared that they don't label this kind of assault "rape" for the following reasons: 1) they aren't certain about what constitutes normal sexual relations versus being "forced," 2) they felt guilty and responsible for the sexual assault; 3) they didn't have a word to describe their experience. They did not conceptualize the term "rape" within a marital context.

In general, women tend to perceive themselves as being more responsible for and less harmed by forced sex when the offender is a husband/long-term partner rather than a stranger. And many women blame themselves for the attack, believing they provoked their husband in some way. Here's a more comprehensive list of reasons why women don't report marital rape, or even understand that what has happened to them was rape:

- *Misunderstandings about a woman's role in marriage and marital responsibilities.* Like Mary Ann, many women believe it is their "wifely duty" to have sex with their husband whenever (and often however) he wants. They believe they are obligated by their marriage vows to submit to all sexual acts, and therefore, these acts are not rape. Some women believe they are wrong or frigid for not wanting sex.

- *Sexual inexperience and uncertainty about what constitutes "normal" and "forced" sexual relations.* Many women whose husbands sexually assault them haven't had much experience with other sexual partners, or their sexual partners have also been abusive. Therefore, they believe that forced sex is normal—not "real rape."

- *Religious and cultural influences.* Culture and religion can have a profound influence on the decisions and actions abused women have to consider. For example, in Latino culture:

  - Women are often designated with the roles of "wife" and "mother." It is socially unacceptable to be divorced, to marry more than once, or to remain single and have children out of wedlock. For these reasons, it may take some time, if ever, for a woman who is being raped by her husband to consider leaving him.

  - Catholicism is prevalent in Latino culture, and religious beliefs can contribute to women's inability to escape any form of domestic violence. Latinas often accept their situations with resignation, believing their life is the way God wants it to be.

  - Inaccessibility to information and resources in their native language may prevent many Latinas from seeking appropriate services to aid her. For example, in Mexico, a law called "abandono de hogar" punishes women who leave their home, even to flee violence. Women convicted of "abandoning the home" often lost custody of their children. Some Mexican women who immigrate to the US erroneously believe that this law applies here.

The Damage Caused by Marital Rape

In general, lower penalties apply to marital rape than to stranger rape. This is based on the myth that because the husband and wife already have an intimate relationship, the act of forced intercourse is less traumatic for the victim. But current research dispels the myth that sexual assault in marriage is less traumatic than stranger rape. Family-violence researcher Kersti Yllo argues, for example: "The shock, terror, and betrayal of wife rape are often exacerbated rather than mitigated by the marital relationship." And Raquel Kennedy Bergen's research indicates that victims of marital rape appear to suffer particularly severe psychological consequences.

Marital rape can be just as dangerous as, if not more dangerous than, stranger rape. Marital rape often involves severe physical violence, threats of violence, and the use of weapons. Men who batter and rape are particularly dangerous men and are more likely to severely injure their wives and potentially even escalate the violence to murder than batterers who do not rape their wives. It is also important to point out that marital rapes can occur many times over many years (Russell, 1990).

Victims of marital rape describe a deep personal violation of trust. This is what my client Mona shared with me about her experience of marital rape: "If a stranger raped me it would feel very different—I wouldn't take it so personally. He doesn't know me and I don't know him. But with my husband it becomes personal. I say to myself, 'This person knows me intimately, he knows my feelings, he knows what raping me will do to me and he does it anyway. It's such a shock, such a betrayal.'"

Another client, Veronica, told me this after being raped by her husband: "I was raped by a stranger when I was in my twenties and I managed to compartmentalize the experience—I was at the wrong place at the wrong time. I didn't blame myself, exactly, I just determined I would be more cautious in the future. I didn't worry about it happening again. But I didn't ever imagine my own husband would do this to me. After the first time he raped me I was in a constant state of terror from that point on. I was always waiting for him to do it again and I couldn't get over it."

As David Finkelhor and Kersti Yllo note, a woman who is raped by a stranger lives with a memory of a horrible attack; a woman who is raped by her husband *lives with her rapist*.

Not only is there no evidence that victims of wife rape are less likely to experience the same consequences as victims of stranger rape, there is considerable evidence that the psychological consequences for wife rape victims are more severe. For example, studies have shown that suicidal ideation and nervous breakdown rates were higher among victims who had experienced complete rape when compared to victims of attempted rape—and sexual assaults between intimate partners are more likely to result in completed rape than assaults by strangers (Ullman & Siegel, 1993).

Researchers including Brown (1993) have found that PTSD is most likely to develop when traumatic events occur in an environment previously deemed safe. Living with a person who has sexually assaulted her, there is no place in which a woman may feel safe from future assaults.

According to RAINN (Rape, Abuse & Incest National Network), marital rape may result in more damage than stranger rape because victims are pressured to stay with their abusive partner, victims may have difficulty identifying the act as a crime or their partner as a criminal, there are potential negative impacts on children living in the home, and there is a higher likelihood of repeat assault.

Often, though not always, sexual assault by intimate partners is accompanied by other forms of domestic violence. Sexual assault is one of the abusive behaviors used by a batterer to establish and maintain power and control over his partner. According to Carol Adams, "Women are often raped as a continuation of beating, threatened with more violence if they fail to comply with their husband's sexual requests, or forced to have sex to oblige the abuser's need to 'make up' after a beating." (Buchwald, et al, 1993).

And so we can see that for numerous reasons, marital rape can actually be more, not less, damaging to the victim than stranger rape.

Other Consequences of Marital Rape

In addition to all the emotional and physical consequences noted above, there are still other negative consequences of marital rape. Physical damage includes: pelvic pain and tearing, painful intercourse in the six months following the attack, vaginal bleeding, anal bleeding, leaking of urine, miscarriages, stillbirths, and unwanted pregnancies. Victims also frequently experience the following psychological problems:

- Anxiety and depression

- Lack of sleep

- Eating disorders

- Lack of interest in sex

- Fear of men

- Other social phobias

- Substance abuse

- Suicidal ideation

- PTSD

Battered women who have been sexually assaulted by an intimate partner have also been found to have more PTSD symptoms, tend to increase their use of alcohol, illicit drugs (usually cocaine), and nicotine, and be more likely to threaten or attempt suicide.

How Women Cope

Women report that most attempts to talk their husbands out of raping them were ineffective, as was running away and hiding. Some did threaten to leave, some did leave temporarily, some did leave and divorce, and some did use violence. Overall, the decision to choose appeasement (giving in or avoiding one threat by submitting to a less harmful one) over outright resistance appeared to be most effective. Women chose appeasement based on the following: the perception of the husband's strength, the presumption that if the wife resisted she would be hurt even worse, (especially if there was a history of battering), the experience that resistance prolonged the assault, the hope that appeasement would protect the children, the understanding that unless she was ready to leave she would have to face the man again, the belief that it was good to "keep the peace," and the belief that she was wrong or at fault.

After being repeatedly raped for four years, my client Lucia decided she had to leave her husband. "I knew I had to leave or I was going to go crazy," she told me during our first session. "For the first year I blamed myself, thinking that there was something wrong with me because I didn't want sex as often as my husband. He told me I was cold and frigid and I came to believe him. I thought he had the right to force me because he was my husband. As time went by, though, I began to hate him. I got to the point where I couldn't stand to have him touch me. In fact, I jumped when he touched me and was always on-guard around him.

"As the years went by my vagina was always sore and it even hurt when I urinated, but I didn't have any way of stopping him and I have two kids and no way to support them. I started to have nightmares and eventually got to the point where I couldn't sleep. I was always afraid he was going to force himself on me in the middle of the night.

"I had a girlfriend whose husband beat her until finally, one day, she took her kids and went to a battered woman's shelter. When I broke down and told her what was happening to me she said, 'You're being battered, but instead of beating you he rapes you.' She talked me into calling the shelter and they told me that yes, marital rape is domestic violence and they agreed to let me stay in the shelter and help me get a job."

If you are currently being raped in your relationship, it is important for you to come out of denial and face the danger you are in. Because insisting that it stop will likely have no impact on your partner's behavior, the only way to say "No!" is to leave the relationship. Call your local domestic violence hotline and tell them your story. There are counselors and advocates available to help you. If you need shelter, marital rape is considered to be domestic violence and qualifies you to go into a shelter.

Goals of Chapter 13

The primary goal of this chapter was to make certain that you are aware that you can be raped by a spouse or intimate partner, and to understand that instead of it being less damaging than stranger rape, it is actually more dangerous and more damaging.

No! Exercise

If you are being raped by your spouse or intimate partner, you will need to practice saying "No!"—not so you can say it to your partner, since he probably won't pay any attention to your "no," but so you will become more empowered.

Imagine standing up to your partner and saying "No!" Even if you are terrified of him, practicing saying "No!" will help empower you to walk away.

- Say "No!" to being treated like you are your partner's property.

- Say "No!" to being forced to have sex when you don't want to.

- Say "No!" to being forced to have sex in ways that repulse you.

Yes! Exercise

- Say "Yes!" to being treated with respect.

- Say "Yes!" to deserving a good life, a life without violence

- Say "Yes!" to freedom.

Chapter 14

Saying "No!" to Sexual Harassment—From Street Harassment to Sexual Harassment at Work

In this chapter, I will provide empowering strategies for handling sexual harassment, whether you experience it on the street, on the job, at school, or in a training setting. We'll start with street harassment—a type of harassment that has received very little attention, even though women and girls are subjected to it constantly.

Street Harassment

"Catcalls make us feel unsafe. Catcalls remind us that, at any moment, even when we feel safe, we could be assaulted. Even if we were all superwomen, capable of dodging all harm, catcalls tell us that we're only objects, waiting to be objectified by the next brazen creep who walks by."

—Valerie Burn, Cat Call Season

Gender-based street harassment is an even bigger problem than harassment at work or school, since most women will face street harassment at various points in their lifetime, beginning when they are just young girls. The definition of gender-based street harassment is unwanted comments, gestures, and actions forced on a stranger in a public place—without their consent, and is directed at them because of their actual or perceived sex, gender, gender expression, or sexual orientation. It includes unwanted whistles; leering; sexual comments and demands; sexist comments; name-calling; persistent requests for someone's name, number, or destination; following; flashing; public masturbation; groping; sexual assault; and rape. It can also include obscene gestures, forced conversation, and threats.

At the very least, street harassment limits a woman's mobility and access to public spaces. This is what one client shared with me: "I can't believe what I have to do to avoid being harassed on my way to work. I have to go way out of my way to avoid certain streets where I know there will be construction sites or a man loitering outside. And I have to wear a jacket, even in warm weather, in order to avoid getting comments about my big breasts."

The effects of street harassment go beyond behavioral changes to avoid harassment and a lowering of a woman's sense of independence. Teachers and parents see young women shrink into themselves and become less outgoing and confident, more conscious of their bodies, and—worst of all—filled with shame, humiliation, and hopelessness. Girls learn early on that they are subjects to be observed, categorized, and consumed by men. They are objects to be desired and to arouse disgust. At all times, when they are in public, they are subject to judgment and appraisal, and in this sense they feel powerless.

Street harassment begins around puberty for most girls:

- In a 2014 national survey of street harassment in the USA, half of harassed persons were harassed by age seventeen. (www.stopstreetharassment.org).

- An informal international online study of 811 women in 2008 found that almost one in four women surveyed had experienced street harassment by age twelve (seventh grade) and nearly 90 percent had experienced it by age nineteen. (www.stopstreetharassment.org).

While street harassment often occurs on a more frequent basis for teenagers and women in their twenties, the chance of it happening never goes away; in fact, I've had women in their eighties share stories with me about recent experiences with this harassment.

Strategies to Help You Stand Up to Street Harassment

There is no "right" way to deal with harassers. Every situation and person is different, and often you only have a second or two to assess your safety and decide what to do. Here are some strategies you can consider and choose from when you are faced with street harassment:

- *Assess the situation.* If you feel unsafe, ignore the harasser, walk away, or call for help.

- *Respond.* If you feel safe enough to do so, assertively and firmly respond to the harassment to let them know that their actions are unwelcome, unacceptable, and wrong. Be direct, name the behavior, and state that it is wrong. Now is an opportunity to put all that you have learned in this book to good use!

- *Use strong body language and look the harasser in the eyes*; speak in a strong, clear voice. Project confidence and calm.

- *Be firm and direct.* Don't start by saying, "Excuse me," "I'm sorry," or "Please,"—say directly, "Stop doing _____." Don't apologize for how you feel or what you want. Don't make an excuse or ask a question. Just make strong statements.

- *Do not escalate the situation* by swearing, insulting or personally attacking the harasser, or losing your temper.

- *Don't get into a dialogue,* try to reason with them, or feel you need to answer their questions. Do not respond to diversions, questions, threats, blaming, or guilt-tripping. Stay on your own agenda, stick to your point, and then leave.

- *Decide ahead of time what you feel comfortable saying.* Here are some comebacks women have reported using that feel empowering to them:
  - *Name the behavior and state that it is wrong.* For example: "Do not whistle at me, that's harassment," or "Do not touch my butt, that is sexual harassment."

- *Tell them exactly what you want.* For example: "Move away from me," or "Stop touching me."

- *Ask them if they would want their mother, sister, daughter, girl-friend, or wife treated like they are treating you.* For example, "I'm someone's daughter. How would you like it if someone said that to your daughter or your sister or your mother?"

- *Make an all-purpose anti-harassment statement in a neutral but assertive tone.* "Stop harassing women. They don't like it. No one likes it. Show some respect."

- *Use an A-B-C statement, starting with what the problem is, then stating the effect and what you want.* For example: "When you make kissing noises at me it makes me feel uncomfortable. I want you to say, 'hello' from now on if you want to talk to me."

- *Identify the perpetrator.* For example: "Man in the red shirt, back away from me." (This is especially useful if other people are nearby, like on a bus).

- *Attack the behavior, not the person.* Tell them what it is that they are doing that you do not like ("You're standing too close") rather than blaming them as a person ("You are such a jerk").

These suggestions were found on the StopStreetHarassment website. For more suggestions, refer to the site or download METRAC's free phone app. It generates suggestions for responses based on where you are and who is harassing you.

Take Creative Actions

Some women like to get their point across by taking a more creative response. Here are some examples from the StopStreetHarrasment website:

- If the harasser is in a car, write down the license plate of the car. Even if you can't see it, pretending to write it down can scare the perpetrator into stopping their behavior. If the harassers are aggressive or threatening and you do write down the license plate number, you can report them to the police.

- Buy a notebook and write "STREET HARASSMENT" in bold letters on the cover. Take out the notebook when you are harassed and ask the harasser to repeat himself so you can write it down. Make a big show of asking for the date and time, noting the location, etc. If they ask why you're writing things down, you can say you are keeping a record of harassment.

- Tell the harasser that you are conducting a street harassment research project or survey. Take out a notebook and start asking them questions such as, "How often do you do this?" or "How do you choose which people to harass?" or "Are you more likely to do this when you are alone or when you're with other people?"

Take Actions that Create Real Consequences for the Harasser

- Report the harassment to their employer. If the harassers work for an identifiable company, such as a construction company, call or write the company to let their employers know that their employees are harassing people on the job and why that is unacceptable.

- Report the person to someone in authority, such as a bus driver or subway employee.

Stand Up to Make a Change

- *Hand the harasser a flyer.* If speaking to the harasser feels too scary, you can hand him information about harassment. Go to www.stopstreetharassment.org for examples from Cards Against Harassment, Appetite for Equal Rights, Street Harassment Project, and Stop Street Harassment.

- *Intervene when someone else is being harassed.* Interject to help a person out of this type of situation and let the harasser know that others do not condone their actions. Ask the person being harassed if they want help and what they'd like you to do, or simply check in to see if they're okay.

- *Share your stories.* Talk about your street harassment experiences with family, friends, coworkers, and acquaintances. A lot of people don't realize how often it happens and how upsetting it is. If more people knew maybe it wouldn't happen as often and there would be less victim-blaming.

- *Share your stories online.* Post your street harassment story or tactic suggestions at www.stopstreetharassment.org website or on your own web/ social media accounts to raise awareness about the problem and/or offer advice to others.

Sexual Harassment at Work or School

"The women's movement got us into the workplace, but it didn't make us safe once we got there."

—Ann Curry

The following behaviors are considered to fall under the category of sexual harassment in a work or school setting: Inappropriate touching, invasion of privacy; sexual jokes; lewd or obscene comments or gestures; exposing body parts; showing graphic images; unwelcome sexual emails, text messages, or phone calls; sexual bribery, coercion, and overt requests for sex; sexual favoritism; being offered a benefit for a sexual favor; being denied a promotion or pay raise because you didn't cooperate.

According to the US Equal Employment Opportunity Commission, it is unlawful to harass a person because of that person's sex. As listed above, harassment can include unwelcome sexual advances, requests for sexual favors, and other verbal or physical harassment of a sexual nature. But it can also include making offensive remarks about a person's sex. Although the law doesn't prohibit simple teasing, offhand comments, or isolated incidents that are not very serious, harassment is illegal when it is so frequent or severe that it creates a hostile or offensive work environment or when it results in an adverse employment decision (such as the victim being fired or demoted). The harasser can be the victim's supervisor, a supervisor in another area, a coworker, or someone who is not an employee of the employer, such as a client or customer.

The law recognizes two general categories of sexual harassment: 1) *quid pro quo* behavior—performing sexual favors in exchange for keeping or doing well in your job, and 2) a *hostile work environment—the* creation of an abusive environment that affects the ability of an employee to do his or her work because of gender. The bottom line: you have the right to not be subject to unwelcome sexual behaviors in the workplace or school setting.

If you are being sexually harassed at work, you are not alone. Up to 70 percent of women suffer sexual harassment on the job. A *Cosmopolitan* survey conducted in 2015 found that one in three women had been sexually harassed in the workplace, 38 percent of whom said the harassment came from a male boss. More than 70 percent had not reported the abuse. A more recent survey conducted by YouGov in 2017 came up with the same results; one in three women reported being sexually harassed at work.

Sexual harassment at school or a training program is also a huge problem. My client Jan experienced the first type of sexual harassment—quid pro quo—when she was in college. She was working as a teacher's assistant to a very well regarded professor whom she admired greatly. She was learning a great deal from working with him and she enjoyed their time together. Unfortunately, after only a few weeks of working together, he started being "a little too handsy," as she described it. "He was a very attractive man and honestly," Jan said, "I probably developed a crush on him. But he was married and he was my mentor and I just knew it wouldn't be a good idea to allow the relationship go any further."

As time went by, she found his behavior more and more disturbing. He often sat much too close to her and he seemed to be looking for reasons for them to work late. She finally decided to have a heart-to-heart talk with him.

"I told him that while I was flattered by his attention, I would appreciate it if he respected my boundaries and stopped coming on to me," Jan said. "I was shocked at his response. He told me that he didn't think I was working out as his TA, and that he was going to have to replace me. I couldn't believe my ears—or my eyes. He suddenly transformed from being this charming, likable guy into this cold, hard man. I knew he was telling me that unless I went along with his antics, I could kiss my position good-bye. It was a real dilemma for me.

"I somehow managed to talk myself into thinking that it wasn't so bad. He wasn't raping me or anything. And I certainly was no virgin. I didn't want to lose my position and I was afraid of the kind of review he would write for me. So I complied. I let him kiss me and touch my breasts and I ended up giving him head. It was so disgusting. I hate myself for being such a coward and for putting my academic career ahead of my integrity."

Sexual harassment is about an abuse of power. It is about someone in power taking advantage of that power by behaving in inappropriate or abusive ways, or there being a general environment in which a culture of inappropriate sexual behavior is allowed to exist. It doesn't matter what kind of job you have; you can be sexually harassed anywhere. You can be an executive or a waitress, drive a bus or work in law enforcement; you can work in a factory or for a multi-million dollar company. You can be in the military or work as a nurse or doctor. You can be pretty or not so pretty; you can be assertive or passive. Harassment can occur regardless of any of this.

Angie is eighteen. She works at a local restaurant during the day and goes to junior college at night. She explained to me that the kitchen staff at work was constantly sexually harassing her. "I can't walk by one of the cooks without him saying something about my body or about wanting to do something sexual to me," she said. "I just hate it. It makes me feel so small. I complained to the owner of the restaurant but he just laughed it off. In fact, he was even insulting. He said, 'You should be happy you have such a great body. Take it as a compliment.' "I don't know what to do. I'm afraid if I quit I won't be able to find another job. I guess I just have to put up with it."

Angie is not alone. There are many women who stay in jobs where they are being sexually harassed because they need the paycheck. In Angie's case, in addition to the harm that the constant sexual comments were having on her self-esteem, there was an even bigger problem: Angie hadn't come into therapy because of the sexual harassment. She was already a member of a sexual abuse survivor's group I was conducting at the time. The sexual harassment on its own would have been damaging enough to any woman, but the fact that

Angie had been sexually abused as a child made it far worse. She already had difficulty trusting men, she already had been traumatized by a man, and now it felt as if she were being retraumatized all over again.

Aside from out-and-out sexual assault, sexual harassment in the workplace can be the most damaging type of sexual offense against women. A woman cannot experience sexual harassment without suffering psychological wounds. Multiple studies have found that sexual harassment can have serious effects, including:

- Depression—victims may experience self-doubt, which can lead to self-blame and depression. The hopelessness of the situation can also lead to depression.

- Anxiety,

- Sleep disorders,

- Loss of self-esteem,

- PTSD—studies have found a link between victims of sexual harassment and PTSD, which causes the victim to relive the harassment and avoid situations where it could happen again.

- Medical consequences—research found that victims of sexual harassment often suffer from high blood pressure, which can contribute to cardiovascular disease. A Canadian study of 4,000 women also found that workers who had neck pain were more than one-and-a-half times more likely to have experienced sexual harassment.

- Suicidal behavior—studies suggest that sexual harassment can lead to suicidal behavior. Females studied reported saying they made suicidal attempts after suffering from some sort of sexual harassment.

There is another damaging effect of sexual harassment in the workplace. It is called insidious trauma—small traumas happening every day. This is what my client Flora reported to me about the cumulative damage she experienced at having been sexually harassed by her boss for five years: "Almost every day it was the same thing. The constant sexual innuendos, the dirty jokes, the lecherous looks. I got so I couldn't look men in the eye for fear of finding they were looking at me like my boss did. I felt like I had to constantly be on guard with him and this transferred to how I acted around other men. I stopped going out with my girlfriends to bars because I felt so uncomfortable being around men and because I actually became afraid of them. My boss was always looking for an opening, a way he could get physically close to me so he could touch me, rub up against me. He got so he didn't even pretend anymore. He got braver by the day. Before I quit he was actually rubbing up against my butt with his crotch. It was disgusting."

Flora came to see me because she couldn't seem to get over her experience of being sexually harassed by her boss. "Even though it's been a year now and I have a new job, I can't get his face out of my head," she told me. "When a man comes into my office, I jump. And if a man comes up behind me, I let out a scream. I want to work on getting over what happened to me. I want to work on being able to move on."

Flora's experience is not unusual. I've had many clients who have been sexually harassed who present with many of the same symptoms as women who were sexually abused as a child or raped as an adult: depression, hyper-arousal, fear of men, insomnia, flashbacks, and nightmares.

In addition to it causing damage to self-esteem and self-concept, depression, and anxiety, sexual harassment interferes with a woman's ability to do her job and threatens her very livelihood. And because it is usually performed by men in power--specifically, men who abuse their power—it can limit the amount of power and control a woman feels, and in some cases, in actuality.

Countess women have experienced devastating real-life consequences due to sexual harassment. They have lost jobs and careers. They have been demoted and passed over for promotion. Some women have halted their career due to being sexually harassed. The hardest hit are young women, whose confidence and self-esteem are especially fragile.

As we have come to recognize, in spite of improved sexual harassment laws and reporting rules, women in business—even high-powered women such as former Fox News host Gretchen Carlson—continue to be sexually harassed in the workplace. Carlson, the co-anchor of *Fox & Friends* for seven years, was the woman who eventually brought down Fox News Chair and CEO Roger Ailes—one of the catalysts for the #MeToo Movement. Carlson, who has started a nonprofit to help other women, Gift of Courage, shared on an ABC news special, "Women deal with this all the time. The problem is in every industry."

It's difficult enough to speak up against street harassment. But speaking up and saying "No!" is far more difficult when your job is on the line. Fear of the repercussions is the primary obstacle in women's way when it comes to taking care of themselves and saying "No!" to sexual harassment—fear of losing their job, of not finding another job, of losing their credibility, for their physical safety. These fears can cause women to feel there is nowhere to turn, feel trapped, and even feel hopeless. For this reason, I'm going to offer you numerous suggestions to help you face these fears and then decide what you feel is right for you in terms of speaking up.

As a precaution, before taking a new job, think ahead to the possibility that you might be sexually harassed there. The reason for this is that it is very common for women to freeze when they get sexually harassed. Some explain this paralysis as being due to how surprised they were by the action; they say they never imagined such a thing would happen. Don't let this be you. Read other women's stories about sexual harassment so you aren't shocked by anything.

As we discussed earlier, the other reason women often freeze is because they were sexually abused in childhood or sexually assaulted in adulthood, and freezing is a common behavior when you are retraumatized. With this in mind, walk through what you would do if harassment on the job happened to you in advance. Sending a "loud and clear" message at the first sign of sexual harassment can serve two purposes: 1) it can establish that the offense was unwanted from a legal perspective, and 2) it can potentially nip the problem in the bud.

Top Ten Suggestions for How to Handle Sexually Harassing Behavior:

1. *Take Offense.* Being compliant in abusive situations doesn't work. Unfortunately, many women find that being assertive doesn't work either. They are labeled "ball-busters" or "man haters." This leaves women in a no-win situation. If they don't say anything, the behavior continues, and if they speak up, they are called names. Forget about staying silent and

telling yourself it doesn't hurt you. *It does hurt you. Every time a man sexually harasses a women it hurts her.* I've worked with clients who are still shell-shocked many years after being sexually harassed. They constantly play back the events in their minds and constantly wonder whether they did something wrong or if they could have prevented it.

2. *Speak Up.* Staying silent sends the unintended message that the behavior is okay. Some harassment situations, usually ones involving the way someone speaks to you or touches you without your permission , can be stopped by a confident retort such as:

   "No!"

   "Don't"

   "Stop it!"

   "That makes me feel uncomfortable."

   "That wasn't funny."

   "Don't rub my shoulders."

   "Don't talk to me like that."

   "That's offensive."

3. *Recognize that it may not be enough to speak up.* Not every person who is confronted, even in a polite manner, is going to respond well, especially if the power imbalance is great. There are situations that require more than a confident retort, such as when a more serious violation has taken place or when your boss propositions you. And in cases where it is your superior who is doing the harassing, you might not be strong enough to go up against him. In cases like this, you may need to seriously consider filing an official complaint. (See items #9 and #10 on this list and the information on filing a complaint later on in this section for help with this.)

4. *Call it by its name.* Gretchen Carlson wrote about an experience she had early on in her career with a top public relations executive: "When he suggested we get dinner, I thought nothing of it. I got in his car, and he immediately grabbed the back of my head and pushed my face so hard into his crotch I couldn't breathe." When a friend declared to Gretchen, "That was assault!" she was surprised. "Thinking about it now," she says, "I wonder why I didn't call it what it was?" As Carlson wrote about in her

wonderful book, *Be Fierce: Stop Harassment and Take Back Your Power*:
"When a powerful person in a professional setting sexually assaults you,
you feel all of your self-confidence drains out of you in a nanosecond.
You question who you are. It almost feels as if you have to start over from
scratch to build up your sense of worth."

5. *Avoid potentially compromising situations.* Experts suggest that if someone higher up asks you to dinner, you should assume the person may
   have an ulterior motive. They also suggest that women tape any conversation with a higher up who seems to be suggesting a sexual relationship or
   speaking to them in a sexual manner in order to avoid the "he said" "she
   said" defense later on.

6. *Don't blame yourself.* It is extremely common for women to blame themselves when a boss or other man in an authority role makes a pass at them.
   They believe they "brought the unwelcome attention on themselves."
   Harassment isn't something you ask for. It doesn't happen because of
   something you did or did not do. It's about what someone else did to you.

7. *No more pretending it didn't happen.* Call it what it is, sexual harassment or sexual assault. Name the men for what they are: "predators."
   Acknowledge the harm that was done to you.

8. *Tell someone you trust.* Women who are sexually harassed often feel
   depressed, lonely, and isolated—not only at work but also at home,
   because they keep the harassment a secret from their loved ones. This is
   not healthy. You need a support system more than ever, and telling others
   about your experience will help you to feel stronger and increase your
   resolve. Even if the experience you're coming forward about happened
   years ago, telling people about what happened will help you heal.

9. *Document problems.* The first time you experience inappropriate behavior, even if it seems minor, write it down in a journal. Don't keep the journal on your work computer or in your office, where your employer can
   gain access. (Note: if you are fired you will lose access to your computer,
   your office, and email and social media accounts that were set up by your
   company.) Make your journal as detailed as possible, noting names, dates,

and witnesses. This serves as contemporaneous "proof" if you make a claim. For example:

March 2, 2018, 1:30 p.m. Paul R. asked me if I'd had a "boob job" because my breasts looked so much larger than before.

April 20, 2018, 10:15 a.m. Danny S. slapped my bottom when he passed me in the break room.

May 10, 2018, 12:00 p.m. Paul R. and Bob A. were looking at porn online. When I asked them to turn if off they just laughed and said, "We're all adults here." Jill T. also observed this and commented that it made her uncomfortable.

In addition, send emails to yourself detailing your experiences. Again, keep it at home or on your person. Also collect written proof. If the harasser texts you, emails you, or sends you cards or notes, keep copies and include the date and time. Screen shots of texts, print them, and store them in your safe file. If you receive inappropriate voice mails, keep these as well. If there are offensive signs, posters, or drawings on display at your workplace, take photos and print them. Keep copies of your performance reviews and other personnel documents to use in case your employer tries to make an issue of your job performance.

10. *Tape your interactions.* A tape recording could provide you with your best chance of proving your case. However, using a tape recorder can be very tricky legally. Check the laws in your state to find out if you have the right to make one-party recordings. Currently there are eleven states (including California) in which it is illegal to record a conversation without consent of all parties.

If You Decide to File a Complaint

Bottom line: the most effective way of dealing with sexual harassment is *to tell the perpetrator to stop.* But unfortunately, standing up to a sexual harasser doesn't necessarily stop him from continuing his inappropriate and abusive behavior. For this reason, many women have found that their only recourse is to file a sexual harassment claim. The following advice has helped many women successfully make their way through this process:

- Report the harassment to your HR representative at work, but don't assume that HR at your company will help you. You need to remember that the HR representative works for the company and he or she is there to protect the company—not the employee. Nevertheless, you need to make a report to HR as your first step.

- Unfortunately, the Supreme Court requires that you must report sexual harassment before you can sue. You have to give the employer a chance to correct the situation. Make sure you've followed the company sexual harassment policy, if there is one, and report your concern to the correct person. If one of the people you would normally be required to report it to is your harasser, your employer should have alternative people you can report it to.

- Either make the report in writing or follow up in writing. Write something like, "This is to confirm our conversation on June 15, 2018, in which I reported sexual harassment by my supervisor, Joe Rose. I reported the following instances of sexual harassment to you: [list them]. Please take prompt action to investigate this matter and address the situation." Always keep a copy of any correspondence with HR or your company.

- Don't agree to a mediation session between you and the perpetrator. This is a trap. Mediation can be an appropriate method to resolve disputes involving a difference of opinion about work issues, but in a sexual harassment case it amounts to further abuse, especially if the accused is someone in a position of power over the accuser. It also sends the message that this is a conflict that both parties are equally responsible for working out.

- An employer doesn't have to fire the harasser or tell you what action was taken. They only have to make it stop. If your harasser does it again or retaliates, report it. Once the company is on notice that a person is a harasser, it will be strictly liable if it doesn't stop him or her.

- File a complaint with the EEOC. If you've already reported harassment at work and your employer won't take action, filing with the Equal

Employment Opportunity Commission is the next step. You are protected from retaliation if you file a charge of discrimination with the EEOC. This isn't to say your employer won't still retaliate, but if they do, you can report the retaliation to EEOC and possibly sue.

- Find a good lawyer. Contact an employment lawyer in your state to see if you can get someone who understands sexual harassment. It is frequently your word against the harasser's, so you'll want someone to bolster your case.

- Get out. If your company won't do anything and you don't feel safe there, start looking for a position elsewhere. Don't let the harasser bully you out of a job before you're ready, but don't stay if you feel trapped, either. I know this can be a tremendously difficult step, especially if you have children to support. You may need to take a lesser job for a while, but your emotional well-being is worth more than money. You'll be amazed how relieved you'll feel once you are out of a bad situation.

- Above all, stand up for your right to a safe workplace. It's the law. And if those of us who are sexually harassed don't report it, there will be other victims and the behavior will likely get worse.

Remember to Say "No!"

Harassment is about power and control, and it is often a manifestation of societal discrimination like sexism, homophobia, classism, and racism. No form of harassment is ever okay; everyone should be treated with respect, dignity, and empathy.

In this chapter, I've shared with you suggestions on how to deal with sexual harassment in the workplace or academic environment. But as helpful as I hope these suggestions may be, the most helpful and powerful message is this—the best way to avoid or get out of a sexual harassment situation is to say "No!"

I'm not being sarcastic or overly simplistic. Nor am I overlooking just how difficult it can be to stand up to a person in power, or denying the possible consequences of taking such an action: a ruined reputation; the loss of your

job; the loss of your career; an inability to feed your family. But saying "No!"—
whether it be to the first inappropriate comment or sexual advance or to a continuing compromise of your integrity—is the most effective strategy you can
use and the most empowering way to stop the harasser, the bully, the predator.

If you can't say "No!" keep working on yourself until you can. Get help,
get support. Do everything and anything so you can stop this devastating
form of sexual violence from robbing you of your self-esteem, your image of
yourself, your integrity, and your sanity.

Goals of Chapter 14

My main goal for this chapter was to introduce you to the issue of sexual
harassment, whether it be street harassment or harassment in the workplace
or academic environment. It is important that you have a basic understanding of what constitutes sexual harassment and that you learn some effective
strategies for handling it.

No! Exercise

Envision a recent situation in which you were harassed, either on the street,
at work or at school.

Pay attention to how your body reacts as you remember the situation.
Does it become tense or tight? Do you have a difficult time breathing? Do you
break out in a sweat?

Now notice the emotions that come up for you. Do you feel afraid? Angry?
Ashamed?

Say "NO!" out loud to all the negative reactions and feelings you have
when you think of this harassment incident. Repeat it as many times as you
feel like saying it.

Now complete the following sentence stem, preferably out loud: "I'm
saying 'No!' to _____." For example:

- "I'm saying 'No!' to obscenities being yelled at me as I walk down the
  street."

- "I'm saying 'No!' to feeling afraid every time I walk into my boss's office."

If you are currently being sexually harassed at work or school, I urge you to read as much as you can on the subject and to work with a therapist if you need more support. I've had limited space in this book to discuss the important topic of sexual harassment and couldn't possibly go into all you need to know about what steps to follow if you file a case in this chapter. Please see the "Recommended Reading" appendix at the end of this book for more resources.

Chapter 15
If You Are Ready to Report Sexual Assault or Abuse

Only one thing is more frightening than speaking your truth. And that is not speaking.

—Audre Lorde

By this point you may feel ready to report the sexual assault you experienced as an adult or the sexual abuse that you suffered as a child. You may now believe that this is the best way for you to use your voice to say "No!" in order to help other potential victims.

You're right. The truth is, reporting sexual violence is actually one of the best ways for you to speak out against sexual violence and to help prevent other victims from being assaulted by the same offender. Reporting can also help you to recover, because in a sense you are standing up to the attacker and saying "No! I'm not going to let you get away with it."

There is no way around it—it will be very difficult for you to report a sexual assault to the authorities. But as scary as it may be to think about taking this step, there are a few things you can do to make it less frightening and less stressful:

- *Call RAINN's National Sexual Assault Hotline at 800-656-HOPE (4673).* RAINN can tell you about available local resources, and may even be able to provide you with an advocate who will accompany you when you make your report.

- *Know where and how to report.* You can call your local police or visit a police station in person. Most police departments have officers or detectives who are trained to interact with victims of sexual assault. Depending upon where you live, the police department may even be able to send an officer to your home to draft an initial report and determine the immediacy of the case. If there is still danger or a possibility of the sexual violence occurring again, police will ensure your safety and well-being.

- *Know what to expect.* The interview process can be difficult, primarily because detectives will need to ask deeply personal questions. The detective needs to follow a set of standards for sexual assault investigations based on best practices. This will include trying to get as many details as possible by asking you to describe the assault in detail and getting information that includes what you thought, how you felt, and what you feared at the time of the assault, as well as how resistance was communicated. Silence is not consent, and they understand this. It will be important that you let them know what "no" looked or felt like for you.

- *Take some time beforehand to go over the details of what you want to say.* For example: the date and time of day the assault occurred, any physical description of the attacker you might remember, anything the attacker said to you, any other characteristics of the attacker (his smell, what he was wearing). For childhood sexual abuse: the years the abuse took place, the last names of the person or persons involved in the abuse, if you know them; where you were abused (e.g., home, school, camp) and the names of other people at the location at the time of the abuse. It may be difficult to remember these details and you will likely be uncomfortable thinking about them, but having this information readily available will be worth the discomfort. Not only will you feel more confident and comfortable if you are prepared to answer these questions, you are also likely to be treated with more respect by the person taking the information. Also, the more information you can share, the better able the authorities will be to confront your attacker or, in some cases, to find the abuser and witnesses.

- *Have someone take you to the interview.* You will be nervous and probably need their support. It is considered best practice to allow a victim to have an advocate or support person with her during the interview. Let the officer or detective know who you would like to be present. If you are planning on driving to the interview, have someone else do the driving. It will be a lot safer than driving yourself. Even if you are not allowed to take that person into the interview room with you, having someone in the waiting room with you will probably feel really good, especially after you've completed the interview.

- *Don't take the reactions of the person who is interviewing you personally.* Most detectives have gone through trainings on how to communicate effectively with victims of sexual assault. While hard questions need to be asked, it should be done in a compassionate manner to avoid re-victimizing the victim. If the detective you are working with seems too businesslike, remember that these detectives are subjected to the issue of sexual assault and abuse all the time and, frankly, they can become somewhat jaded. Just because the person looks at you impersonally or speaks in a tone that you experience as impersonal, it does not mean they don't believe you or that they are judging or criticizing you. Police workers are just doing their job, trying to get all the information down as accurately as possible.

- *Speak up.* Hopefully you will be fortunate enough to get a detective who is sensitive and compassionate, which will make it a lot easier for you to share this difficult information. But if the person seems overly distant, unfriendly, or harsh in any way, you can ask for another detective. If you prefer speaking to a female detective, you can request one.

- *Try to remember, you are not the criminal.* You are reporting a criminal. Even though a police station can be intimating and you may feel like you've done something wrong, you haven't. You did nothing wrong. You are the victim of a serious crime.

- *Take care of yourself.* Although it is important for the interviewer to get the information, it is not more important than your well-being. It is okay to show emotion when you report, including crying or getting angry. There may also be times when you shut down out of fear or because you become overwhelmed. If you begin to get overwhelmed or to dissociate, just tell the interviewer you need to take a break. You can go into the rest-room and put water on your face and take a few breaths. If you feel like you are not in your body you can ground yourself (see exercise located toward the end of Chapter 1). Also, looking in the mirror can help bring you back into the present.

- *Soothe yourself with kind, compassionate statements.* If you are doing inner-child work, you can talk to your inner child in a soothing tone and tell her she is okay, you are with her and you will protect her. Or you can just tell yourself the same comforting things. Here are some examples of soothing and compassionate statements you can say to yourself:

  - "I know it feels terrible to bring all this back up but remember, it is over. You are safe now."

  - "It is understandable that you are afraid. Anyone would be afraid in this situation."

  - "You're doing great. Just remember that you, not the criminal, are the victim here."

  - "I know this is hard, but it is almost over. You'll be out of here soon and back home to where it feels safe and secure."

What Happens After You Make the Report

After the interview, an investigation will be conducted to collect evidence and locate the suspect. According to RAINN, victims can decide whether they would like to move forward with the investigation after the initial report to law enforcement. However, the decision to press criminal charges is up to the state. Although uncommon, a prosecutor may move forward with charges based solely on available evidence, even if the victim chooses not to be involved.

The police will let you know if someone is caught and charged and whether or not they have been released on bail. You should tell the police if you are worried that the person who assaulted you will harass or attempt to intimidate you.

Don't assume nothing is happening if you don't hear from the authorities. Unless you are an adolescent reporting ongoing sexual abuse or an adult reporting that other children are in imminent danger (they are living with the abuser, the abuser is babysitting children, or the abuser is a teacher or works with children in other ways), the authorities won't necessarily act on your report right away. This may be because they are overloaded with other cases or because they are investigating the case further behind the scenes. If a significant amount of time has gone by (several months) and you are not aware of any action having been taken, you have a right to call the authorities and ask them about the status of the case.

If the authorities are able to find your attacker or abuser, they must investigate the situation. If prosecutors believe there is enough evidence, your perpetrator will go on trial. While not every perpetrator who is reported goes to jail, it is important to note that a large number of those arrested for child sexual abuse are convicted and serve time in prison or jail. In the US, for example, sexual assault has mandatory prison sentences of two, five, or ten years depending on the conduct and the victim's age. Because of the rigid sexual assault laws in the US, child sexual abuse offenders now typically serve about 90 percent to 100 percent of their sentence.

In the case of childhood sexual abuse many offenders have been put on trial for molesting children. But many also agree to a plea deal so that they do not have to go through the humiliation of a trial. Most plea deals include some prison time, although not as much as they would get if convicted. Even when convicted, not all abusers serve prison time. Some are sent to mental hospitals or treatment centers for sex offenders, and some are given probation.

Whatever the outcome of your reporting, know that you did the right thing by making your disclosure. Even if your abuser manages to evade the police or to sway a jury into believing that he is not guilty, there is now a record of your disclosure. This means that if another person comes forward accusing your abuser of sexual assault or childhood sexual abuse, the authorities will take that person's accusations far more seriously than they would if there was no such prior report. And even if your abuser is not convicted of a crime, the humiliation of being exposed as a rapist or child molester will certainly affect him in very negative ways.

The Statute of Limitations and Civil Suits

It is important to understand about the statute of limitations when it comes to reporting sexual assault or abuse to the authorities, since the reporting is often done years after the abuse occurred. Statutes of limitations can vary from state to state. For a state-by-state listing of statutes of limitations for sexual assault, go to https://victimsofcrime.org.

In addition to criminal charges, victims of child sexual abuse can also file a civil suit against their perpetrator. You will need to check with the authorities in order to discover what the laws are in your state or country surrounding the statute of limitations for a civil suit. For example, in the state of Massachusetts, an extension of the child sexual abuse statute of limitations was recently passed. Victims of child sexual abuse now have until they reach the age of fifty-three to sue their perpetrator (before this, the statute of limitations expired at the age of twenty-one).

Unburdened and Proud

It takes tremendous courage to report sexual abuse or assault, but in the end most people feel relieved of the burden of secrecy they've been carrying around. And many feel a sense of pride in doing something they believe may help to stop future rapes of women or molestation of children. You have a right to feel proud for stepping forward and speaking your truth. It isn't easy but it is a powerful way of saying No! to sexual assault and child sex abuse.

Please keep this in mind: Every time one more victim finds her voice, that person brings more light into the world. And every time a victim brings abuse into the light, she helps prevent more abuse from happening.

Allow your voice to be heard. Allow your voice to break free from its silent prison of pain and proclaim your human right to be heard.

Goals of Chapter 15

The goal of this chapter was to provide you with some important information and support if you've decided to make a report. It is a difficult step to take and you will need all the support you can get. You will also need to be as prepared as you can be. Hopefully, this chapter has provided you with enough information for you to feel more prepared and enough encouragement for you to feel you are not alone.

No! Exercise

Say No!

- No! I will not remain quiet any longer!
- No! I will not carry this horrible secret any longer!
- No! I did nothing wrong.
- No! I don't deserve this shame—I'm giving it back to the perpetrator

Yes! Exercise

- Yes! I can do this!
- Yes! I have the right to speak my truth!
- Yes! I can stand up for myself and all women and girls!
- Yes! It's important to tell my story—no matter what happens.

Conclusion
Passing It On—
Continue to Stand Up

When the whole world is silent, even one voice becomes powerful.

—Malala Yousafzai

N ow that you've completed this book, I hope that you feel more empow-ered to stand up for yourself, especially when it comes to sexual assault, harassment, and sexual pressure. I hope you are determined to say "No!" loudly and clearly to anyone who tries to impose his will on you or tries to coerce you or force you to do anything you do not want to do.

I hope you are well on your way to being healed of any vestiges of shame and any tendency to blame yourself for any sexual violations you have expe-rienced in life. I hope you have gained compassion for your suffering and that you have come to own your righteous anger.

I hope you feel proud of the work you've done to make yourself stronger, to heal yourself in your wounded places, and to build up your self-esteem and self-confidence so that you can continue your fight to have what you deserve: safety, equality, and respect.

I hope you have come to appreciate, love, and respect your precious body, and become determined to never allow anyone to violate it.

And I hope you feel emboldened to reach out to help other women and girls to become more empowered, to believe and fight for their right to decide what they want to do sexually and with whom—to know that their body is their own and that no one has the right to attempt to overpower them.

And mostly, I hope this is not the end of the road for you in terms of your efforts to heal yourself and others. Think of survivors of sexual victimization as a tribe and yourself as one of the tribe's elders. For far too long, women have had to endure the effects of sexual violation all alone. This is very sad because there is a remarkable community of survivors waiting to connect with others. Become part of that group of wise, empowered women. There is tremendous power in collective stories and struggles.

There are many opportunities for you to pass along hope and support to the next wave of women who will be victimized. Reach out your hand to help someone who is just beginning her journey of healing and empowerment. Become active in the organizations that aid and support survivors of child sexual abuse, adult sexual assault, victims of street harassment, and, of course, sexual harassment in the workplace and school settings. I list some of these organizations in Appendix B of this book.

We not only need to be advocates for ourselves and other women, we also need to be advocates for the next generation of young girls. There are many opportunities for you to pass on what you have learned to the next generation. Become a positive role model of strength, self-worth, and courage for every young girl you know. Teach your daughters that they have a right to stand up for themselves and say "No!" to unwanted touches and sexual approaches. Teach them to honor and respect their bodies and to never do anything just to go along with the crowd or try to keep a boyfriend. Help them build up their self-esteem by encouraging them to focus on other attributes aside from how they look—their intelligence, their sense of humor, their creativity, their compassion for others. Most important, teach your daughters to have compassion for their own suffering. Help them understand that they don't need to pretend that something doesn't bother them when it does and that by acknowledging that something is hurtful, embarrassing, or damaging, they will actually strengthen their resolve to not allow it to happen again. Teach them to respect other girls instead of seeing them as rivals. Emphasize that all females suffer in similar ways and we need to support one another.

Because of the internet, there is no longer the choice of protecting your children from information about sex until they are older. They probably already know about subjects like masturbation, homosexuality, pornography, etc., so make sure they are getting accurate information from you. Make sure you include information about child sexual abuse, sexual assault, and the dangers of internet stalking. In essence, warn your children about the dangers all around them.

Don't just focus on teaching your daughters about sex; teach your sons as well. And make certain that you teach your sons about how to be good men—how to respect girls, how to treat them, and how to protect them. Become a positive role model of a strong woman who doesn't allow men to dominate, take advantage of, or abuse her. Teach your sons that there is no excuse for aggressive, bullying behavior and that they need to be kind and considerate toward others. Teach them that they do not have to prove their manhood by overpowering others, on or off the football field. Teach them that there is no excuse for violence and that they have the ability to control themselves.

Also teach both your boys and girls how to love themselves just as they are and that they don't have to define themselves by judgments of others. Have frank discussions about bullying and cyberbullying and make it safe for them to come and talk to you at any time if they feel bullied. Let them know that you are open to having a nonjudgmental, confidential conversation about anything they encounter.

Think about the young girls all over the world who are being sexually abused every day. Feel compassion for them and let your voice speak out for them. Express your righteous anger and let it overshadow their silence. Let your compassion and your strength and fury lift them up and inspire them to stand up for themselves. Become part of the change this world needs.

Together, we can stand up against sexual assault. We can stand up to sexual harassment in the workplace and in school settings. We can stand up to sexual pressure and coercion. Together, we can stand up as warriors and show the world that we are a force to be reckoned with—a force that cannot be broken or beaten or disappeared.

We each can do this in small ways and big ways. We can make changes that might appear to be small but which snowball into gigantic changes. Do your part, whatever it may be. Your voice matters. Your voice demands to be heard.

As Senator Elizabeth Warren said so eloquently in Emma Gray's *A Girl's Guide to Joining the Resistance,* "If not you, then who? If not now, then when? We need more women to speak up and make their voices heard. Young women have valuable experiences and perspectives. We need you in this fight."

There are many ways to stand up against sexual assault, sexual harassment, and sexual pressure:

- Support women who have been sexually assaulted or abused. Donate time and money to rape crisis centers.

- Speak out in support of women who have come forward about their sexual assault. Instead of joining in with others who question or doubt them, send them the message that you believe and support them.

- Tell your story of sexual assault or child sexual abuse. Not only is there a lot of power in telling your story but you encourage other women to come forward to tell their story.

- Speak up whenever you hear or see another woman being disrespected, mistreated or abused. Speak up at work, at school, and among your friends when you see or even hear about the mistreatment of another woman.

- Join Women's Marches and demonstrations. There is a lot of power in protest. The election of Donald Trump as president galvanized many people to stand up for women's rights, as well as human rights in general. It has now been reported that there were a half a million women (and men) at the Women's March in Washington DC the day after Trump's inauguration, and a total of 4 million at similar marches throughout the US. These marches empowered many women. It helped them feel less alone. It motivated them to fight for their rights. Recently we witnessed the power of protest concerning the nomination of Judge Brett Kavanaugh to the Supreme Court. Women marched in Washington and protested outside their senator's headquarters. It was reported that we haven't seen as much anger from women since the 2016 election.

- Allow yourself to express your righteous rage at the mistreatment of women. Don't be afraid of your rage and don't feel like you have to push it down in order to be a "nice girl."

- Join and support organizations that are working toward ending sexual violence in all its forms (see list in Appendix A of this book).

- Donate money to the organizations and politicians that support the change you want to see.

- Back legislation to change the nondisclosure laws in the workplace.

- Instead of waiting for someone else to step up to the plate, initiate change by becoming politically active.

- Run for office on the local level, and especially in your industry.

- Support and vote for candidates who work to protect women and women's rights.

STAND UP AND SAY "NO!"

"No!" to women being raped and children being molested. "No!" to women being harassed on a daily basis on their job or at school. "No!" to women leaving their job because they can't abide the constant harassment. "No!" to women being blackmailed into putting up with rude, crude, abusive behavior from their bosses or teachers. "No!" to young girls being grabbed by the breasts or buttocks in the school yard. "No!" to girls being raped by so-called "friends" at parties. "No!" to college girls being drugged and gang-raped at fraternity parties. "No!" to girls and women being afraid to report sexual abuse and assault for fear of not being believed. "No!" to our voices and our stories being swept under the rug. "No!" to men treating us like second class-citizens, to men dismissing us, laughing at us, disrespecting us.

Say "NO! NO MORE!"

Appendix A
Recommended Reading

On rape culture:

Transforming a Rape Culture, edited by Emilie Buchwald, Pamela R. Fletcher, and Martha Roth

Asking for It: The Alarming Rise of Rape Culture—and What We Can Do About It, by Kate Harding

Not That Bad: Dispatches from Rape Culture, edited by Roxanne Gay

On healing from trauma of sexual abuse and assault:

Trauma and Recovery: The Aftermath of Violence—from Domestic Abuse to Political Terror, by Judith Herman

The Courage to Heal: A Guide for Women Survivors of Child Sexual Abuse, by Ellen Bass and Laura Davis

The Right to Innocence: Healing the Trauma of Childhood Sexual Abuse, by Beverly Engel

The Art of Healing from Sexual Trauma: Tending Body and Soul through Creativity, Nature, and Intuition, by Naomi Ardea

Resurrection after Rape: A Guide to Transforming from Victim to Survivor, by Matt Atkinson

The Sexual Trauma Workbook for Teen Girls: A Guide to Recovery from Sexual Assault and Abuse, by Raychell Cassada Lohmann and Sheela Raja

On shame and self-compassion:

Shame: The Power of Caring, by Gershen Kaufman

It Wasn't Your Fault: Freeing Yourself from the Shame of Childhood Abuse with the Power of Self-Compassion, by Beverly Engel

Self-Compassion: Stop Beating Yourself Up and Leave Insecurity Behind, by Kristin Neff

The Mindful Path to Self-Compassion, by Christopher Germer

On Nice Girls:

The Nice Girl Syndrome: Stop Being Manipulated and Abused—and Start Standing Up for Yourself, by Beverly Engel

On Anger:

Honor Your Anger: How Transforming Your Anger Style Can Change Your Life, by Beverly Engel

Waking the Tiger: Healing Trauma, Peter Levine

Rage Becomes Her: The Power of Women's Anger, Soraya Chemaly.

Good and Mad: The Revolutionary Power of Women's Anger, Rebecca Traister

On Protecting Yourself:

The Gift of Fear and Other Survival Signals that Protect Us from Violence, by Gavin De Becker

On Enjoying Sex:

Sensual Sex: Awakening Your Senses and Deepening the Passion in Your Relationship, by Beverly Engel

The Sexual Healing Journey: A Guide for Survivors of Sexual Abuse, by Wendy Maltz

On Sexual Harassment:

Back Off! How to Confront and Stop Sexual Harassment and Harassers, by Martha Langelan.

Be Fierce: Stop Harassment and Take Back Your Power, by Gretchen Carlson

Stand up for Yourself without Getting Fired, by Donna Ballman

Stop Street Harassment: Making Public Places Safe and Welcoming to Women by Holly Kearl

On Joining the Resistance:

Nasty Women: Feminism, Resistance, and Revolution in Trump's America, by Samhita Mukhopadhyay and Kate Harding

Brave, by Rose McGowan

A Girl's Guide to Joining the Resistance: A Feminist Handbook on Fighting for Good, by Emma Gray

Appendix B
Organizations to Join and Support

DARKNESS TO LIGHT (d2l.org, 1-866-FOR-LIGHT)
24/7 assistance providing local resource referrals and answering questions.

HOLLABACK! (ihollaback.org)
A global movement to end street harassment, powered by a network of grassroots activists. Encourages people to work together to understand street harassment, ignite public conversations, and develop innovative strategies to ensure equal access to public spaces.

IT'S ON US (itsonus.org)
Launched in 2014 by President Barack Obama and the White House Council on Women and Girls, this is a national movement to end sexual assault that encourages people to stand up and be a part of stopping sexual assault on campus, through campaigns and events at hundreds of schools and extensive social media messaging.

JOYFUL HEART FOUNDATION (joyfulheartfoundation.org)
Organized to transform society's response to sexual assault, domestic violence, and child abuse, and to support survivor's healing and end violence.

KNOW YOUR IX (knowyourix.org)

A survivor and youth-led organization that aims to empower students, specifically focused on sexual violence, harassment, and abuse on US college and university campuses, as well as in high schools.

NATIONAL SEXUAL VIOLENCE RESOURCE CENTER (nsvrc.org)

Provides leadership in preventing and responding to sexual violence through collaboration, sharing, creating resources, and promoting research.

PROTECT OUR DEFENDERS (protectourdefenders.com)

A national organization dedicated to ending the epidemic of rape and sexual assault in the military, and combating a culture of pervasive misogyny, sexual harassment, and retribution against victims.

RAPE, ABUSE, AND INCEST NATIONAL NETWORK (rainn.org)

The nation's largest anti-sexual violence organization, RAINN created and operates the National Sexual Assault Hotline in partnership with more than a thousand local sexual assault service providers across the US and operates the DoD Safe Helpline for the Department of Defense. RAINN also carries out programs to prevent sexual violence, help victims, and ensure that perpetrators are brought to justice.

STOP STREET HARASSMENT (stopstreetharassment.org)

A non-profit organization dedicated to documenting and ending gender-based street harassment worldwide.

STUDENT COALITION AGAINST RAPE (studentcoalitionagainstrape. wordpress.com) Educates high school and college students about their rights under the law, tracks problematic police departments and school administrations, and supplements high school health education with up-to-date information on gendered and student-on-student violence.

References

Introduction

General statistics—RAINN (Rape, Abuse and Incest National Network)

2014 Sexual Harassment Study. www.stopstreetharassment.org

Chapter 1: Empowerment from the Inside Out

General statistics—RAINN

Street harassment statistics—www.stopstreetharassment.org

Intimate partner abuse—RAINN

www.endrapeoncampus.org

Women of Color Network Facts and Stats: Domestic Violence in Communities of Color, June 2006

Huffingtonpost.com 2014

SMU Research news. Blog.smu.edu/research

Chapter 2: Why Is It So Difficult for Women to Say No?

Engel, Beverly. *The Nice Girl Syndrome: 10 Steps to Empowering Yourself and Ending Abuse,* Hoboken, New Jersey, John Wiley & Sons, 2008.

Gilligan, Carol. *In a Different Voice: Psychological Theory and Women's Development,* Cambridge, MA: Harvard University Press, 1993.

Chapter 3: Knowledge is Power

Buchwald, Emilie. *Transforming a Rape Culture*, Minneapolis, MN: Milkweed Editions, 2005.

Harding, Kate. *Asking For It: The Alarming Rise of Rape Culture and What We Can Do About It,* New York, NY: Da Capo Lifelong Books, 2015.

Atkinson, Matt. *Resurrection after Rape: A Guide to Transforming from Victim to Survivo*r. Oklahoma: RAR Publishing, 2016.

RAINN

US Department of Justice

US Equal Employment Opportunity Commission (EEOC)

www.stopstreetharassment.org

National Institutes of Mental Health

The Federal Bureau of Investigation (FBI)

Ndvac.org

Chapter 4: Child Sexual Abuse

Classen, C. C., Palesh, O. G., & Aggarwal, R. (2005). Sexual re-victimization: A review of empirical literature, *Trauma, Violence, & Abuse*, 4 (6), 103-129.

Darkness to Light (www.d21.org)

Filipas, H. H., & Ullman, S.E. (2006). Child sexual abuse, coping responses, self-blame, postrtraumatic stress disorder, and adult sexual re-victimiza-tion. *Journal of Interpersonal Violence*, 5(21), 652-672

Herman, Judith Lewis, *Trauma and Recovery: The Aftermath of Violence—From Domestic Abuse to Political Terror.* New York: Basic Books, 2015.

Noll, J.G., Horowitz, L.A., Bonanno, G. A., Trickett, P.K., & Pullman, F.W. (2003). Re-victimization and self-harm in females who experienced childhood sexual abuse: Results from a prospective study. *Journal of Interpersonal Violence*, 12 (18), 1452-1471.

Oshri, A., Tubman, J. G., & Burnette, M. L., (2012). Childhood maltreatment histories, alcohol and other drug use symptoms, and sexual risk behavior in a treatment sample of adolescents. *American Journal of Public Health*, 102(2), 250-257.

RAINN

Tapia. Survivors of Child Sexual Abuse and Predictors of Adult Re-Victimization in the United States. *International Journal of Criminal Justice Sciences*, Vol 9 Issue 1. January-June 2014.

Van der Kolk, B. A. (1989). The compulsion to repeat the trauma: Reenactment, Revictimization and masochism. *Psychiatric Clinics of North America*, 12, 341-39.

Chapter 5: Shame—The Most Damaging Effect of Sexual Violations

Atkinson, Matt. *Resurrection after Rape: A Guide to Transforming from Victim to Survivor,* Oklahoma City, OK: RAR Publishing, 2016.

Finn, Robert. "Involuntary paralysis common during rape—Legal and TX Implications." *OB/GYN News*, Jan 15, 2003.

Heidt, J.M. Marx, B.P., & Forsyth, J.P. (2005). Tonic immobility and childhood sexual abuse: Evaluating the sequela of rape-induced paralysis. *Behavior Research and Therapy*, 43, 1157-1171.

Chapter 6: Compassion for Your Suffering

Gilbert, P., 2005. *Compassion and Cruelty: A Biopsychosocial Approach. In Compassion: Conceptualizations, Research, and Use in Psychotherapy*, edited by P. Gilbert. London: Routledge.

Longe, O., F.A. Maratos, P. Gilbert, G. Evans, F. Volker, H. Rockliff, and G. Rippon. 2010. "Having a Word with Yourself: Neural Correlates of Self-Criticism and Self-Reassurance." *Neutoimage* 49: 1849-56

Neff, Kristin. *Self Compassion: The Proven Power of Being Kind to Yourself.* New York: William Morrow, 2015

Shapiro, Leah, Mongrain, Myriam. The Benefits of Self-Compassion and Optimism Exercises for Individual Vulnerable to Depression. *Journal of Positive Psychology*, Vol 5, 2010, Issue 5.

Chapter 7: Anger

Levine, Peter. *Waking the Tiger: Healing Trauma.* CA: North American Books, 1997.

Chapter 8: Body-Esteem: A New Way of Viewing Your Body and Your Sexuality

Albertson, Ellen, Neff, Kristin, and Dill-Shackleford, Karen. *Self-Compassion and Body Dissatisfaction in Women: A Randomized Controlled Trial of a Brief Meditation Intervention.* New York, Published online, Mindfulness. Springer Science & Media, 2014.

Fix, Kate, *Mirror, Mirror: A Summary of Research Findings on Body Image.* New York. Social Sciences Research Center, 2018.

Chapter 9: Another Key to Empowerment—No More Ms. Nice Girl

de Becker, Gavin, *The Gift of Fear and Other Survival Signals that Protect Us From Violence.* New York: Dell, 1999.

Engel, Beverly. *The Nice Girl Syndrome: 10 Steps to Empowering Yourself and Ending Abuse.* New Jersey, John Wiley and Sons, 2008.

Gilligan, Carol. *In a Different Voice: Psychological Theory and Women's Development,* Cambridge, MA: Harvard University Press, 1993.

Simmons, Rachel. *Odd Girl Out: The Hidden Culture of Aggression in Girls.* New York: Harcourt, 2002.

Chapter 10: Have Your Wits about You: Strategies that Can Help Prevent Stranger and Acquaintance Rape

Boyle, Kaitlin M. (2015). Social psychological process that facilitate assault within the fraternity party subculture. *Sociology Compass,* 95, 386-398.

de Becker, Gavin, *The Gift of Fear and Other Survival Signals that Protect Us From Violence.* New York: Dell, 1999.

"The Role Alcohol Plays In Sexual Assault on College Campuses." Campus Safety. www.alcohol.org

Passero, Nina (2015) Effects of Participation in Sports on Men's Aggression and Violent Behavior. Applied Psychology OPUS, NYU Steinhardt, 2015.

Chapter 13: When Sexual Pressure Becomes Intimate Partner Abuse

Bachman, R., & Saltzman, L.E. (1995). Violence against women: Estimates from the redesigned survey (BJS Publication No. 154-348). Washington, D.C: U.S. Department of Justice, Bureau of Justice Statistics.

Buchwald, Emilie. *Transforming a Rape Culture.*

Bergen, R. K. (1996). *Wife rape: Understanding the response of survivors and service providers.* Thousand Oaks, CA: Sage

Browne, A. (1993). Violence against women by male partners: Prevention, outcomes, and policy implications. *American Psychologist*, 48(10), 1077-1087.

Campbell & Alford. (1989). The dark consequences of marital rape. *American Journal of Nursing*, 946-949.

Finkelhor, David & Yllo, Kersti. (1985) *License to rape: Sexual abuse of wives.* New York: Holt, Rinehart, and Winston.

Mahoney, P. & Williams, L. (1998). Sexual assault in marriage: Prevalence, Consequences, and Treatment of Wife Rape. In J. Jasinski & L. M. Williams (Eds), *Partner Violence: A 20-Year Literature Review and Synthesis.* Thousand Oaks, CA: Sage

RAINN (Rape, Abuse, and Incest National Network) www.rain.org

Russell, Diana. E. H. (1990). *Rape in marriage.* Indianapolis, IN: Indiana University Press.

Ullman, S. E., & Siegel, J. M. (1993). Victim-offender relationship and sexual assaults. *Violence and Victims*, 8 (2),121-134.

Yllo, K., & LeClerc, D. (1988). *Marital rape.* A. L. Horton & J.A. Williamson (Eds), Lexington, MA: Lexington Books.

Chapter 14: Saying "No!" to Sexual Harassment

Carlton, Gretchen, *Be Fierce: Stop Harassment and Take Back Your Power*, 2017, Hachette Book Group, Inc.

www.stopstreetharassment.org

Chapter 15: If You Are Ready to Report Sexual Assault or Abuse

RAINN

Acknowledgments

I am deeply grateful to all the wonderful women at She Writes Press, especially Brooke Warner, our dedicated publisher, Lauren Wise, our Editorial Manager, and Krissa Lagos, my talented copyeditor.

A big thank you as well to my dear friends Sharon and Patti and my "niece" Rhoda for their helpful feedback on the cover, as well as feedback from M and FL.

And finally, I want to share my heartfelt appreciation to all the clients who work so hard to stand up and say NO! to sexual assault, harassment and pressure. Because of your hard work, courage and determination you inspire me every day and make my work a pleasure.

About the Author

© Gian Cinardo

Beverly Engel is an internationally recognized psychotherapist and an acclaimed advocate for victims of sexual, physical, and emotional abuse. The author of 23 self help books, her latest book is entitled, *It Wasn't Your Fault: Freeing Yourself from the Shame of Childhood Abuse with the Power of Self-Compassion.* Engel is a licensed marriage and family therapist, and has been practicing psychotherapy for 35 years.

Beverly's books have often been honored for various awards, including being a finalist in the Books for a Better Life award. Many of her books have been chosen for various book clubs, including *One Spirit* Book Club, *Psychology Today* Book Club and *Behavioral Sciences* Book Club. Her books have been translated into many languages, including Japanese, Spanish, Chinese, Korean, Greek, Turkish and Lithuanian.

In addition to her professional work, Beverly frequently lends her expertise to national television talk shows. She has appeared on *Oprah, CNN,* and *Starting Over,* and many other TV programs. She has a blog on the *Psychology Today* website as well as regularly contributing to the *Psychology Today* magazine, and has been featured in a number of newspapers and magazines, including: *Oprah Magazine, Cosmopolitan, Ladies Home Journal, Redbook, Marie Claire, The Chicago Tribune, The Washington Post, The Los Angeles Times, The Cleveland Plain Dealer,* and *The Denver Post.* Contact Beverly at *beverly@beverlyengel.com*

SELECTED TITLES FROM SHE WRITES PRESS

She Writes Press is an independent publishing company founded to serve women writers everywhere. Visit us at www.shewritespress.com.

Stop Giving it Away: How to Stop Self-Sacrificing and Start Claiming Your Space, Power, and Happiness by Cherilynn Veland. $16.95, 978-1-63152-958-0
An empowering guide designed to help women break free from the trappings of the needs, wants, and whims of other people—and the self-imposed limitations that are keeping them from happiness.

(R)evolution: The Girls Write Now 2016 Anthology by Girls Write Now
$19.95, 978-1-63152-083-9
The next installment in Girls Write Now's award-winning anthology series: a stunning collection of poetry and prose written by young women and their mentors in exploration of the theme of "Revolution."

Love Her, Love Her Not: The Hillary Paradox edited by Joanne Bamberger
$16.95, 978-1-63152-806-4
A collection of personal essays by noted women essayists and emerging women writers that explores the question of why Americans have a love/hate "relationship" with Hillary Clinton.

Dumped: Stories of Women Unfriending Women edited by Nina Gaby
$16.95, 978-1-63152-954-2
Candid, relatable stories by established and emerging women writers about being discarded by someone from whom they expected more: a close female friend.

This Way Up: Seven Tools for Unleashing Your Creative Self and Transforming Your Life by Patti Clark. $16.95, 978-1-63152-028-0
A story of healing for women who yearn to lead a fuller life, accompanied by a workbook designed to help readers work through personal challenges, discover new inspiration, and harness their creative power.

Think Better. Live Better. 5 Steps to Create the Life You Deserve by Francine Huss
$16.95, 978-1-938314 66-7
With the help of this guide, readers will learn to cultivate more creative thoughts, realign their mindset, and gain a new perspective on life.